THE LIVES OF JESUS

GARLAND REFERENCE LIBRARY
OF THE HUMANITIES
(VOL. 452)

THE LIVES OF JESUS
A History and Bibliography

Warren S. Kissinger

GARLAND PUBLISHING, INC. · NEW YORK & LONDON
1985

Library of Congress Cataloging in Publication Data

Kissinger, Warren S., 1922-
The lives of Jesus.

(Garland reference library of the humanities ; v. 452)
1. Jesus Christ—History and criticism.
2. Jesus Christ—Biography—Bibliography.   3. Jesus
Christ—Biography—Juvenile literature—Bibliography.
I. Title.   II. Series.
BT301.9.K57   1985   232.9   83-48284
ISBN 0-8240-9035-7 (alk. paper)

Cover design by Randy Barlin

Printed on acid-free, 250-year-life paper
Manufactured in the United States of America

To
Cara Jean

CONTENTS

FOREWORD

When Albert Schweitzer published his monumental *Von Reimarus zu Wrede* in 1906, he covered only German lives of Jesus (with the one exception of the French scholar Renan) and, of course, limited himself to the nineteenth century. Since then part of the gap has been filled with a book by Daniel L. Pals on *Victorian Lives of Jesus*, dealing with (mostly) British authors.

But much water has flowed under the bridge since Albert Schweitzer's history of the "Old Quest." That quest was abandoned, at least in Germany, though it was continued in modified form in the English-speaking world throughout the 20th century. Popular lives of Jesus, too, have continued unabated. A "New Quest" arose in Germany in the mid 1950s. And just as Tyrrell accused Harnack of looking down a well for the historical Jesus and seeing the reflection of his own liberal Protestant face, so, too, in our own day, writers have found in Jesus the liberationist, the revolutionist, the psychotherapist, and many other things.

The time is ripe for a comprehensive history of the lives of Jesus, presenting not only the ground covered by Schweitzer and Pals but also the present century. Warren Kissinger is eminently qualified to undertake this. He has shown himself both a learned and lucid expositor of the history of New Testament scholarship in other areas, notably on the Sermon on the Mount and the Parables of Jesus. We welcome this new history and bibliography of the lives of Jesus and commend it without qualification to pastors and students and to the general reading public interested in biblical studies.

Reginald H. Fuller
Professor of New Testament
Virginia Theological Seminary
Feast of St. James of Jerusalem, 1984

PREFACE

I long ago concluded that bibliographers are among the most masochistic, daring, and foolhardy individuals. They seemingly have few if any qualms about "throwing caution to the winds" or "rushing in where angels fear to tread." This is particularly true of anyone who would attempt to compile a bibliography on Jesus. Hugh Anderson, commenting on nineteenth-century Protestant theology, notes that the gospel materials bearing on the life of Jesus were so assiduously studied that within a few generations an estimated 60,000 biographies had been produced. Anderson appropriately asks: "Who of sufficient range of intellect and breadth of vision is to survey and measure an enterprise so massive, to bring some order into the chaos of the Lives of Jesus?" (*Jesus*, Hugh Anderson, ed. [Englewood Cliffs, N.J.: Prentice-Hall, 1967], p. 16).

It is not surprising, therefore, that few major bibliographies on Jesus have been attempted. The most notable and comprehensive is Samuel Gardner Ayres' *Jesus Christ Our Lord*, which was published in 1906. Ayres' work comprised only English titles, was partially annotated, and was classified. It contained over 5,000 entries. His classification was divided into twenty-three categories, such as Pre-existence of Christ, Christ in the Old Testament, Christ as fulfillment of prophecy, Christ's life on earth—general, Person and work of Christ, Teaching of Christ, Resurrection of Christ. In the Introduction to his bibliography, Ayres noted: "The work has been done in the hope that someone at some future time will do the same kind of work in other languages and combine them all in one grand tribute to the claims of Christ" (Samuel Gardner Ayres, *Jesus Christ Our Lord* [New York: Armstrong, 1906], p. 6).

Doubtless, Ayres' hope was far too ambitious. To compile what has been written about Jesus will probably always remain

xi

an "impossible possibility." However, one can proceed step by step by concentrating on a given area of the life, person, and work of Christ. But even then the task is well-nigh unmanageable.

One can illustrate further the monumental dimensions of the enterprise by examining the subdivisions under "Jesus Christ" in the Ninth Edition of *Library of Congress Subject Headings*. In addition to such headings as Jesus Christ—Biography; Jesus Christ—Person and offices; Jesus Christ—Nativity; Jesus Christ—Passion, there are about 125 subdivisions, plus divisions within subdivisions.

In the bibliography that follows, I have attempted to single out works that are "biographies" or "lives" of Jesus. Consequently, I have excluded studies that focus on partial or single episodes in Jesus' life, such as the nativity, the passion, the baptism, the temptation, the miracles, the parables, and the teachings of Jesus. Two previous bibliographies that I compiled dealt with the teachings of Jesus—one with the Sermon on the Mount, the other with the parables. Excluded also are primarily Christological works that deal with the person and work of Christ. It becomes apparent immediately, however, that neat divisions and categories are impossible. For example, a "biography" of Jesus will doubtless contain Christological elements, and vice versa.

Another voluminous genre excluded is that of the "harmony," which seeks to construct a continuous narrative of the life of Jesus by "harmonizing" the gospels. The *British Museum General Catalog of Printed Books* (1937) contains forty-four pages of harmonies, or about 660 entries. The *National Union Catalog Pre-1956 Imprints* contains thirty-one pages of harmonies in English.

The bibliography is divided into two sections—one consisting of general biographies, the other of juvenile biographies. It is representative of the Lives of Jesus corpus in that it contains both critical-scholarly and popular works. Monographs in European and non-European languages are included as well as films and filmstrips.

Instead of annotations, which so readily become repetitious and are divorced from a broader interpretive context, I have introduced the volume with an essay dealing with the history and criticism of the Lives of Jesus, extending from the patristic period to the present. This survey treats the various interpreters and movements that have been influential in the attempt to know who Jesus was and is. It is my hope that this overview will provide a background and perspective from which the various Lives of Jesus can be better understood and evaluated.

In view of the above observations, it is evident that this bibliography on the Lives of Jesus is far from exhaustive. Though it contains a good proportion of the "scholarly" works, it offers but a representative sample of the myriad popular and devotional Lives of Jesus. It represents a beginning upon which others can build and expand. Moreover, it is offered in the belief that it will contribute to a deeper understanding and appreciation of that one whom many view as teacher, prophet, idealist, and visionary dreamer, but whom others acknowledge as Lord and Savior.

I am particularly grateful to Reginald H. Fuller for reading the introductory essay and offering critical and constructive suggestions, and to numerous colleagues at the Library of Congress who read all or part of the manuscript, assisted with language problems, and offered support and encouragement.

Warren S. Kissinger
University Park, Maryland
December 1984

The Lives of Jesus

PART I
HISTORICAL OVERVIEW

The Gospel of John concludes on a hyperbolic note, with
the writer stating that if everything were written about the
things that Jesus did the world itself could hardly contain
the books that would be written. After more than nineteen centuries, the voluminosity of books about Jesus has grown to the
extent that one is almost tempted to take these words literally. Without doubt, more has been written about Jesus than
about anyone else in all history. The extent of this literature is so vast that it almost defies systematic treatment and
categorization. It reflects every kind of theological system,
and emotions ranging from intense piety and devotion to scorn
and hatred.

A historical study of the Lives of Jesus is instructive
because it concerns more than nineteen centuries of theological
history and development. It is marked by phases and movements
that were dynamic and creative and that evidenced patient and
painstaking effort. This history is characterized by progress
and movement, so that its earlier preoccupation with religious
and theological considerations gave way in more recent times
to historical and existential concerns.

Prior to the eighteenth century, it was generally assumed
that the teaching of the church and the four gospels provided
a reliable account of the life and teachings of Jesus. Though
there were discrepancies in the gospels, these could be reconciled and harmonized so that a historical Life of Jesus emerged.
Jesus himself left nothing in writing, and there was a notice-
able gap in the gospels between his birth and the beginning of
his Galilean ministry, a situation that led many writers of
Lives of Jesus to use their imagination most freely in "filling
in the gaps."

Apart from the four gospels, there are only minor references
to Jesus in contemporary literature. These are found in Tacitus,
Suetonius, Pliny the Younger, and Josephus. The Jewish Talmud
contains some polemical and derogatory remarks about Jesus.
However, none of these sources adds anything to the gospel accounts. Adolf Harnack notes that apart from the gospels of the
New Testament just about everything we know concerning Jesus'
history and teaching "may easily be put on a small sheet of
paper, so little does it come to."[1]

In addition to the above, there are several "gospels" that
were discovered in Egypt several decades ago. None of these

furnishes any account of the life of Jesus. One of them, the
Gospel of Thomas, contains sayings and parables of Jesus and
has been a useful source for parable research. There are
fragments of other apocryphal gospels, such as the Gospel of
the Nazaraeans, the Gospel of the Ebionites, the Gospel of the
Hebrews, the Gospel of the Egyptians, the Gospel of Thomas,
and the Gospel of Peter. These are later than the New Testament gospels, and the information they contain about Jesus is
generally considered to be fanciful and legendary.

Thus, we are left with the four gospels as the sources for
our information about Jesus. They are a relatively brief corpus, and one would assume that the writing of a Life of Jesus
would entail a minimum of difficulty. But this has not been
the case, especially since the eighteenth century. The question of the authenticity and reliability of the sources, and of
the relationship between the kerygma and history, are persistent
problems that have not yielded to easy resolution. Despite the
persistent claims that Jesus can be readily known, there is a
dimension of mystery about him that is not easily penetrated.
In spite of the myriad Lives of Jesus and the erudite research
into his life and person, there is still a haunting truth
about the closing words of Albert Schweitzer's *Quest of the
Historical Jesus*: "He comes to us as one unknown, without a
name, as of old, by the lakeside, he came to those men who
knew him not."

Harmonies

The earliest attempts to write Lives of Jesus were in the
form of harmonies, which presented a continuous narrative by
"harmonizing" the four gospels. The first harmony of this kind
was probably Tatian's *Diatessaron*, composed soon after A.D. 150.
"Diatessaron" is a Greek musical term meaning "a harmony in
four parts."

Tatian (*ca.* 110-172), an Assyrian from Nisibitis on the
Euphrates, was a Christian apologist and Gnostic. In A.D. 150,
he came to Rome, where he was converted and later became a
pupil of Justin Martyr. He is best known for his *Diatessaron*,
which was used as a liturgical book in the Syrian church until
the fifth century.

The original language of the *Diatessaron*, whether Greek or
Syriac, is unknown. F.C. Burkitt suggests that it might have
been originally in Latin. There are no extant manuscripts of
the whole *Diatessaron*. In the fourth century, Ephraeum Syrus
wrote a commentary on the *Diatessaron*, and an Armenian translation of this was discovered in 1836. A considerable portion
of the Syriac original came to light in 1957. There are extant

two late Arabic manuscripts of the *Diatessaron*, a medieval
Dutch harmony that is dependent upon it, and the Latin Codex
Fuldensis, which has the order of the *Diatessaron*, though the
text has been assimilated to the Vulgate.

There are a number of critical questions attending the
Diatessaron. One deals with the original order of the narrative. The various versions differ significantly in the sequence of incidents. It appears that Tatian dealt quite
freely with the gospel sequences. He tended to combine narratives found in one gospel with similar incidents elsewhere,
even when they did not appear in the same order in the separate
gospels or even if they differed in detail. Harvey K. Mc-
Arthur notes:

> By way of summary it may be said that Tatian attempted
> to create a unified "Life" of Jesus by including prac-
> tically everything from the four gospels; he combined
> incidents if they were at all similar without too much
> concern for differences in chronology or detail; and,
> consciously or unconsciously, he allowed the chronologies
> of Matthew and John to dominate his pattern.[2]

Although Augustine is best known for his theological contribution to the western church, he was also a biblical critic.
His *De Consensu Evangelistarum*, or *The Harmony of the Gospels*,
(*ca.* 400) had a great influence in the Middle Ages and upon
subsequent harmonization.

Augustine's basic purpose in writing his harmony was apolo-
getic--to vindicate the gospel against critical assaults of
the heathen. It is laid out in four divisions. In the first
book, Augustine refutes those who have asserted that Christ
was only the wisest among men and who have aimed at detracting
from the authority of the gospel by insisting on the absence
of any written composition from the hand of Christ himself.
He further objects to those who have affirmed that the disciples
went beyond Jesus' teaching about his divinity and about the
duty of abandoning the worship of the gods.

In the second book, Augustine's purpose is to enter upon a
careful examination of the Gospel of Matthew up to the account
of the Last Supper. He compares Matthew with Mark, Luke, and
John and "exhibits the perfect harmony subsisting between them."

Book 3 continues this process of harmonization from the
account of the Supper to the end of the gospels. Book 4 inves-
tigates those passages in Mark, Luke, and John that have no
parallels in Matthew.

A number of observations can be made about Augustine's
harmony. There is less frequent allegorizing in *The Harmony*
than in many of Augustine's other works, where allegorization
appears to be one of his favorite methods of exegesis. Further-

more, his principles of harmonizing are generally characterized
by simplicity and good sense.

Augustine held a high view of biblical inspiration, and
subsequently his purpose was to defend the authenticity of the
gospel writers. Thus, discordant versions of one incident are
explained as different instances of the same circumstances or
repeated utterances of the same words. However, Augustine reflected a measure of flexibility in his analysis of the materials by contending that the order of events in the gospels was
sometimes the order of recollection rather than the order of
history; that when the gospels reported conversations it was
adequate for them to report the sense intended rather than the
precise words; and that, since any one gospel generally reported only part of an event, varying details in other gospels
should be regarded as supplementary and not contradictory.[3]

Compared with Tatian, Augustine did not deal freely with
the gospel sequences and their rearrangement and thus was more
"conservative." He favored Matthew as the basis for his harmonization, although he felt free to adopt the chronology of
the other gospels.

Though there were weaknesses and inconsistencies in Augustine's methods, his achievement was nevertheless outstanding,
given the status of biblical scholarship in his day. One can
appreciate S.D.F. Salmond's remarks:

> However unsuccessful we may now judge some of his en-
> deavors, when we consider the comparative poverty of his
> materials, and the untrodden field which he essayed to
> search, we shall not deny to this treatise the merit of
> grandeur in original conception, and exemplary faithful-
> ness in actual execution.[4]

Poetic Lives

During the fourth and fifth centuries, another type of
literature dealing with the life of Jesus appeared. It was in
Latin and in poetic form, confining itself to the four gospels,
but especially to Matthew. It also reflected a strong affinity
for, and dependence upon, the works of Vergil.

One of the earliest examples of this literature was the
Evangeliorum Libri Quattuor, which was written by Juvencus
about A.D. 330.[5] Little is known about Juvencus except that
he was a well-born Spanish priest. Drawing primarily on
Matthew, Juvencus closely paraphrased the gospels, especially
Jesus' words, and there is a minimum of flights of poetic imagi-
nation in his writing. As noted above, these poetic Lives of
Jesus were strongly influenced by Vergil. This is evident in
Juvencus' meter, vocabulary, and mythological allusions. His

dependence upon Matthew is evident in that 2,600 of the 3,211 hexameters are based on the first gospel. In the *Evangeliorum Libri Quattuor*, Juvencus attempted to present the story of Jesus as an epic in Vergilian form.[6]

About the middle of the fourth century, Proba, a convert to Christianity, composed the *Cento*.[7] The term "cento" originally meant a cloak made of patches, and then came to be applied to compositions constructed from words and lines taken from the poets and put together to express content other than the original. Proba's *Cento* is a compressed Life of Jesus because nearly half of it deals with the events ranging from the creation to the flood. The portion on Jesus concentrates on his birth and passion. The entire work contains 694 hexameter lines. Though Pope Gelasius refused to give the *Cento* the sanction of the church, it appears to have been much read during the Middle Ages, since there are many existing manuscripts and the mention of many others.

A third example of the poetic Life of Jesus is the *Carmen Paschale*, by Sedulius, an early fifth-century Italian poet.[8] Probably written in Greece before A.D. 431, it is basically an account of biblical miracles. The *Carmen Paschale* is composed in five books of hexameters. Book 1 describes miracles of the Old Testament and also emphasizes the importance of the Trinity, condemning the heretical doctrines of Sabellius and Arius. Book 2 recounts the baptism and temptation of Jesus and the call of the disciples. Book 3 relates the miracles of Jesus from the marriage at Cana to the quarrels of the apostles about their rank in heaven. Book 4 continues the narration of the deeds of Jesus and concludes with his entry into Jerusalem and the raising of Lazarus. Book 5 retells the passion and the resurrection.

Sedulius used allegory rather freely in treating his subjects. He usually followed Matthew and Mark but used all four gospels in Book 5. As with Juvencus, Vergil served as a model for his verse.

Medieval Period

The actual life and humanity of Jesus continued to be a vital concern during the medieval period. One of the most popular and widely disseminated works was the *Meditations on the Life of Christ* (*Meditationes vitae Christi*). It was believed to have been written by Saint Bonaventura and was published with his works until the eighteenth century. Today, Bonaventura's authorship is rejected, and modern scholars agree that the author must have been a Franciscan monk living in Tuscany during the second half of the thirteenth century.

The popularity of the *Meditations* is evidenced by the fact
that over 200 Latin, Italian, and French manuscripts are extant. The most complete English version, translated from the
Latin by Isa Ragusa, is based on Ms. ital. 115 in the Biblio-
thèque Nationale in Paris, an illustrated manuscript dating
from the fourteenth century.[9]

The *Meditations* was originally written as a devotional guide
for a nun named Cecilia. The author praises her virtues, which
derive from her fervent meditation on the life of Jesus. The
readers of the *Meditations* are urged to do likewise:

> You will never find better instruction against vain and
> fleeting blandishments, against tribulation and adversity,
> against the temptations of enemies and vices, than in the
> life of Christ, which was without blemish and most per-
> fect. Through frequent and continued meditation on his
> life, the soul attains so much familiarity, confidence,
> and love that it will disdain and disregard other things
> and be exercised and trained as to what to do and what
> to avoid.[10]

Thus, the *Meditations* cannot be strictly regarded as a Life
of Jesus because its intent is contemplative and devotional.
However, the author adheres closely to the gospel chronology.
His chief intent is to draw readers into the events so that
they will become "eye witnesses." The narrative events are
told "as they occurred or as they might have occurred according to the devout belief of the imagination and the varying
interpretation of the mind."[11] Though these remarks would lead
one to believe that the author is prepared to use his imagination freely, this is not the case. The devotional element is
predominant, but the human side of Jesus is in evidence, so
that one can indeed speak of the *Meditations* as a Life of Jesus.

As with other early Lives, the author of the *Meditations*
emphasizes the infancy and the passion narratives. He states
that it would take too long to convert into meditations all
the things that Jesus said and did.[12] Among the notable
omissions are the Sermon on the Mount and other major discourses of Jesus, such as those contained in Matthew 13 and
John 14-17. It appears that the author was interested in presenting incidents or "visual aspects" rather than speeches.
Concerning the Sermon on the Mount, he observes:

> Read it often and diligently and commit to memory the
> things said in it, for they are spiritual. But now I
> will not continue in this, for it would take too long
> and these expositions do not always seem to benefit medi-
> tations, although I shall intersperse such moral facts
> and sayings of saints for your instruction as occur to
> me.[13]

In a summary statement concerning the *Meditations*, Harvey McArthur writes:

> The differences between the fourteenth and the twentieth centuries are so great that it is difficult to evaluate the *Meditations*. Yet in its day it was clearly a moving and effective document. Even in our times he who reads with sympathy is aware of its power.... But in the main, this is an effective presentation of the life of Jesus with special reference to the Franciscan virtues of poverty and humility.[14]

Another work that was extensively copied and used, that provided its author a prominent place among spiritual writers of the fourteenth century, was *De gestis Domini Salvatoris*, by Simone Fidati.

Born in Cascia in central Italy at the close of the thirteenth century, Fidati became a member of the Order of Hermits of St. Augustine. Regarded as one of the learned theologians of fourteenth-century Italy, Fidati was also a renowned preacher. As a young man, he pursued the study of the sciences. However, after meeting "a man who had a reputation for living a holy life," Fidati gave up sciences and devoted himself exclusively to theology.[15]

Fidati began work on the *De gestis Domini Salvatoris* in 1338 at the request of his friend and follower Thomas Corsini. At the time of his death in 1348, the *De gestis* was not completed. Subsequently, John of Salerno gathered Fidati's notes and added them to the material already written, and composed a table of contents for the entire work.

The arrangement of the *De gestis* differs from that of the *Meditationes vitae Christi* and the *Vita Christi* of Ludolphus in that it is arranged topically rather than chronologically. Sister McNeil notes: "He does not seem to have profited by the numerous harmonies of the gospels into one synthetic account, for he arranges the *De gestis* topically and because of this feature, the chronological sequence of Christ's life is greatly obscured."[16] Fidati's primary aim was not to present a historical account of Jesus' life but to present the teaching drawn from his life and actions as a guide to Christian living. His concern was an ethical emphasis. It was the moral interpretation of scripture in which Fidati was chiefly interested.

Divided into fifteen books, the *De gestis* is of vast proportions. Fourteen of these books deal with the life of Jesus and the moral lessons to be drawn from his actions and doctrine. Book 15, dealing with Christian justice, was probably added by John of Salerno. Though the books are divided topically, they do form a rough chronological exposition of the whole life of Jesus.

Unlike most medieval writings on the life of Jesus, Fidati based his material upon the authority of the scriptures alone. Fidati seems to have been familiar with the patristic writings, but he does not quote a single authority by name except the scriptures. Sister McNeil observes that this does not imply that he was an original thinker. Rather, he selected what was pertinent and useful in developing his own moralizations on the gospel texts. He clothed quotations from the Fathers in "indistinct circumlocutions and fanciful terminology."[17]

Fidati's treatment of the life of Jesus appears to be a combination of a chronological harmony and a commentary on the gospels. He uses all four gospels in selecting the events of Jesus' life. Where more than one gospel records a given incident, he synthesizes the various accounts.

The influence of the *De gestis* was widespread during at least two centuries of the medieval period. It was translated into the vernacular and is still extant in numerous manuscripts.[18] Though the *De gestis* was primarily a moral commentary on the gospels and not a Life of Christ in the strict sense, nevertheless it makes a definite contribution to Life of Jesus research. The events of Jesus' life are treated with reverence, but unlike many medieval spiritual writers, Fidati stresses the divinity of Christ rather than his humanity.

Commenting on the *De gestis*' influence and significance, Sister McNeil writes:

> The secret of its influence lies in the fact that it is an exposition of the gospels emphasizing the moral instruction to be drawn from our Lord's teaching, for these are lessons that are timeless.... While these characteristics, together with its length, repetitions, digressions, and obscurity hinder the work from being appreciated by the modern reader, the book suited the taste of its fourteenth-century readers, and served a practical purpose in that period.... the *De gestis* fulfilled the author's twofold aim: "to perfect the interior man in Christian life and doctrine, and to adapt the exterior man to Christian ways."[19]

Though both the *Meditationes vitae Christi* and the *De gestis Domini Salvatoris* were widely recognized and used, their popularity was surpassed by the *Vita Christi* of Ludolphus.

Little is known about the early life of Ludolphus. According to some sources, he was a Dominican for thirty years before becoming a Carthusian. In 1343, Ludolphus became prior of the charterhouse at Coblenz, where he served until 1348. From Coblenz, he went to the charterhouse of Mainz and later to Strassburg, in 1377.

Ludolphus' most-renowned work was the *Vita Christi*, which was probably written in Mainz sometime after 1348. It is a

voluminous production that is far more than a mere biography
of Jesus drawn from the gospels. The author's purpose was to
supply not a narrative account but a book of meditations.
It consists of 2,500 octavo pages and would take several weeks
to read. Not a Life of Jesus in the modern sense, it is rather
a devout, meditative work intended for slow spiritual reading.

The *Vita Christi* contains an incredible number of references
(more than 100) to patristic and secular writings.[20] Ludolphus
begins with the gospel texts and then interweaves material from
other writers. The style is rambling, and he frequently di-
gresses into moral and allegorical interpretations. An original
feature of the work is the devotional prayers that conclude
each chapter. These reflect the author's devout meditations
on the life of Jesus.

The *Vita Christi*'s influence in the fourteenth century and
beyond is attested by the many contemporary and later manuscripts,
which caused Heinrich Boehmer to conclude that the *Vita Christi*
was the most influential work of German mysticism in the fourteenth and fifteenth centuries.[21]

The main body of the text is divided into two parts. Part 1
treats the public life of Jesus from the baptism to the healing
of the blind man of Bethsaida. The second part begins with
Peter's confession of Christ's divinity and deals with the
passion. However, Part 2 contains fifty-seven additional chapters on Jesus' public life. It is evident that Ludolphus departed from the prevailing pattern of giving primary attention
to the nativity and the passion.

As an exegete, Ludolphus differentiated particular aims of
the four evangelists. Matthew's purpose is to show that Jesus
is the Messiah and the one promised by the prophets; he provides twenty-two proofs to support this contention. Mark
dwells on the miracles of Christ, and he offers twenty proofs
that Jesus is King, supreme in power and might. Luke offers
six proofs that the saving and healing character was dominant
in the life of Jesus. Luke includes many parables on mercy
and forgiveness. Ludolphus finds that John has nineteen proofs
that Jesus is the son of God.[22] Other marks of Ludolphus'
exegesis are his frequent allegorizing, his recourse to moral
explanations, and his fondness for symbolism of numbers.

Among the sources that Ludolphus used was the *Meditationes
vitae Christi* of pseudo-Bonaventure. He uses textual material
from more than sixty chapters out of a total of 100 from the
Meditationes. Sister Bodestedt offers the following comparison
between the two works:

> The *Vita* is by far a more learned work than the *Medi-
> tationes* as is evident from the wealth and diversity of
> its source material. It is more abstract. The pseudo-
> Bonaventure considers the expository nature of the Sermon

on the Mount as rather foreign to meditation, whereas
Ludolphus devotes as high as six per cent of his work
to it.... In narrative and descriptive power the *Meditationes* surpasses the *Vita*. Both works had great influence. The former inspired the literature and art of
the late Middle Ages, the latter lives on in the *Spiritual
Exercises*.[23]

Sixteenth-Century Harmonies

The late fifteenth and sixteenth centuries were marked by
an upsurge in the publication of gospel harmonies. The reasons
for this development are not clear. One that has been suggested is that the growing awareness of non-Christian religions
called for a renewed apologetic. The Reformation emphasis on
the centrality of the scriptures may have played a part.
Another reason may have been the new interest in ancient languages and texts that the Renaissance inspired. A technical
reason for this proliferation of harmonies may have been the
development of movable type in the fifteenth century. Whatever
the reason, harmonies flowered in the sixteenth century. Their
importance can be gauged by the fact that some of the most pres-
tigious figures of the Reformation were compilers of harmonies.
Among them were Bucer, Osiander, Calvin, and Flacius. Harvey
McArthur estimates that as many as thirty-five gospel harmonies
appeared in the sixteenth century, more than had been written
in the fourteen preceding centuries.[24]

A new development in the sixteenth century was the emergence
of a new harmony format--the arrangement of the gospels in
parallel columns. Prior to this time, harmonies consisted of
the gospel texts woven together into a single consecutive
narrative. The differences between these two types is frequently designated by the terms "synopsis" and "harmony," the
latter being reserved for the consecutive narrative. McArthur,
in his discussion of the two types, speaks of the "integrated
harmony" and the "parallel harmony."[25]

The new format represented an advance in gospel study. The
writers of "integrated harmonies" were clearly aware of the
problems of harmonization, but their readers were not. However, with the introduction of the "parallel harmony," both
harmonist and reader could see and appreciate the problems.
McArthur notes: "The parallel harmony allowed the reader to
evaluate the problems of order and the proposals of the har-
monists with respect to those problems." The parallel harmony
was a significant step toward the critical approach to the
gospel texts that was to come in the eighteenth and nineteenth
centuries.

One of the most influential sixteenth-century harmonies
was Andreas Osiander's *Harmoniae evangelicae libri quattuor*
(1537). Two principles governed his methodology. Each gospel
should be presented in its own sequence, and differing details
between two versions of an incident should be viewed as separate
incidents, even though they occur at the same chronological
points in the gospels. This second axiom led to some rather
bizarre exegesis. For example, Osiander concluded that Peter
denied Jesus not three times but nine times.
A more flexible and "critical" approach to harmonization
is reflected in John Calvin's *Commentary on a Harmony of the
Evangelists*. Calvin was indifferent to Osiander's view of the
integrity of the chronological order in the separate gospels.
Moreover, he was more inclined to regard parallel incidents as
single events. McArthur observes that there appears to be a
tension between Calvin's abstract statements concerning the
doctrine of scripture and the assumptions implicit in his his-
torical-exegetical work. His theory was rigid, but his practice
was flexible.[26]

Modern Period

Prior to the eighteenth century, Lives of Jesus, whether in
the form of harmonies or poetry, whether apologetic or devotional, assumed two basic presuppositions. The first was that
the classical creeds, church teaching and tradition, and the
Bible itself presented the authentic view of Christ. He was
fully God and fully man, born of the Virgin Mary, crucified,
resurrected, and ascended into heaven, whence he shall come
again in triumph and judgment. Jesus was the "Christ of
faith," the "dogmatic" or "theological" Christ whom God sent
into the world to redeem it.
The second presupposition was that the gospels were trustworthy historical records that revealed a true picture of who
Jesus was, what he said, and what he did. Though the gospels
differed in details, these differences could be reconciled and
harmonized so that a fuller and more complete view of Christ
emerged from reference to all four of the gospels.
To be sure, there were scattered exceptions to this pattern. The first modern Life of Jesus was written by Hieronymus
Xavier in 1602. It was composed in Portuguese and later translated into Persian for the use of the Mogul King Agbar. In
the seventeenth century, the Persian text was translated into
Latin by the Reformed theologian Louis de Dieu in an attempt
to discredit Catholicism. Albert Schweitzer observed that it
was a skillful falsification of the life of Jesus, in which the
omissions, and the additions from the Apocrypha, were inspired

by the sole purpose of presenting to the open-minded ruler a
glorious Jesus in whom there should be nothing to offend him.[27]
     During the Reformation period, Laelius Socinus (1525-1562)
and Michael Servetus (1511-1553) denied the divinity of Christ
and regarded him as only a prophet and founder of a religion.
However, they found no problems in the life of Jesus, nor did
they apply the methods of historical criticism to the gospels.
     During the latter half of the seventeenth century, there
arose in England a school of thought called deism. It was
rationalistic and sought in nature and in reason a basis for religion and belief in God apart from revelation. It sought to
"free men's minds" from the bondage of dogmatic, ecclesiastical,
and institutional Christianity. The deists denied the gospel
miracles and tried to rationalize them. They rejected dogmatic
views about Jesus, insisting that he was a great prophet and
nothing more. They gave preference to the Gospel of John over
the synoptics because it was more philosophical, contained
fewer miracles, and placed more stress on Jesus' religious and
ethical teaching than on his messianic claims. Among the most
prominent English deists were John Toland (1671-1723), Peter
Annet (d. 1768), and Thomas Woolston (1669-1721).[28]
     From England, deism spread to France and Germany during
the eighteenth century, influencing such notables as G.E.
Lessing, Voltaire, and Hermann Samuel Reimarus. It is to the
latter that we now turn.

                        Hermann Samuel Reimarus

     Prior to Reimarus, neither the question "What is the his-
torical value of the gospels?" nor its corollary, "What was
the historical character of Jesus?," was raised. He was the
first to do so.
     Reimarus was born in Hamburg in 1694. After studying theol-
ogy, ancient languages, and philosophy at the University of
Jena, he joined the philosophical faculty in Wittenberg. In
1727, Reimarus became professor of Hebrew and oriental languages at Hamburg Academic Gymnasium.
     At his death, Reimarus left a manuscript of 4,000 pages
that is an apology for natural religion. Between 1774 and
1778, G.E. Lessing published seven portions of this work as
Fragmente des wolfenbüttelschen Ungenannten. The last two
fragments deal with the life of Jesus. The one that is best
known and concerns us here is "Von dem Zwecke Jesu und seiner
Jünger."[29]
     In retrospect, Reimarus' work was epoch making because he
was the first to present a historical conception of the life of
Jesus. He likewise pioneered in recognizing problems related

to the life of Jesus that were only recovered and developed
many years later.

   According to Reimarus, Jesus' message had a dual emphasis:
the necessity of repentance and the proclamation of the Kingdom
of God. His intention was to awaken Jewish nationalism and
to place himself at the head as the Messianic King. The Christian view of the Son of God and the atonement was a creation
of the disciples and did not correspond to Jesus' own views.
Jesus had no interest in revealing "articles of faith and mys-
teries." Jesus always remained a Jew and had no intention of
founding a new religion. He urged nothing more than purely
moral duties, a true love of God and one's neighbor; on these
points he based the whole content of the law and the prophets
and commanded that the hope of gaining his kingdom and salvation be constructed on them.[30]
   Jesus' attempt to free his people from political oppression
ended in failure. Out of this seeming failure the disciples
conceived a plan of action. Within twenty-four hours of the
crucifixion, they took the body of Jesus away. They waited
fifty days, during which time they claimed that Jesus had
spoken with them, had eaten with them, and at last had parted
from them, ascending into heaven that he might soon return in
glory.[31]
   In keeping with his deistic orientation, Reimarus rejected
two other fundamentals of orthodox faith--miracles and prophecy.
Miracles by themselves cannot establish a single article of
faith. They are the "invention" of the disciples and are
secondary and unessential to faith. Those who would establish miracles "seek to work upon the credulity of ignorant and
weak-minded people."[32]
   As for Old Testament prophecies, Reimarus sought to show
that they are "worthless and false." They never came to pass
and in reality refer to quite other things than those ascribed
to them. Not a single sentence from the Old Testament applied
by Matthew and others to the history of Jesus was written in
the sense ascribed to it. In short, "One cannot refer to a
single quoted prophecy that is not false."[33]
   As might be expected, Reimarus' work produced a considerable
sensation and was offensive to orthodox belief. Approaching the
gospels as a rationalist, Reimarus stripped Jesus of his metaphysical and dogmatic being and saw him as only a prophet and
moral teacher. His rationalizing of the resurrection and the
miracles were likewise controversial.
   Yet Reimarus is important for later Lives of Jesus research
in two areas. He placed much emphasis upon Jesus' hopes for
the future. It was this element in Reimarus that Albert Schweitzer naturally found so significant. He wrote: "His work is perhaps the most splendid achievement in the whole course of the his-

torical investigation of the life of Jesus, for he was the
first to grasp the fact that the world of thought in which
Jesus moved was essentially eschatological."[34] For Schweitzer,
however, Reimarus saw the eschatology in a wrong perspective.
He believed that Jesus' intention was to be a political ruler,
the son of David. As we shall see later, Schweitzer's view
was not political but apocalyptic.

Reimarus' second and more important contribution was his
recognition of the discontinuity between the teaching of Jesus
and that of the apostles. In emphasizing the development that
took place between the death of Jesus and the formation of the
church, Reimarus anticipated an issue that became a basic presupposition of form criticism.

Reimarus was far ahead of his time, and the critical problems he raised fell into oblivion and were not taken up again
until a long time after his death. As Schweitzer puts it:
"Thus the magnificent overture in which are announced all the
motifs of the future historical treatment of the life of Jesus
breaks off with a sudden discord, remains isolated and incomplete, and leads to nothing further."[35]

Rationalistic Lives

The work of Reimarus did not influence the movement that
followed. From the middle of the eighteenth century to about
1830, there appeared a series of "rationalistic" Lives of Jesus.
The spirit of rationalism is to accept only those religious
views that can be justified at the bar of reason. Moreover,
the origin of religion is interpreted by this same principle.
In examining this period, Schweitzer writes of an earlier
rationalism—whose representatives were Johann Jakob Hess,
Franz Vollkmar Reinhard, Ernst August Opitz, Johann Adolph
Jakobi, and to a lesser degree Johann Gottfried Herder—and
the fully developed rationalism of Heinrich Eberhard Gottlob
Paulus. A third and last phase of rationalism, according to
Schweitzer, was seen in Karl August Hase, Friedrich Ernst
Daniel Schleiermacher, and David Friedrich Strauss.[36]

For the earlier rationalists, the question of miracle was
not yet central. The teaching of Jesus and religion in general
are authentic because of their inner reasonableness, rather
than any outward evidence. These earlier rationalists did
not hesitate to reduce the number of miracles by explaining
those that rest on "natural causes." However, their interest
was not to eliminate all supernaturalism from the life of
Jesus. Schweitzer notes that the older rationalists were
wholly unhistorical. They were interested in history to the
degree that they found their rationalistic ideas in the past.

The problem of Jesus was solved for them by bringing him near
to their own time, portraying him as the great teacher of virtue
and showing that his teaching was identical with the intellectual truth that rationalism deified.[37]
Herder, like Reimarus, was ahead of his time. He was the
first and only scholar prior to Strauss who saw that a Life of
Jesus cannot be harmonized from all four gospels. Rather, a
choice must be made between the synoptics and John. In his
two books, *Vom Erlöser der Menschen: nach unseren drei ersten
Evangelien* (1796) and *Von Gottes Sohn, der Welt Heiland: nach
Johannes Evangelium* (1797), Herder held that the synoptic gospels are Palestinian and historical. They are marked by Palestinian ideals and beliefs and present Jesus as the Jewish
Messiah. The Fourth Gospel is more doctrinal than historical
and rests more of Greek ideas and beliefs. Its aim is to present Jesus as the savior of the world rather than the Jewish
Messiah. In the Fourth Gospel, miracles have only symbolic
value, illustrating religious and philosophical ideas. It was
composed later than the synoptic gospels.
Herder likewise suggested that of the synoptic gospels Mark
is the earliest. It is the cornerstone of all the gospels because it gives only the simplest unadorned details. Herder believed that the basis for the synoptics was a primitive oral
gospel narrated in brief form by the apostles in Aramaic. In
his gospel, Mark made little change from the primitive Aramaic
gospel. The second gospel was that of Luke, who added supplementary matter he had acquired. Matthew followed, adding what
he thought necessary.[38]
In his views on the gospels and their construction, Herder
was more than a generation ahead of his time. He was a pioneer
in the path later followed by Strauss and subsequently by
modern critical scholarship.
Before turning to Paulus, let us consider two other "rationalists" who wrote fictitious Lives of Jesus--Karl Friedrich
Bahrdt and Karl Heinrich Venturini.
Between 1784 and 1792, Bahrdt published an eleven-volume
work, *Ausführung des Plans und Zwecks Jesu*, and during 1800-
1802 Venturini wrote *Natürliche Geschichte des grossen Propheten
von Nazareth*, in four volumes. Schweitzer notes that Bahrdt
and Venturini were the first to apply, with logical consistency,
a non-supernatural interpretation of the gospel miracle stories.
Likewise, rather than being content with the simple reproduction
of the successive sections of the gospel narrative, they endeavored to grasp the inner connection of cause and effect in
the events and experiences of the life of Jesus.[39]
Since this connection was absent from the gospels, Bahrdt
and Venturini supplied it themselves. Jesus was instructed by
a secret order, the Essenes. According to Bahrdt, he became a

tool of the Essenes, who stage-managed the miracles. The
miracles were clever illusions produced by the Essenes. The
resurrection was also "staged" and was imaginary. Luke, the
physician, gave Jesus powerful drugs that enabled him to endure
the utmost pain and suffering and also resist death for a long
time. After a short time on the cross, Jesus was rushed into
an Essene cave, where he was resuscitated. Venturini's account
of the resurrection differed somewhat from Bahrdt's, but for
both the Essenes were prominent, and the event of the resurrection, as well as all the other miracles, was explicable by
natural causes. However, to the uninitiated they appear to
be miraculous and supernatural.[40]

The rationalistic tendency attained its most thorough
development in Paulus' *Das Leben Jesu als Grundlage einer reinen
Geschichte des Urchristentums* (1828). The first part gives a
section-by-section, historical exposition of the gospels. The
second part is a synopsis interspersed with supplementary
material. Schweitzer observes that there is no attempt to
present the life of Jesus as a connected whole. The basic plan
for the work is taken from the Fourth Gospel.[41]

The main interest in Paulus' Life of Jesus is in the explanation of miracles, although this was not his intention.
There are two basic points about miracles: that unexplained
alterations of the course of nature can neither overthrow nor
attest a spiritual truth, and that everything that happens in
nature emanates from the omnipotence of God. The biblical
miracles are the result of secondary causes that the eye-wit-
nesses did not understand. Their knowledge of the laws of
nature was inadequate so that they did not understand what
actually happened.[42]

Except for the birth of Jesus, Paulus rationalized the
miracles by attributing them to natural causes. The miracles
of healing, for example, resulted from Jesus working through
his spiritual power upon the nervous system of the sufferer,
or sometimes he used medicine that he alone knew about.

The nature miracles suggest their own explanation. Jesus
walking on the water is an example. The disciples had an il-
lusory conception of what happened. Jesus walked along the
shore and in the mist was taken for a ghost by the distraught
occupants of the boat. As for the feeding of the multitudes,
the rich among them shared their abundance, and Jesus began to
distribute his own and the disciples' provisions to the people
sitting near them. The example was contagious, and soon there
was plenty for everyone.

The resurrection is in the same category. Jesus was laid
into the tomb while in a deathlike trance. The cool grave and
the aromatic unguents continued the process of resuscitation.
The storm and the earthquake aroused Jesus to full consciousness.

The earthquake also rolled away the stone from the tomb, enabling Jesus to come forth. He lived with his followers for forty days. They never knew where Jesus finally died, and so they described his departure as an ascension.[43]

Schweitzer concludes his discussion of the rationalistic Lives of Jesus by referring to the "last phase of rationalism," represented by Karl August Hase and the renowned theologian Friedrich Schleiermacher. They still clung to the rationalistic explanation of miracle. However, they were content to leave a question mark instead of offering a solution. Moreover, they went beyond rationalism because they endeavored to grasp the inner connection of the events of Jesus' ministry.[44]

Hase was a professor at Jena for many years. Schweitzer is laudatory in his evaluation of him. He believes that Hase was more than a theologian; he was one of the finest monuments of German culture. In his *Das Leben Jesu zunächst für akademische Studien*, Hase divided Jesus' life into two periods. In the first, he accepted almost without reservation the popular ideas regarding the messianic age. In the second, he abandoned these ideas and developed his own distinctive views. Schweitzer notes that Hase was the first to speak of two periods in Jesus' life, and that through the influence of Theodor Keim and Heinrich Julius Holtzmann it became the prevailing view and determined the plan of all Lives of Jesus down to Johannes Weiss. Schweitzer also credits Hase with the creation of the modern historico-psychological picture of Jesus.[45]

Friedrich Schleiermacher

Schleiermacher's *Das Leben Jesu*, published after his death in 1864, was reconstructed from a student's notebook of a course of lectures that Schleiermacher delivered in 1832. He was the first person to lecture publicly on the topic of the Life of Jesus. Books had appeared on the life of Jesus, but Schleiermacher was apparently the first to make the life of Jesus a distinct part of academic studies. He began his lectures in 1819 and repeated them five times during the next thirteen years.

Schleiermacher's *Das Leben Jesu* reflected the concern of the theologian more than that of the historian. His understanding of biography was that one must grasp the inner quality of a person's life-development as a unity. Schleiermacher set forth the relationship between the outer and the inner, between the historical and the theological, thus:

> And so we shall be able to follow no other rule than
> this: everything that appears in Christ's individuality

as a life-moment appears as a deed and an action, and
it must be able to be apprehended in its historical connection in a purely human way; but nevertheless, we conceive it as the expression or effect of God which was
internal.[46]

As for the question of the sources of a Life of Jesus,
Schleiermacher pointed out that the four canonical gospels
are our main source, but they are inadequate for the construction of a detailed biography of Jesus. There are essentially
two sources--the Gospel of John and the three synoptic gospels.
Of the two, Schleiermacher preferred John, but it too is inadequate. He wrote:

> The Gospel of John has always given me the impression
> that in a decisive way it bears the character of a co-
> herent, comprehensive presentation, but not to the ex-
> tent that what it reproduces would be sufficient for
> our task, for not only does it entirely disregard Jesus'
> earlier life but also admittedly has many gaps, and
> therefore a Life of Jesus cannot be reconstructed from
> it as it actually should be; and yet it constitutes all
> our material![47]

Schleiermacher divided Jesus' life into three periods that
must be kept separate from each other. The first period is
what happened before Jesus' public ministry. However, we have
the fewest coherent accounts of this period, and we actually
know nothing at all of what immediately preceded his public
ministry. Consequently, the two major periods in Jesus' life
were his public life until his arrest and the period from the
arrest to the ascension. Schleiermacher's description of
these periods comprises the major part of his work.[48]

In his discussion of Schleiermacher, Schweitzer characterizes him as a master dialectician. His dialectic was directed
toward a presentation of the dogmatic Christ rather than the
historical Jesus. One aspect of Schleiermacher's dialectic
concerned the external and the internal features of Christ's
activity. As noted above, Schleiermacher was concerned primarily with the internal. A basic element of the internal was
Christ's consciousness of God. One reason for Schleiermacher's
preference of the Gospel of John was that John presents Christ's
God-consciousness most forcefully. Christ stood in a unique
relationship to God in that God had entered his life and he
was conscious of God's presence in a very special way. Thus,
it was natural that Christ should represent himself as the
truth and as the source of truth for others. Salvation was
grounded in him and in his ability to communicate his consciousness of God to others.[49]

In reference to miracles, Schleiermacher arranged them in an ascending scale of probability, with the miracles of healing as most plausible because they are analogous to the removal of pathological conditions by mental influence. Schleiermacher preferred John to the synoptics because the former usually includes individual miracles in his account only to the extent that they give rise to other acts or to Jesus' discourses, which are a necessary element of his gospel.[50]

In his preference for the Gospel of John, Schleiermacher was at variance with the prevailing view of subsequent gospel criticism. One can sympathize with Schweitzer's observation that Schleiermacher's antipathy to the synoptists depended more upon his dogmatic presuppositions than upon his critical analysis of the gospels.[51] It was David Friedrich Strauss, more than anyone else, who altered the situation by rejecting the historicity of John and preferring the synoptics for a reconstruction of the life of Jesus.

David Friedrich Strauss

The year 1835 was an important one in Lives of Jesus history. It marked the publication of David Friedrich Strauss' *Das Leben Jesu, kritisch bearbeitet*, which appeared in four editions between 1835 and 1840. Without a doubt, it aroused more excitement and controversy than any work about Jesus before or since. The negative reaction to Strauss' *Leben Jesu* was so intense that he was relieved of his academic post at Tübingen. He returned home to Ludwigsburg, where he taught philology for a time. In the fall of 1836, he departed for Stuttgart and began a freelance career of writing and research. His professorial career was at an end.

Against the background of Hegelian dialectic, Strauss rejected both the supernaturalistic and the rationalistic interpretations of Jesus, proposing a new mode, the mythical, for considering the life of Jesus. Both the supernaturalists and the rationalists held that the gospels contained authentic history. For the former, this history was supernatural, while for the latter it was unadulterated, though only natural. Both views had to be relinquished, and the inquiry had first to be made whether in fact, and to what extent, the gospel records are historical.[52]

Judaism and Christianity, like all religions, have their myths. Religion can be defined as the perception of truth, not in the form of an idea, but as imagery. Myths are expressions in storylike form of temporally conditioned religious ideas.[53]

Strauss attempted to describe myth by examining two grada-
tions of myth in the gospels. The *evangelical mythus* is a
narrative relating directly or indirectly to Jesus, which may
be considered not as the expression of a fact but as a product
of an idea of his earliest followers. The transfiguration and
the rending of the veil of the temple are examples of *evangelical
mythi*.

The *historical mythus* has for its basis a definite individual fact that reflects religious enthusiasm and has been surrounded by mythical conceptions drawn from Christological ideas.
Examples are Jesus' pronouncements concerning "fishers of men"
or the barren fig tree. The baptism also falls into this
category.

The mythical view deals with the unhistorical, which the
myth embodies. It may have formed gradually by tradition or
have been created by an individual author. In each case, however, it is the product of an *idea*. Strauss' intention was
not to reject the historical elements that the gospels contain.
Rather, it was the unhistorical to which his understanding of
myth exclusively referred.[54]

But how shall one distinguish between the historical and
the unhistorical? Strauss viewed as unhistorical those occurrences where not merely the particular nature and manner are
critically suspicious, their external circumstances represented
as miraculous and the like, but also those occurrences where
the essential substance and groundwork are either inconceivable
in themselves or are in striking harmony with some messianic
idea of the Jews of that age.

Strauss' judgment as to when an occurrence is historical
appeared less certain than his judgment of unhistoricality.
If the form only, and not the general contents of the narration, exhibits the characteristics of the unhistorical, it is
at least possible to suppose a kernel of historical fact. But
we can never confidently decide whether this kernel of fact
actually exists, or of what it consists, unless it can be discovered from other sources.

The boundary line between the historical and the unhistorical in the gospels will remain fluctuating and unsuscep-
tible of precise attainment. Strauss cautioned those who expect that the "first comprehensive attempt to treat these
records from a critical point of view" would be successful in
drawing a sharply defined line of demarcation.[55]

Strauss had no intention of producing a Life of Jesus
based on the gospel materials that criticism had judged "historically sound." The Christian faith is independent of criticism. The supernatural birth of Christ, his miracles, his
resurrection and ascension remain eternal truths in spite of
doubts about their historical authenticity.[56]

In his treatment of miracles, Strauss distinguished between two types. The first is miracle in the strict sense of supernatural intervention and the exercise of divine power over nature or animals. The second involves cures of human beings based on ordinary powers of nature, such as medicinal and psychical. Strauss analyzed the cures of Jesus in an order of descending probability. All the miracles are products of mythical tradition. In certain instances of mental or nervous disorders, a historical kernel can be uncovered that enables one to offer a natural or psychological explanation.[57]

As Strauss saw Jesus' religious consciousness, Jesus believed himself to be the Messiah and came to identify himself with the messianic Son of Man. As Jesus' life drew to a close, he predicted that soon after the destruction of Jerusalem and the temple he would visibly come in the clouds of heaven as the Son of Man and terminate the existing dispensation. Jesus came to accept the necessity of suffering and death as part of his messianic office. This would be the means by which the messianic age would be ushered in through the supernatural power of God, rather than by political revolution. It was this eventuality for which Jesus sought to prepare the disciples.[58]

One of Strauss' most significant contributions to Life of Jesus research was his preference for the synoptic gospels over the Gospel of John, a view that has largely prevailed to the present time. Of the synoptic gospels, Strauss preferred Matthew, believing that it represents the closest approximation to truth. The Gospel of John is so preoccupied with dogmatic concerns that its historical value is dubious.[59] But though Strauss held definite views about the historical value of the gospels, he had no definite theory about their composition or their relationship to each other. Advance in these areas occurred in 1838, when Christian Gottlob Wilke and Christian Hermann Weisse, working independently, concluded that Mark was the earliest of the synoptics and had been used as a source by both Matthew and Luke.[60] The priority of Mark continues as the overwhelming majority opinion of critical gospel research.

With the advent of gospel criticism, it became commonplace to question the historicity of the miracles and of other events in the life of Jesus, such as the birth stories, baptism, and temptation. It remained, however, for Bruno Bauer to deny the historicity of Jesus himself.

Bruno Bauer

Bauer was born in 1809. In 1834, he became Privat-Docent in Berlin but moved to Bonn in 1839. Between 1840 and 1850, he published a number of volumes on the criticism of the gospels.

Bauer came to the conclusion that the Gospel of John together
with the synoptic gospels were literary creations. At first,
he rejected the idea that the evangelists invented the gospel
history and the personality of Jesus. Later, however, he became more radical.

Bauer's original intention was to reinstate the person of
Jesus into a living relation with history and rescue him from
the status to which the theologians and apologists had assigned
him. But Bauer became intrigued by the idea that Jesus Christ
may have been the product of the imagination of the early church.
What if the whole of Christianity was nothing but a literary
invention, not only the incidents and discourses but also the
person of Jesus? What if the only historical reality were a
late imaginary embodiment of a set of exalted ideas?

At last, Bauer turned to Rome and Alexandria for his explanation of Christianity's origin. There never was a historical Jesus. He was an imaginary being--a combination of
motifs drawn from Seneca, the Roman philosopher, and Philo,
the Jewish Alexandrian philosopher. The spirit of the new religion came from the West, but Judaism provided its external
frame. The experiences of the early church were attributed
to one great personality. Moreover, the contemporary religious
and philosophical ideas represented by Seneca and Philo were
adopted by early Christianity and were also ascribed to the
same single personality. It was out of this milieu that the
personality of Jesus emerged, but he had no real existence because he was the postulation of the evangelist.

Schweitzer categorizes Bauer's work as "the first skeptical
Life of Jesus." He ranks him with Reimarus and holds that they
were unique in their grasp of the extremely complex problems
surrounding the life of Jesus.[61]

Ernest Renan

The first life of Jesus to be published in a Catholic
country was Ernest Renan's *La Vie de Jésus* in 1863. It was
widely disseminated and had an enormous influence. Maurice
Goguel reports that ten editions appeared in its first year of
publication and three others in 1864. In 1864 a popular
abridged edition came out, and fifteen editions appeared that
year. Since then, there have been many other French editions
as well as translations into other languages.[62] The *Vie de
Jésus* engendered a larger critical literature than any other
Life of Jesus ever published. Its literary style attracted a
vast multitude of readers. Goguel notes that Renan's book is
as easy to read as Strauss' is difficult. Consequently, it
was read by many people who were unfamiliar with exegetical research.[63]

Like Strauss, Renan was controversial. The *Vie de Jésus* was placed on the Index of forbidden books, and the church offered prayers to counteract its influence. Renan rejected the conventional supernaturalistic view of the scriptures. He identified himself with Strauss and the rationalists in denying the occurrence of miracles. Unlike Strauss, Renan believed that the historian could recover sufficient material from the gospels in order to construct a Life of Jesus.

Though many critics speak of Renan's work as a literary masterpiece, they question its scholarly importance. Goguel quotes Colani, who observed that Renan thinks too much of beauty and not enough of the truth.[64] Klausner says that the *Vie de Jésus* owed its influence to its elegant style and its excellent arrangement, which lent unity to the inconsequent fragments of the gospels. Its psychological illustrations are often important and illumine narratives and facts that at first sight seem to have little value. But more important, according to Klausner, is the attention devoted to the geography of Palestine and especially the poetical picture of Galilee. Otherwise, it is not important. "It is rather a historical novel than a work of scholarship."[65]

In the introduction to the *Vie de Jésus*, Renan analyzed the gospels as sources for a Life of Jesus. As noted above, he rejected the notion of a divine origin of the scriptures. The gospels are in part legendary because they are full of miracles and of the supernatural. Renan concluded that the gospels are neither biographies nor fictitious legends; they are legendary biographies.

Of the synoptic gospels, Renan favored Luke because it is a work written entirely by the same hand and is of the most perfect unity. He did not find the same quality of individuality in Matthew and Mark. They are impersonal compositions in which the author totally disappears.

Renan diverged from Strauss in his evaluation of the Gospel of John, regarding it as a historical document and preferring it to the synoptics. Renan wrote that those who attempted to write a Life of Jesus without any predetermined theory as to the relative value of the gospels, letting themselves be guided solely by the sentiment of the subject, will be led in numerous instances to prefer the narration of John to that of the synoptics. He noted further that the author of the Fourth Gospel is in fact the better biographer.

Though the gospels reveal the spirit of Jesus, argues Renan, they have been embellished with legendary accretions. With the desire to picture Jesus, there was also the attempt to explain him. This is evident in the attempt to prove that in Jesus the messianic prophecies had been fulfilled. Consequently, only the most general features about Jesus can be

accepted as authentic. Renan observed that among the anec-
dotes, discourses, and celebrated sayings handed down by the
historians there is not one strictly authentic.
As for miracles, Renan was rationalistic and pragmatic.
None of the biblical miracles took place under scientific conditions. Miracles only happen in times and places where they
are believed and in the presence of persons disposed to believe
them. No miracle ever occurred in the presence of people capable
of testing its miraculous character. Miracles are rejected not
because of some theoretical reason but because of universal
experience. We do not say that miracles are impossible, but
we say that up to this time a miracle has never been proved.
Renan summarized his views about miracles with a "principle of
historical criticism." A supernatural account cannot be admitted as such because it always implies credulity or imposture.
The duty of the historian is to explain it and seek to ascertain
what share of truth or of error it may conceal.

Such skepticism about the sources for a Life of Jesus did
not deter Renan, because he had access to other "sources."
It was here that his imaginative and aesthetic faculties came
into play. In addition to the documentary evidence, Renan had
seen firsthand the places where the events occurred. In 1860
and 1861, he had directed a scientific exploration of ancient
Phonecia. He was able to travel frequently to Galilee, and he
traversed in all directions the country of the gospels. Scarcely
any important locality of the history of Jesus escaped him.
This was a revelation to Renan, and instead of the abstract
figure presented in Matthew and Mark he saw "living and moving
an admirable human figure." It was as if Renan had access to
a "Fifth Gospel," which though "torn" was still legible.[66]

Renan's work has a literary charm and romantic quality that
is compelling and unmistakable. Jesus becomes a sort of gentle
dreamer who wanders through Galilee, entranced with the goodness
of life. Who is not captivated by a Jesus described in such
terms as these:

> He returned, then, into his beloved Galilee, and found again
> his heavenly Father in the midst of the green hills and
> the clear fountains--and among the crowds of women and
> children, who with joyous soul and the song of angels in
> their hearts, awaited the salvation of Israel.... Thus
> as often happens in very elevated natures, tenderness of
> the heart was transformed in him into an infinite sweet-
> ness, a vague poetry, and a universal charm.[67]

The Jesus who emerges from Renan's *Vie de Jésus* was born
in Nazareth of poor parentage; he was brought up amid the
natural beauties of Galilee, which contributed much to his dis-
position; he became conscious of a close relationship with God;

"he lived in the bosom of God by constant communication with
him." However, he never succumbed to the "sacrilegious idea"
that he was God. God, conceived simply as Father, was all the
theology of Jesus.
    Jesus acquired a band of loyal followers. Influenced
by the apocalyptic views of John the Baptist, Jesus came to
regard himself as the Messiah. He became filled with revolu-
tionary zeal and abandoned the "innocent aphorisms" and the
"beautiful moral precepts" of his earlier career. He accepted
the messianic role and encouraged people to believe that he
was a miracle worker. Jesus was no longer himself, because
his sense of mission overwhelmed him. He came at last to Jerusalem, where his doom was imminent. He was finally crucified
as a martyr--the fate of a gentle teacher who was betrayed not
only by the cruelty of evil men but by his own inflated dreams
of his mission.
    With Jesus' death, the life of Jesus concludes for the his-
torian. But he left such an impression in the heart of his
disciples and of a few devoted women that it appeared to them
that he was still living and consoling them. The circumstances surrounding the resurrection can never be ascertained.
However, the imagination of Mary Magdalen was the decisive
factor. Renan wrote: "Let us say that the strong imagination
of Mary Magdalen played an important part in this circumstance.
Divine power of love! Sacred moments in which the passion of
one possessed gave the world a resuscitated God!"[68]
    Such in brief outline was Renan's *Life of Jesus*. It did
little to advance historical criticism of the gospels. Renan's
chief interest was not so much with the documents or sources
as with the impression they made upon him. He was more the
artist than the critic. His *Vie de Jésus* is marked by his
own personal interpretation. The imagination and intuition
of the artist supplements and embellishes the paucity of the
historical evidence. As Goguel views it, "Renan's one achievement was that he brought forward the problem of the life of
Jesus in such a way that henceforth it was impossible to with-
draw it from this leading position."[69]
    On the whole, Schweitzer's treatment of Renan is negative.
He makes the interesting comparison between the German and
French attraction to Renan. Germans find in Renan German
thought in a novel and piquant form. Conversely, the French
discover ideas belonging to a world that is foreign to them,
ideas that they can never completely assimilate but that yet
attract them. However, the *Vie de Jésus* reflected a basic
weakness. It was written by one to whom the New Testament
was something foreign. Renan was not accustomed to "breathe
freely in its simple and pure world." Instead, he "perfumed
it with sentimentality" in order to feel at home in it.[70]

Under Renan's aesthetic and naturalistic guise, the Jesus
of the New Testament is transformed. He is no longer the
supernatural miracle worker, or one immersed in eschatology,
or the Christ of the creeds. Rather, he is the epitome of
human sublimity. Let us recount Renan's evaluation of Jesus
in his conclusion of the *Vie de Jésus*:

> The sublime person we may call divine, not in the sense
> that Jesus has absorbed all the divine, or has been
> adequate to it, but in the sense that Jesus is the one
> who has caused his fellowmen to make the greatest step
> toward the divine.... There are pillars that rise
> toward the sky, and bear witness to a nobler destiny.
> Jesus is the highest of these pillars which show to man
> whence he comes, and whither he ought to tend. In him
> was condensed all that is good and elevated in our nature.
> He was not sinless.... But whatever may be the unexpected
> phenomena of the future, Jesus will not be surpassed.
> His worship will constantly renew its youth, the tale of
> his life will cause ceaseless tears, his sufferings will
> soften the best hearts; all the ages will proclaim that,
> among the sons of men, there is none born who is greater
> than Jesus.[71]

Liberal Lives

Following Renan, there were many Lives of Jesus written
from the liberal viewpoint. Schweitzer designates them as
"the liberal Lives of Jesus." Among them were books by David
Friedrich Strauss, Daniel Schenkel, Karl Heinrich Weizsäcker,
Heinrich Julius Holtzmann, Theodor Keim, Karl Hase, Willibald
Beyschlag, and Bernhard Weiss. Though these works were quite
diverse in their views about the sources and about Jesus' person and thought, they did possess a certain likeness. They
tended to modernize Jesus and clothe him in contemporary
thought forms. Klausner notes that these "Liberal Lives"
became non-historical. Jesus was not primarily a Messiah but
a religious man and an ethical teacher. His eschatological
pronouncements were either eliminated or spiritualized, since
they were "foreign" to the "spirit of the age." Jesus became
more antagonistic to ancient Judaism, more replete with new
ethical ideas—and less historical.[72]
But perhaps most typical of all was the recourse of these
scholars to psychological reconstruction and interpretation
in order to compensate for the insufficient connection between
the incidents recorded in the gospels. Schweitzer observes
that they resorted to the modern "psychological" method of
reading between the lines of the Marcan narrative, which most
of them accepted as the best outline of the life of Jesus.[73]

British Lives of Jesus

Our examination of the Lives of Jesus since the time of
Reimarus has been almost exclusively of German works. Renan
has been the lone exception. Most interpreters of the modern
Lives of Jesus and of the quest of the historical Jesus have
followed Schweitzer's work which, except for Renan, deals with
German scholarship. A significant departure from this pattern
is Daniel L. Pals' *The Victorian "Lives" of Jesus*, which was
published in 1982. He surveys the British Lives of Jesus,
especially after about 1860.

Pals makes some interesting comparisons between the German
and the British Lives of Jesus. German critics came nearer
achieving a tradition of pure scholarship. British writers,
even when unorthodox, tried to turn scholarship into public
literature. They endeavored to bridge the gap between scholarship and the common reader. Pals observes that the Victorian
Lives of Jesus scholars did not depart from the strong conviction that the claims of genuine biblical science, orthodox
faith, and popular religious edification could be united without
strain or sacrifice.[74]

One of the most widely discussed, controversial, and influential British Lives of Jesus was published anonymously in 1865
under the title *Ecce Homo: A Survey of the Life and Work of
Christ*. Eleven years later, John Robert Seeley, Professor of
Latin in University College, London, was discovered to be the
author. It passed into new editions almost every other year
up to 1888 and beyond. It was reviewed extensively, and there
were at least nine essays and responses published in book form.
One of the major criticisms of *Ecce Homo* was that it lacked
theological content. Seeley's intention was "to lay aside the
vexing theological issues of the biblical story and begin with
those human, historical phenomena which are easiest to grasp."[75]
Pals characterizes *Ecce Homo* as edging its way quietly between
the skeptical productions of continental criticism and the
devotional, conservative works that prevailed in Britain.
It produced its own unique, enticing image of Jesus.[76]

Pals suggests that Seeley did for Great Britain what Renan
did for the continent. He lifted discussion about Jesus out
of the academic environment and brought it into the broad
forums of public discussion. *Ecce Homo* convinced scholars
that a definitive historical Life of Jesus could be written
for Victorian believers. Seeley was a pathfinder who laid out
an approach to the life of Jesus that subsequent writers could
follow.[77]

Following 1860, the number of Lives of Jesus increased
rapidly. One of the most ambitious works was William Hanna's
The Life of Our Lord upon Earth, which ran to six volumes. It

was practical and devotional in nature.

In addition to the more conventional works, there were rationalistic Lives of Jesus by Richard Davies Hanson and Thomas Scott. These writings, according to Pals, did not measure up to their German counterparts in seriousness or scholarship. They were "present-day controversialists, carrying on a contemporary argument in historical guise." Jesus turned out to be a "first-century, socially progressive free-thinker." The form of these Lives was identical with that of the religious Lives, since their aim was popular persuasion.[78]

The most "successful" Victorian Life was Frederic William Farrar's *The Life of Christ*, published in 1874. In a short time, more than thirty editions appeared, and sales mounted to 100,000. It remained popular through the 1890s. Pals observes that Farrar's work combined true faith and real scholarship and that it reflected the novelist's psychological insight and literary style. In addition, like Renan's, Farrar's travels through the Holy Land afforded him a "Fifth Gospel," which enabled him to see Jesus amid the scenic romance of Palestine. Pals notes that Farrar, more than any other Victorian, was sensitive to the magical power of the life and landscape of the Near East. Moreover, no one exceeded him in recreating these scenes with such a wealth of colorful and descriptive imagery.

Farrar's approach to the sources was conservative in comparison with critical German scholarship. He viewed the Gospel of John as an authentic and historical source for a Life of Jesus. The gospels were basically trustworthy, and, given the circumstances of their composition, they were strikingly accurate.

So influential was Farrar's *The Life of Christ* that Pals says that from 1874 to the end of the century almost every successful British Life was to draw heavily upon the model shaped by Farrar. According to Pals, Farrar's work represented a fusion of orthodoxy, scholarship, appealing style, a venerable human Christ, and the glow of antiquarianism and oriental romance.[79]

Of the several works that appeared in the years immediately after Farrar's *Life of Christ*, the most important was *Life and Words of Christ*, by Cunningham Geikie. It was published in two volumes in 1877.

Theologically, Geikie was traditional and orthodox. The novelty of his work was the painstaking care with which he filled in the historical scene and the context. He was a student of late Judaism and the political and geographical context of Jesus' time. Pals' evaluation of *Life and Words of Christ* is that it tended to psychologize characters and did not give serious attention to critical questions about his sources.[80]

Like Farrar's *Life of Christ*, Geikie's *Life* was highly popular. There were new editions and impressive sales well into the first decade of the twentieth century. By the time of Geikie's death, sales of *Life and Words of Christ* exceeded 100,000.

More modest in length than Farrar's and Geikie's were Lives by three Scotsmen. James Stalker, a Scottish Free Church pastor from Aberdeen, published his *Life of Christ* in 1879. It represented a simple retelling of the life of Jesus with orthodox theological presuppositions. By about 1915, sales had reached 100,000.

In 1880, *Studies in the Life of Christ* was published by A.M. Fairbairn, a distinguished Congregational theologian. It consisted of a series of essays arranging the life of Jesus chronologically. Fairbairn's basic intention was to reaffirm orthodoxy and to substantiate the reliability of the gospel texts.

The third Scot was William Robertson Nicoll, whose *The Incarnate Saviour* appeared in 1881. Pals notes that Nicoll stayed close to the biblical events and accepted the traditional view that the four gospels are complimentary and equally valid as historical sources. He made only modest attempts at anything approaching historical criticism. The Lives by Stalker, Fairbairn, and Nicoll were within the Victorian pattern of combining orthodox theology with a serious, though appealing, interpretation of Jesus.[81]

The final British Life that we shall note is Alfred Edersheim's two-volume *Life and Times of Jesus the Messiah* (1883). Edersheim was a converted Jew who was born in Vienna and who studied under Hengstenberg and Neander in Berlin. After emigrating to Scotland, he converted to Christianity and for a time was a Presbyterian pastor.

Edersheim's intimate and extensive knowledge of Judaism lent a dimension to his work unparalleled by other British Lives of Jesus. Pals observes that Edersheim's work had expanded his already formidable grasp of the Jewish world to a point where no other English-speaking scholar was a match for him. He treated the Jewish world in depth and often devoted pages to seemingly minor details, such as rabbis' clothing or the precise character of Jewish writing materials.

Edersheim's erudition, however, did not extend to a criticism of the gospels to the extent of his German contemporaries. He viewed the gospels as authentic and accurate and as the product of the apostles themselves, or, in the case of Mark and Luke, as the result of direct access to the apostles as a supplement to their own reminiscence.

Not only was Edersheim a conservative critic, he was also a strict adherent to theological orthodoxy. He accepted the authenticity of miracles and viewed them as crucial to the gospel record and as an affirmation of Christ's divinity. He also defended inspiration, atonement, resurrection, and supernaturalism.

Though Edersheim's *Life and Times of Jesus the Messiah* is
a lengthy and scholarly work, it gained a wide readership.
He was partly successful in the difficult task of popularizing
scholarship. The book was in print for twenty-five years,
and printings were made at regular intervals until 1908.
These were supplemented after 1890 by an abridged edition.[82]

Pals observes that the impact of the Lives of Jesus on
Victorian society and religious sensibilities was deep and
even decisive. Not only did the human Christ become more
real, but the Lives played a pivotal role in British Christianity's acceptance of biblical higher criticism. Pals writes:
"In the last quarter of the Victorian era they stood out as
the most visible and publicly comprehensible exhibit of the
benefits which newer historical scholarship offered the religious community. They provided a bridge of reassurance over
which the churches passed undamaged—though not unshaken—to
the acceptance of biblical higher criticism."[83]

Nineteenth-century Lives of Jesus research, with its attempt to recover the "real Jesus," is one of the most impressive undertakings in religious scholarship. Albert Schweitzer
notes that in retrospect German theology will stand out as a
great, a unique, phenomenon in the mental and spiritual life
of our time. He adds that the greatest achievement of German
theology is the critical investigation of the life of Jesus.
It laid down the conditions and determined the course of the
religious thinking of the future. Schweitzer concludes that it
is impossible to overestimate the value of what German research
into the life of Jesus has accomplished. It is a uniquely great
expression of sincerity, one of the most significant events
in the whole mental and spiritual life of humanity.[84]

But a time of questioning and doubt inevitably arose. As
the century drew to its close, fundamental challenges were
being leveled against the Life of Jesus presuppositions and
methodology. At the very moment that scholars were coming
closer to the historical Jesus than ever before, and were
already welcoming him into their own time, he began to fade
from their sight and to return to his own time. It was not,
however, orthodoxy that threatened the liberal Lives of Jesus
movement but the work of historical criticism.

History of Religions School

During the final decade of the nineteenth century, there
arose in Germany a movement that, though short-lived, had a
significant influence upon the interpretation of Jesus and the
origin of Christianity. It was the so-called History of Religions School (*Religionsgeschichtliche Schule*). Among those

related to this movement were some of the most eminent names in German biblical scholarship: Wilhelm Heitmüller, Hermann Gunkel, Wilhelm Bousset, William Wrede, Johannes Weiss, and Ernst Troeltsch.

The History of Religions School posed two basic questions that had a vital bearing upon the liberal view of Jesus. They questioned the claim that the full and final revelation of God has been mediated through the facts of history. History is a transient and relative phenomenon. Jesus comes from an era quite different from our own. Why should we base our faith upon so remote and uncertain a foundation as the historically demonstrable facts of the life of Jesus?

A second problem concerned the relationship between Christianity and other religions. Except for examining the influence of Judaism and the Old Testament, liberal scholarship had treated Christianity as an isolated entity. Why had the Hellenistic background of the New Testament been ignored?[85]

The History of Religions School attempted to illuminate the wider religious and cultural milieu from which Christianity emerged. It placed Jesus in his own time and sought to explain him by reference to its presuppositions. The School consistently regarded primitive Christianity as a product of ancient thought, as a result of the religious development of its time. Christianity was profoundly influenced by dynamic religious movements from the East. It was a syncretistic religion composed of the most disparate elements, Jewish, Greek, and oriental. There were rabbinic Judaism and Hellenistic Jewish enlightenments, Stoic ethics, Greek mystery religions, asceticism, Gnosticism, intellectual reflection, ecstatic mysticism. Such was the soil in which primitive Christianity was said to have grown up.[86]

In view of this analysis of early Christianity, the significance of the historical Jesus was minimized. In his book *Kyrios Christos*, Wilhelm Bousset maintained that Jesus became "Lord" in the context of Hellenistic influences and that this took place in a way analogous to the pagan worship of cult deities. Just as the pagan cultic communities assembled before their "Lord"--whether Serapis, Mithras, or Dionysus--and worshiped him, so too the Christians worshiped their "Lord," Jesus. They confessed his name, baptized in his name, and gathered around his table to eat and drink his flesh and blood.

Thus, history gave way to cultic practice. What Jesus had said and what he had done were unimportant. In place of the unique historical figure, there emerged the constantly present head of the cult, the symbol. Bousset wrote: "What is purely historical can never be of any effect, but only the present living symbol in which one's own religious conviction is presented in a transfigured form."[87]

The inevitable question arises as to why Jesus was not abandoned in favor of a myth or metaphysical principle. Why be concerned with history at all? The eminent religious sociologist Ernst Troeltsch spoke to this issue. He maintained that each religious community has need of a concrete center point, a cultic "symbol," a "means of union and illustration." But community and cult are dependent upon a historical person. People need more than myth; they want real, vivid life. Symbols of faith must be grounded in a real person. Consequently, Jesus is necessary for the religious life, not for reasons of dogma but for reasons of social psychology. In Troeltsch, therefore, historicism makes way for both metaphysics and sociology.[88]

Another outgrowth of the History of Religions School was the dichotomy between Jesus and Paul. Hermann Gunkel asserted that it is not the gospel of Jesus that is a syncretistic religion, but the primitive Christianity of Paul and John. William Wrede characterized Paul as the "perverter" of the gospel of Jesus. He wrote: "Jesus knows nothing of that which for Paul is everything"; and of Paul: "In comparison with Jesus he is a new phenomenon, as new as is possible with their one great common foundation. He is much further removed from Jesus than Jesus himself is removed from the most noble figure of Jewish piety." Thus, Paul is "the second founder of Christianity." The choice becomes "Jesus or Paul." There is a religion *of* Jesus and a religion *about* Jesus, and the two are radically different. There is a marked discontinuity between the historical Jesus and the Christ of faith.[89]

Martin Kähler

In 1892, there appeared a work that was to have a pronounced impact upon subsequent gospel criticism and the Lives of Jesus movement. It was Martin Kähler's *Der sogennante historische Jesus und der geschichtliche, biblische Christus.* Like Reimarus, Kähler was ahead of his time. There is no mention of Kähler in Schweitzer's *Quest of the Historical Jesus*, which appeared fourteen years later. However, motifs that Kähler developed influenced form criticism and the later kerygma theology of Rudolf Bultmann and his followers. Writing in 1964, Paul Tillich, who was one of Kähler's few surviving pupils, expressed delight in the fact that "a kind of Kähler revival is taking place." Kähler's work has appeared in six German printings and in a 1964 English translation by Carl E. Braaten.

Kähler sets himself unequivocally against the "quest of the historical Jesus." He writes:

I wish to summarize my cry of warning in a form inten-
tionally audacious: *the historical Jesus of modern authors
conceals from us the living Christ.* The Jesus of the
"Life of Jesus movement" is merely a modern example of
human creativity, and not an iota better than the no-
torious dogmatic Christ of Byzantine Christology. One
is as far removed from the real Christ as is the other.
In this respect historicism is just as arbitrary, just
as humanly arrogant, just as impertinent and "faithlessly
gnostic" as that dogmatism which in its day was also
considered modern.[90]

What is the meaning of the term "historical Jesus"? Kähler
says that originally it was used to set the biblical Christ
over against the dogmatic Christ. Later, it was believed that
one had to go behind the preaching of the apostles to their
sources in order to find the historical Jesus. It was discovered, however, that the gospel writers were themselves
authors and that the gospels consequently reflected biases
and distortions. Therefore, the only remaining course was to
embark on the quest of the historical Jesus who was faintly
discernible behind the primitive Christian reports. Kähler
observed that it was this enterprise that many of his contemporaries were pursuing with great zeal. His task was twofold:
to criticize and reject the wrong aspects of this approach to
the life of Jesus, and to establish the validity of an alterna-
tive approach. For Kähler, the latter was the more important.[91]

Kähler maintained that the entire Life of Jesus movement
was a "blind alley." We have no sources for a biography of
Jesus that measure up to the standards of contemporary historical science. The psychological approach suffers the same
limitations because the New Testament presentations were not
written for the purpose of describing how Jesus developed.
There is a uniqueness about Jesus that sets him above our
psychologizing and our principles of analogy. The distinction
between Jesus Christ and ourselves is one not of degree but
of kind. Kähler believed that the inner development of a
sinless person is as inconceivable to us as life on the Sandwich
Islands is to a Laplander.[92]

Kähler admitted that historical research can help to explain and clarify particular features of Jesus' actions and
attitudes, as well as many aspects of his teaching. The historian can also describe the historical institutions and
forces that influenced the human development of Jesus. But
such insights are never adequate for the production of a biographical work in the modern sense. What happens, therefore,
is that the "biographers" of Jesus resort to imagination in
order to reconstruct the early period of Jesus' life and to

explain the course of his spiritual development during his
public ministry. The result is that some "outside force" must
rework the fragments of the tradition. "This force is nothing
other than the theologian's imagination--an imagination that
has been shaped and nourished by the analogy of his own life
and of human life in general."[93] Many of Kähler's contemporaries were "on guard against dogma." However, they failed
to discern the dogmatic elements when a Christology appeared
in the form of a "Life of Jesus." This too was dogma--dogma
now disguised as history, dogma refracted through the spirit
of the writers themselves.

How then do we come to know Jesus? If the way is through
historical science, only a relatively few will have access
to him because only they can carry on the work of historical
science and are sufficiently trained to evaluate such work.
Historical research requires the mastery of a sophisticated
technique and significant erudition. If this is the path to
Jesus, the vast majority are excluded.

For Kähler, the real Jesus is not the "historical Jesus"
but the "historic Christ." Kähler helped to create a distinction, which continues in German theology, between *historisch* and *geschichtlich*. The "historical Jesus" is not the
earthly Jesus, as such, but the Jesus who is the object of
historical-critical research. The "historic Christ," on the
other hand, is the object of faith, the content of preaching,
and the one confessed by the believing community as Lord,
Messiah, and Redeemer.

Carl Braaten points out the distinction between *Historie*
and *Geschichte* in the following pairs of terms: objective
history and existential history, outer history and inner history, or even writing history and making history. Following
the practice of Reginald H. Fuller in his translation of
Kerygma und Mythos I (*Kerygma and Myth*. London: SPCK, 1964),
he translated *historisch* as "historical" and *geschichtlich*
as "historic." There is a difference between a "historical"
fact and a "historic" event. A historic event has great significance for the future and is remembered by posterity as
determinative in the continuous life of people. A historical
fact may be completely insignificant to anyone and registered
as a mere disconnected jot in an ancient chronicle.[94]

It is the historic Christ who is decisive for Kähler.
"The risen Lord is not the historical Jesus *behind* the gospels, but the Christ of the apostolic preaching, of the *whole*
New Testament." To confess Christ is to confess his unique,
supra-historical significance for the whole of humanity. The
real Christ is the Christ who is preached.[95]

The historic Christ or the Christ of faith confronts us
in the pages of the Bible. The biblical Christ is the really

historical Christ and the only figure worthy of our faith.
Moreover, in relation to the Christ in whom we may and should
believe, the most learned theologian must be in no better or
worse a position than the simple Christian. Kähler's dis-
illusionment with historicism was further evidence when he
wrote:

> As the simple scriptural theology of Pietism once de-
> posed the dogmaticians from their papacy of learning,
> so today it is the task of the dogmatician, in defense
> of the plain Christian faith, to set limits to the
> learned pontificating of the historians. They "occupy
> a larger territory than they can maintain." They under-
> take to satisfy the demands of a merely scientific
> curiosity while lacking means adequate to the task; at
> the same time they fail to observe clearly and decisively
> the boundary between the concern of the scientific im-
> pulse and that of faith in Christ.[96]

Kähler was completely skeptical about the possibility of
constructing a biography of Jesus from the gospels. They are
too sketchy, and their authors' interest was not historical
but dogmatic. In an arresting phrase, Kähler characterized
the gospels as "passion narratives with extended introduc-
tions."[97] It is through the gospel accounts that we are able
to come into contact with Christ. But these accounts are not
the reports of impartial and objective observers; rather, they
are the *testimonies* and *confessions* of believers in Christ.[98]
Consequently, we cannot bypass the primitive Christian testimony about Christ and get back to the "real Jesus"--the "Jesus
of history." The historical facts cannot be separated from
their interpretation and proclamation.

Though Kähler's answer to the problem of historical research has proven insufficient in view of the later methods
and conclusions of form criticism, his recognition of the
kerygmatic character of the sayings about Jesus has remained
influential and significant to the present time. His insistence that the certainty of faith is independent from historical research was a much-needed corrective to the historicism
that pervaded the nineteenth-century Lives of Jesus movement.[99]

Johannes Weiss

In the same year (1892) that Kähler's *Der sogennante historische Jesu und der geschichtliche, biblische Christus* was
published, another work appeared that was to have a profound
impact upon subsequent New Testament criticism and theology.
It was *Die Predigt Jesu vom Reiche Gottes*, by Johannes Weiss.

The concept of the Kingdom of God as developed by liberalism was the rule of God in the hearts of persons or the exercise of the moral life to realize the ideal society. Jesus became a moral exemplar and a religious teacher, and the Kingdom of God that he proclaimed became an inner kingdom of values and a timeless ideal.

Weiss begins *Die Predigt* by acknowledging the gratifying and promising aspects of recent theology's serious attention to and emphasis upon the concept of "Kingdom of God." However, he suggested that it is necessary to submit the historical foundations of this concept to a thorough investigation because there is always the danger of stripping biblical concepts of their original historical character by reinterpreting or converting them to new purposes in accordance with new viewpoints. Weiss proposed that a fresh attempt should be made to identify the original meaning that Jesus connected with the words "Kingdom of God."[100]

Weiss' investigation revealed that Jesus' conception of the Kingdom of God was radically supra-worldly and stood in diametric opposition to the world. This means that there can be no talk of an *inner-worldly* development of the Kingdom of God in the mind of Jesus. Liberalism's stripping away of the original eschatological-apocalyptical meaning of the idea was unjustified. It is "unbiblical" to use the term in a sense different from that of Jesus'.[101]

The conception that the Kingdom of God is the supreme ethical ideal or an inner-worldly entity that can be actualized by human initiative is contrary to Jesus' view. Weiss wrote:

> The actualization of the Kingdom of God is *not* a matter for human initiative, but entirely a matter of God's initiative. The only thing man can do about it is to perform the conditions required by God. The Kingdom of God, in Jesus' view, is never an ethical ideal, but is *nothing other than the highest religious Good*, a Good which God grants on certain conditions.[102]

Weiss' eschatological interpretation made it clear that Jesus was not a modern man and that the historical Jesus could no longer be identified with the modern Jesus of the liberal Lives of Jesus. These writers intended to free Jesus from the dogmatic accretions with which theology had surrounded him. But now, as Weiss maintained, Jesus himself was a "dogmatist" who harbored views, at least concerning the Kingdom of God, that were radically at variance with those of liberal theology.

William Wrede

Following the conclusions of Wilke and Weisse in 1838, it was widely believed that the Gospel of Mark was the earliest of the gospels. Furthermore, it was thought that Mark was essentially historical in the usual understanding of that term. Though there were chronological displacements and inaccuracies in matters of fact, alterations in the wording of pronouncements ascribed to Jesus, and even an accretion of later dogmatic views, the liberal Lives of Jesus nevertheless assumed that Mark portrayed an accurate and reliable account of the chronology of Jesus' life. They presupposed that Mark was thinking from the standpoint of a biography of Jesus.

In 1901, William Wrede published *Das Messiasgeheimnis in den Evangelien*--a work that challenged the prevailing view that Mark was historically reliable. After a careful and detailed analysis of Mark, Wrede concluded that Mark did not have a real view of the historical Jesus. Mark's gospel was written with a deliberate theological purpose. His outlook was conditioned by the idea of the "messianic secret," which is a dogmatic and theological concept. As Wrede put it: "A historical motive is really absolutely out of the question; or, to put it positively, the messianic secret is a theological idea."[103]

According to Wrede, Mark is dealing with two conflicting views regarding Jesus' messiahship. One view held by Mark's contemporaries was that Jesus never made messianic claims nor acted as the Messiah during his earthly life, but that he became Messiah through the resurrection. The other view was that since Jesus was destined to be the Messiah he gave evidence of this fact during his earthly ministry. Mark dealt with this incongruity by means of the messianic secret. Wrede wrote:

> Our conclusion is that during his earthly life Jesus'
> messiahship is absolutely a secret and is supposed to
> be such; no one apart from the confidants of Jesus is
> supposed to learn about it; with the resurrection, how-
> ever, its disclosure ensues. This is in fact the crucial
> idea, the underlying point of Mark's entire approach.[104]

Mark's problem was to reconcile the non-messianic material of his sources with his own Christological beliefs. Since the actual record did not express Jesus' messiahship, and since messianic motif originated only with the resurrection, Mark resorted to the dogmatic device of the messianic secret to explain the discrepancy.

In Mark, the demons and the demoniacs recognize Jesus as the Messiah, but he orders them not to make known who he is. He gives the same command to people who have witnessed a heal-

ing. Jesus also engages in a number of esoteric conversations
with his disciples in which he tells them about the nature
of his messiahship and of the need to keep it secret prior to
the resurrection. Wrede pointed to two ideas found in Mark:
Jesus keeps his messiahship a secret as long as he is on earth,
and he does reveal himself to the disciples in contrast to the
people, but to them too he remains in his revelations incom-
prehensible for the time being. Both these ideas, which frequently overlap, have behind them the common view that real
knowledge of what Jesus is begins only with his resurrection.[105]
    Wrede granted that Mark is the oldest gospel and that it
contains a whole series of historical ideas, or ideas in a
historical form. Among these are the fact that Jesus was a
teacher in Galilee who was surrounded by a circle of disciples
whom he instructed, and some of whom were his special con-
fidants. He liked to speak in parables, and he performed
miracles. He was not averse to associating with publicans and
sinners. His somewhat free attitude toward the Law brought
him into opposition with the Pharisees and the Jewish authorities. They succeeded in entrapping him, and finally, with the
cooperation of Roman authorities, Jesus was condemned to death.
    These are the main features of Jesus' life. However, ac-
cording to Wrede, for Mark's view as a whole they are not important. These ideas are "quite general and undefined," and
history is not their dominant characteristic. They give us
only the external framework or a "few trivial sketches."
    Mark must be viewed, not as a historian, but as a dogmatician.
His view of Jesus is dogmatically conceived. Jesus is a supernatural being, and the one pervasive motive (messianic secret)
takes the form of a divine decree lying above and beyond human
comprehension. From the beginning, Jesus' gaze is directed
to the resurrection, the "point of the whole story," which
will reveal to men what has been secret. Wrede concluded:

> These motifs and not just the historical ones represent
> what actually motivates and determines the shape of the
> narrative in Mark. They give its coloring. The interest
> naturally depends on them and the actual thought of the
> author is directed towards them. It therefore remains
> true to say that as a whole the Gospel no longer offers
> a historical *view* of the real life of Jesus. Only pale
> residues of such a view have passed over into what is a
> suprahistorical view for faith. In this sense the Gos-
> pel of Mark belongs to the history of dogma.[106]

    Wrede's departure from one of the fundamental presupposi-
tions of the liberal Lives of Jesus--the historicity of Mark--
is evident. Henceforth, even Mark had to be viewed skeptically
as a historical source for the life of Jesus. Wrede's method-

ology and conclusions had a significant influence upon the later development of form criticism. It is also noteworthy that Albert Schweitzer concludes his *Quest of the Historical Jesus* with Wrede, whose position regarding the possibility of constructing a Life of Jesus, is characterized as "thorough-going skepticism."

Albert Schweitzer

Among the most radical interpretations of Jesus was Albert Schweitzer's *Quest of the Historical Jesus*. Following Johannes Weiss, Schweitzer made eschatology the central motif for his understanding of Jesus' life and message. He maintained that Jesus must be understood eschatologically, that he was an ancient apocalyptist, not a modern social reformer. Richard R. Niebuhr notes:

> To Schweitzer belongs the honor of having restored the Jesus of the New Testament to history and his own age. Thereby he made Jesus to be flesh and blood once more.... He sees that a Jesus radically different from the figure presented in the gospels is simply a fiction. This is the import of Schweitzer's rejection of the free recon-struction of Jesus' life and self-consciousness in which his predecessors indulged so heavily.[107]

Schweitzer's position of "thoroughgoing eschatology" developed in response to a series of lectures at Strassburg University by Heinrich Julius Holtzmann.

Holtzmann was a firm advocate of the priority of Mark. He concluded that the activities of Jesus can be understood from Mark's gospel only. It is Mark that historically is most authentic and genuine. It was this conclusion that Schweitzer came to question and later to reject.

In April 1894, Schweitzer began his year of military ser-vice. However, he was given freedom to continue his work at the university. When he went on maneuvers in the autumn of that year, he put his Greek Testament in his haversack.

On a certain rest day in the village of Guggenheim, Schweitzer, while concentrating on the tenth and eleventh chapters of Matthew, became aware of the significance of these two chapters, which do not have parallels in Mark. In Matthew 10, the mission of the twelve is recorded. Matthew 10:23 was for Schweitzer one of the key verses in his intrepretation of Jesus: "... for truly, I say to you, you will not have gone through all the towns of Israel, before the Son of Man comes." Schweitzer could not accept Holtzmann's explanation that this was not a historical discourse of Jesus but rather

one that was made up at a later period, after his death, out
of various "Sayings of Jesus." Schweitzer raised the question
whether a later generation would have put into Jesus' mouth
words that were belied by the subsequent course of events.
And he concluded that Jesus really did speak of the persecu-
tions that were to befall the disciples and that he also spoke
of the immediate appearance of the celestial Son of Man.

Schweitzer wrote of the end of his first year at Strassburg
and of his new understanding of Jesus:

> Thus was I, at the end of my first year at the Univer-
> sity, landed in perplexity about the explanation then
> accepted as historically correct of the words and actions
> of Jesus when he sent out the disciples on their mission,
> and as a consequence of this about the wider question of
> the conception of the whole life of Jesus which was then
> regarded as history. When I reached home after the
> maneuvers, entirely new horizons had opened themselves
> to me. Of this I was certain: that Jesus had announced
> no kingdom that was to be founded and realized in the
> natural world by himself and the believers, but one that
> was to be expected as coming with the almost immediate
> dawn of a supernatural age.[108]

Thus, Schweitzer replaced the "modern-historical solution" with
what he terms the "eschatological-historical."

A question that had proved most troublesome to the nineteenth-century interpreters concerned the relationship between
the ethical and the eschatological in the thought of Jesus.
One of the most satisfying answers was the assumption of
gradual development in the thought of Jesus. At first, Jesus
may have entertained a purely ethical view, looking for the
realization of the Kingdom of God through the spread and per-
fection of the moral-religious society that he was undertaking
to establish. However, when opposition to him began to put
the completion of the Kingdom in doubt, the eschatological conception forced itself upon him. Jesus was thus brought to the
place where his hope for the fulfillment of the religious-
ethical ideal, which he had regarded as the completion of a
continuous moral development, now had to be replaced with the
view that only God by a cosmic cataclysm would bring to a conclusion the work that Jesus had begun.

Schweitzer rejected any idea of "development" in the thought
of Jesus. The eschatological dimension of his thinking is
present from the very beginning of his ministry, and it forms
the context for all his thought.

> Therefore the eschatological notion cannot have been
> forced upon Jesus by outward experiences, but it must

from the beginning, even in the first Galilean period,
have lain at the base of his preaching! The idea of
Passion is dominated *only* by the eschatological conception of the Kingdom. In the charge to the twelve the
question is *only* about the eschatological--not about
the ethical-nearness of the Kingdom. From this it follows, for one thing, that Jesus' ministry counted *only*
upon the eschatological realization of the Kingdom.
Then, however, it is evident that the relation of his
ethical thoughts to the eschatological view can have
suffered no alteration by reason of outward events but
must have been the same from beginning to end.[109]

Schweitzer's well-known answer to the relationship between
ethics and eschatology was that the ethics of Jesus are "interim-
ethics." His ethics are ethics of repentance in the face of
the imminent coming of the Kingdom of God. Jesus' ethics
were given for that brief interim before the coming of the
Kingdom. This accounts for their radical and uncompromising
character. It also accounts for his silence regarding such
basic ethical issues as one's relationship to the state and
government, marriage and family life, economic life. The relationship between morality and the Kingdom of God is summarized
thus: "Whosoever at the dawning of the Kingdom is in possession
of a character morally renovated, he will be found a member of
the same. This is the adequate expression for the relation of
morality to the coming of the Kingdom of God."[110]
After the return of the twelve from their mission, Jesus
had expected the impending event of the coming of the Kingdom.
But what he had so confidently predicted did not occur. The
disciples returned, and all things were as they had been.
Moreover, they had not experienced the woes and sufferings that
Jesus had told them that they would. This led Jesus into soli-
tude once again to seek light upon the mystery.
Before the Kingdom can come, there must be a time of affliction. Repentance and the constraint of the powers of ungodli-
ness will not avail to bring in the Kingdom. Something more
spectacular is yet necessary. If the Kingdom is to come, the
final affliction must come down upon the future Messiah himself.
The conception of the final affliction contains the thought
of atonement and purification. Those who would enter the Kingdom must be purged from sin and guilt through repentance and
forgiveness. For this guilt impedes and holds back the coming
of the Kingdom.
But the affliction does not appear, and yet atonement must
be made. It occurs to Jesus that he as the coming Son of Man
must accomplish the atonement in his own person. He must humble

himself and suffer and give himself as a ransom for many.
This is the purpose for which he has come (Mark 10:45). In
order to accomplish this, he goes to Jerusalem, there to suffer at the hands of the secular authorities just as "Elijah,"
who went before him, suffered at the hands of Herod. Herein
lies the secret of the passion. "Jesus did actually die for
the sins of men, even though it was in another sense than that
which Anselm's theory assumes."[111]
    Jesus went to his grave without revealing the secret of
the passion. But the Kingdom still did not come. Therefore,
it was incumbent upon the disciples to offer some explanation
or interpretation of the passion. And the theory that the
early church offered was poorer than Jesus' secret. It re-
volved chiefly around one point: the passion and the resurrection from the dead attest that Jesus is the Messiah. And the
passion and the exaltation are foreordained in the scriptures.

> While Jesus' secret brought his death and the dawning
> of the Kingdom into the closest temporal and causal con-
> nection, for the primitive church, on the other hand,
> a past event, as such, constituted the object to be ex-
> plained, since the Kingdom had not arrived and the
> original causal connection was dissolved along with the
> temporal.[112]

What this adds up to is that none of the interpretations of
the significance of the passion (no matter how profound), from
Paul to Ritschl, apprehend the thought of Jesus because they
proceed upon entirely different presuppositions and assumptions. According to Jesus' secret of the passion, forgiveness
of sins is not for those who believe in Jesus Christ but for
those who are inheritors of the Kingdom.
    With the death of Jesus and the secret of the passion,
eschatology also passed out of the picture. "For Jesus and
his disciples his death was, according to the eschatological
view, merely a *transitional* event. As soon, however, as the
event occurred it became the *central fact* upon which the new,
uneschatological view was built up."[113]
    What Schweitzer had done, as he pointed out in the preface
to *The Mystery of the Kingdom of God*, was to write a Life of
Jesus, commencing not at the beginning but in the middle,
with the thought of the passion. The Life that he wrote ran
counter to both traditional orthodoxy and nineteenth-century
thought. He had charted a new possibility, which though extreme, forced subsequent writers about Jesus to reckon with it.
    Schweitzer's construction of the life of Jesus can perhaps
be summarized in these grandiose and esoteric words from *The
Quest of the Historical Jesus*:

There is silence all around. The Baptist appears, and
cries: "Repent, for the Kingdom of Heaven is at hand."
Soon after that comes Jesus, and in the knowledge that
he is the coming Son of Man lays hold of the wheel of the
world to set it moving on that last revolution which is
to bring all ordinary history to a close. It refuses to
turn, and he throws himself upon it. Then it does turn,
and crushes him. Instead of bringing in the eschatological conditions, he has destroyed them. The wheel rolls
onward, and the mangled body of the one immeasurably
great man, who was strong enough to think of himself as
the spiritual ruler of mankind and to bend history to
his purpose, is hanging upon it still. That is his
victory and his reign.[114]

Schweitzer's best-known and most erudite work was *The
Quest of the Historical Jesus*, published in 1906. The motivation for doing research on the life of Jesus came as a result
of a conversation with students at Strassburg University, to
whose faculty he had been appointed in 1902. These students
informed Schweitzer that they had attended a course of lectures by Professor Spitta on the Life of Jesus but that they
had learned practically nothing about previous investigations
into the subject. Thus, Schweitzer decided, with the approval
of Professor Holtzmann, that he would lecture for two hours
weekly during the summer term of 1905 on the history of research on the life of Jesus.

His method of research and the resulting confusion in his
room at Strassburg are characterized by humor and human interest:

When I had worked through the numerous Lives of Jesus,
I found it very difficult to group them in chapters.
After attempting in vain to do this on paper, I piled
all the "Lives" in one big heap in the middle of my
room, picked out for each chapter I had planned a place
of its own in a corner or between the pieces of furni-
ture, and then, after thorough consideration, heaped
up the volumes in the piles to which they belonged,
pledging myself to find room for all the books belonging
to each pile, and to leave each heap undisturbed in its
own place, till the corresponding chapter in the Sketch
should be finished. And I carried out my plan to the
very end. For many a month all the people who visited
me had to thread their way across the room along paths
which ran between heaps of books. I had also to fight
hard to ensure that the tidying zeal of the trusty
Württemberg widow who kept house for me came to a halt
before the piles of books.[115]

The Quest of the Historical Jesus has no parallel in the
history of scholarship on the life of Jesus insofar as magnitude and comprehensiveness are concerned. It is a remarkably
complete survey of the German literature (with the addition of
Renan) of a century and a quarter on the subject of the Lives
of Jesus, from Hermann Samuel Reimarus to William Wrede.
Schweitzer's interest was primarily with a question that he
found beginning with Reimarus: What was the aim of Jesus'
ministry? However, as he moved on and dealt one after another
with the many scholars, the central question became: What was
this author's attitude toward "consistent eschatology"?

    The last part of *The Quest* consists of Schweitzer's own
Life of Jesus and his additional criticisms of the nineteenth-
century Life of Jesus movement. It is in this latter section
that Schweitzer developed his views on "consistent" or "thorough-
going eschatology."

    Schweitzer undertook to make a "critical examination of
the dogmatic element in the life of Jesus." The dogmatic
element is not distinct from the life of Jesus. Rather, the
dogmatic element is the historical element. "For after all,"
Schweitzer saked, "why should not Jesus think in terms of
doctrine, and make history in action, just as well as a poor
evangelist can do it on paper, under the pressure of the
theological interest of the primitive community?"[116]

    Johannes Weiss had not gone far enough, because he applied
the eschatological explanation only to the preaching of Jesus.
What is necessary is to apply the eschatological dimension to
the whole public work of Jesus. Weiss had failed to see that
the eschatological element had not only to do with Jesus'
preaching regarding the Kingdom of God but that the same "dogmatic" element also overshadowed the history of Jesus. Consequently, Schweitzer maintained, the eschatological element
must be projected into the center and into the whole of the
life of Jesus.

    The portrait of Jesus that emerges from Schweitzer's pains-
taking labors was that he was an unworldly, apocalyptic figure
who shared the eschatological and apocalyptic world-view of
late Judaism. Schweitzer destroyed the nineteenth-century
"liberal Jesus"--a Jesus who was a high-souled teacher of
morality, who sought to establish the spiritual reign of God
in men's hearts and thus induce a reign of justice on earth,
and who died a martyr to his lofty cause. According to
Schweitzer, such a figure never existed. This great and noble
effort to find the "real Jesus" resulted in negativism. "There
is nothing more negative than the result of the critical study
of the Life of Jesus."[117]

    The Jesus for whom the nineteenth century quested must
remain for us hidden and unknown. The historical Jesus belongs
to an age that is strange and mysterious to us.

The historical Jesus will be to our time a stranger and
an enigma.... The study of the Life of Jesus has had a
curious history. It set out in quest of the historical
Jesus, believing that when it had found him it could
bring him straight into our time as a Teacher and Savior.
It loosed the bands by which he had been riveted for
centuries to the stony rocks of ecclesiastical doctrine,
and rejoiced to see life and movement coming into the
figure once more, and the historical Jesus advancing,
as it seemed, to meet it. But he does not stay; he
passes by our time and returns to his own.... Jesus
as a concrete historical personality remains a stranger
to our time.... The names in which men expressed their
recognition of him as such, Messiah, Son of Man, Son of
God, have become for us historical parables. We can
find no designation which expresses what he is for us....
He comes to us an one unknown, without a name, as of old,
by the lakeside, he came to those men who knew him not.[118]

This is the only conclusion to which we can come so long
as we rely upon historiography to lead us to Jesus. History
tried to disengage that which is abiding and eternal in the
being of Jesus from the historical forms in which it worked
itself out, in the hope that this vital and dynamic spirit
might be set loose in the world. But all this toil ended in
failure. The historical foundation as built up by rationalistic, by liberal, and by modern theology no longer exists. The
pertinent question therefore becomes: Has Christianity lost its
historical foundation? Has the foundation of Christianity
crumbled with the passing of the "historical Jesus"? Schweitzer's
answer was a resounding, No! Christianity rests upon something
more fundamental than the historical Jesus:

Jesus means something to our world because a mighty
spiritual force streams forth from him and flows through
our time also. This fact can neither be shaken nor con-
firmed by any historical discovery. It is the solid
foundation of Christianity. But the truth is, it is not
Jesus as historically known, but Jesus spiritually
arisen within men, who is significant for our time and
can help it. Not the historical Jesus, but the spirit
which goes forth from him and in the spirits of men
strives for new influence and rule, is that which over-
comes the world.... The abiding and eternal Jesus is
absolutely independent of historical knowledge and can
only be understood by contact with his spirit which is
still at work in the world. In proportion as we have
the Spirit of Jesus, we have the true knowledge of Jesus....
His spirit, which lies hidden in his words, is known in
simplicity, and its influence is direct.[119]

Thus, Schweitzer concluded his criticism of the historical
study of the life of Jesus with a Jesus-mysticism. Gone are
both the Nicene Christ and the historical Jesus of liberal
theology. In their place is the timeless "spirit of Jesus,"
which is dependent upon neither theological dogma nor historical
methodology but which in its immediacy and power has the po-
tentiality of remaking us and our world.

Julius Wellhausen

Though Julius Wellhausen is best known for his pentateuchal
source criticism and his conclusion that the Pentateuch is a
composite document, he also contributed significantly to New
Testament studies. Along with Wrede, Wellhausen demonstrated
the difficulty of constructing a Life of Jesus from the gospels.
As noted above, Wrede held that the Gospel of Mark was a dogmatic and theological document. Wellhausen extended Wrede's
insight to all the synoptic gospels. The work of Wrede and
Wellhausen was a precursor of the later development of form
criticism.

In 1903 and 1904, Wellhausen wrote brief commentaries on
each of the synoptic gospels and furnished proof that the
gospels cannot be used as sources for a Life of Jesus. They
offer only testimony to the messianic faith of the early church.
These commentaries were followed in 1905 with *Einleitung in
die drei ersten Evangelien*, in which Wellhausen summed up his
conclusions. In the introduction, he maintained that the
gospel material was selected with dogmatic intent and that
the evangelists were wholly responsible for its content. Jesus
thought of himself as only a teacher and did not identify himself with the coming of the Messiah. Though he accepted the
messianic title conferred on him by the disciples, he did so
only as an accommodation to popular Jewish belief.

Wellhausen described the composition of the gospels and
their historical authenticity as follows:

> The ultimate source of the gospels is oral tradition,
> but this contains only scattered material. The units,
> more or less extensive, circulate in it separately.
> Their combination into a whole is always the work of
> an author and, as a rule, the work of a writer with
> literary ambitions.... The passion story need not be
> excluded from the judgment that the Gospel of Mark as
> a whole lacks the distinctive marks of a history....
> Mark does not write *de vita et moribus Jesu*. He has no
> intention of making Jesus' person manifest, or even in-
> telligible. For him it has been absorbed in Jesus' divine
> vocation. He wishes to demonstrate that Jesus is the
> Christ.[120]

The Jesus who emerges from Wellhausen's evaluation of the gospels is not the dogmatic Christ nor yet Schweitzer's eschatological figure. He is a Jew who always sought to remain a Jew. "Jesus was not a Christian, but a Jew." He did not introduce a new faith but taught the doing of God's will. As with the Jews, the will of God for him was found in the Law and in the rest of the scriptures. However, Jesus pointed to a way of fulfilling the Law that was at variance with Jewish piety. His intention was not to destroy the principles of Judaism. Perhaps suspicion was directed against him because he regarded the end of the world as imminent. The break with Judaism resulted from the crucifixion and was first manifested in Paul. But in Jesus' own teaching and attitude, it was dormant because he wished to remain within Judaism. It was the gospels and Paul who conceived the historical Jesus in dogmatic terms. Wellhausen added: "We cannot go back to him, even if we wanted to.... He would not have become a historical figure had it not been for his death. The impression left by his career consists in the fact that it was not ended but abruptly interrupted after it had scarcely begun."[121]

Theories of Non-Historicity

David Friedrich Strauss had espoused the mythical view in his Life of Jesus, and Bruno Bauer had maintained that Jesus was an imaginary being representing a combination of Roman and Jewish motifs, but even more radical views of the non-historicity of Jesus developed during the later nineteenth and early twentieth centuries. These views evolved quite independently from those set forth by Bauer a number of decades earlier.

The first claims that Jesus may never have existed appeared in the eighteenth century. Voltaire referred to "some disciples of Bollingbroke, more ingenious than learned," who believed that the obscurities and contradictions in the gospels led to a denial of Jesus' existence. These ideas were not expressed in writing but were set forth at the close of the eighteenth century by Constantin Volney and Charles Dupuis. They held that Jesus was neither man nor God, but represented a solar deity like those worshiped in ages past. After considerable attention, these views passed into oblivion.[122]

During the last twenty years of the nineteenth century, a "radical Dutch school"--represented by such critics as Allard Pierson, Jan Carel Matthes, Samuel Andrianus Naber, J. Van Loon, for a time Abraham Dirk Loman, and later Gerhardus Bolland--denied the existence of Jesus. Their criticism was directed largely to the Pauline Epistles, which they dated as late as the second century. From their conclusions, from

the uncertainty of the gospel tradition, and from the absence
of all external evidence, they felt justified in rejecting the
historicity of Jesus.[123]   The Dutch school has been largely
ignored, and their theories have had little influence outside
the Netherlands.

It was during the opening years of the twentieth century
that the theories of non-historicity reached their most intense
and widespread discussion. Goguel observes that these recent
theories agreed in scarcely anything except in that which they
denied. Among these critics were John Mackinnon Robertson,
Peter Jensen, Heinrich Zimmern, William Benjamin Smith, Gilbert
Thomas Sadler, Albert Kalthoff, Arthur Drews, Salomon Reinach,
Paul Louis Couchoud, and Robert Stahl.[124]

Of the above, Arthur Drews was the staunchest apologist
and did the most to popularize the theory of non-historicity.
It was in a work on the philosophy of religion (*Die Religion
als Selbstbewisstein Gottes*, 1905) that Drews suggests that
the cult of Jesus was a relic of superstition and should be
purged from religion. He welcomed William Benjamin Smith's
conclusions about a pre-Christian Jesus and combined them with
an astral system. He also found a connection between Christ
the Lamb of God (*Agnus Dei*) and the Vedic god *Agni*.

It was in his two-volume *Die Christusmythe* that Drews set
forth most fully his views on the non-historicity of Jesus.
An abbreviated and amended version of the second part of this
work, entitled *The Witness to the Historicity of Jesus*, was
published in 1912. Drews observed that the basic issue regarding the Christ-myth controversy is a struggle over religion.
Those who believe that the historical Jesus is necessary for
faith have a faulty and immature understanding of religion.
Religion is subjective, and religious progress consists of
making faith more intimate, in transferring its center from
the objective to the subjective world, by "a confident sur-
render to the God within us." To ground one's belief in a
historical instrument is to regress to a stage of mental development that has been superseded by the inner life. Drews
wrote: "Those who cling to a historical Jesus on religious
grounds merely show that they have never understood the real
nature of religion, or what 'faith' really means in the religious sense of the word."[125]

To understand the story of Jesus and all that is related
to him, argued Drews, one must turn to Isaiah 53. This is the
"solid nucleus round which all the rest has crystallised."
The prophet describes the "servant of Jahweh," who voluntarily
submits to suffering in order to expiate the sin and guilt
of the people. This theme of the persecution and the suffering
of the just man is also found in Plato's *Republic* and in The
Wisdom of Solomon. In Deuteronomy 21:22-23, the most shameful

death was "to hang on a tree." In addition, Drews found parallels in Job's experience of suffering and humiliation with
the figure of Jesus depicted in the gospels. It is, however,
in Isaiah and The Wisdom of Solomon that one finds the "germ-
cell" of the figure of Jesus and the Christian theory of redemption.

Drews believed that Christianity originated from the
Gnostic sects who knew an astral Jesus whose mythic "history"
was composed of passages from the prophets, Isaiah, the twenty-
second Psalm, and The Wisdom of Solomon. This pre-Christian
Jesus was transformed in the second century after the destruction of Jerusalem. As the new faith spread to wider circles,
the astral features of the Jesus-myth were lost, and people
regarded the myth as real history and began to seek a basis
for the story of Jesus in the real course of events. Thus,
the mythical Jesus was converted into the historical Jesus--
an abstract scheme into a living personality. "The more the
new faith spread among the people, the more the gnosis was
adapted to their intelligence, and thus the supposed historicity
of the Savior was substituted for the mythical and astral character of their religious ideas."[126]

Drews was insistent that the mythical view provides the
best explanation for the origin and genius of Christianity.
The actions and words of Jesus have a mythical character and
are derived from antecedent sources, so that one cannot with
good conscience affirm the existence of a historical Jesus.

If, then, the historical Jesus cannot be regarded as the
founder of Christianity and the one who inspired its adherents,
what can we substitute for him as the determining principle
of the whole movement? For Drews, the question of the historicity of Jesus is not merely a historical, but an eminently
philosophical, question. It is the difference between two
opposed philosophical systems. The one maintains that the
idea is the ultimate determining principle of the world-process,
and great personalities of history are the servants, instru-
ments, and realizers of its content. The other holds that
personalities as such are the determining factors of the
world-process, something ultimate and original. It is the
idealistic philosophy of history, as represented by Plato and
Hegel, that best explains the essential character of Christ
and of Christianity.

Drews was critical of liberal theology because it elevated
the historical Jesus to a central significance for Christian
life and faith. But since religion is basically subjective,
the purely historical conception of Jesus cannot satisfy the
religious consciousness of our age. It is the *idea* that attains consciousness in people and stirs them to action. It
is the living power of the divinity within them that makes

them what they are. Christianity is centered in an idea or an
ideal rather than in historical occurrences. Drew noted: "The
ideal Christ, not the historical Jesus of modern liberal
theology, was the founder of the Christian movement, and made
it victorious over its opponents.... From the first we find
Christianity as the religion, not of the historical man Christ,
who merely passed through history, but of the *super-historical
god-man Jesus Christ*.[127]

Drews' major contention was that religion is debased when
the ideal becomes enmeshed in history and when a historical
person attains a position of absolute significance. The true
aim of religion is to free people from dependence on the world
and therefore from the dependence and relativity of temporal
existence.

Basic to all the deeper religions, Drews noted, is the
idea of a suffering god, sacrificing himself for humanity and
obtaining spiritual healing for people by his death and subsequent resurrection. In pagan religions, these ideas were
conceived naturalistically in that myths were related to the
cycles of nature. Christianity advanced beyond nature religions,
spiritualizing these ideas and applying them to the man Jesus
Christ. The many savior-gods were blended in the idea of the
one god-man who became connected with a historical reality.
However, the historical embodiment of the Christian idea of redemption is ruined when, as in liberal theology, it is made
the express object of scientific inquiry and historical criticism. To ground Christianity in a single historical personality is to retreat to a geocentric and anthropocentric
view of its origins and to relate it to a superstitious concept of Christology. "What was once the prerogative of
Christianity--that it superseded the polytheism of pagan
antiquity, and conceived the idea of the divine Savior in
the singular and historical--is today the greatest hindrance
to faith."[128]

The religion that is compatible with modern thought views
the idea of a religious significance of Christ as both super-
fluous and mischievous. It "loads the religious consciousness
with doubtful historical ballast" and gives the past an
authority over the religious life of the present. Thus, Drews
insisted, belief in the historical reality of Jesus is the
chief obstacle to religious progress. He concluded that modern
humanity has "the task of again universalising the idea of
divine redemption, or enlarging the idea of a god-*man*, which
is common in Christendom, to the idea of a god-*humanity*."[129]

Contrary to both orthodox and liberal theology, Drews
rejected the reality of the historical Jesus and of historical
revelation. Instead, he held an idealistic view of history
and a view of religion that is naturalistic and pantheistic.

In a concluding statement, he observed:

> The divinity lives in history, and reveals itself there-
> in. History is, in union with nature, the *sole* place
> of divine activity. The divinity, however, does not
> chain itself to history, in order to unite past and
> future to a single historical event; but one continuous
> stream of divine activity flows through time. Hence
> it cannot wish that men shall be bound up with some such
> simple event; in virtue of its divine character the de-
> tail may at any point of history be raised above the
> conditions of time and nature. To bind up religion
> with history, as modern theologians do, and to represent
> a *historical religion* as the need of modern man, is no
> proof of insight, but of a determination to persuade
> oneself to recognise the Christian religion alone.[130]

Other Liberal Lives of Jesus

Adolf Harnack

Along with Friedrich Schleiermacher and Albrecht Ritschl,
Adolf Harnack was a leading exponent of liberal Protestantism.
Though Harnack never wrote a Life of Jesus as such, he delivered
a series of lectures at the University of Berlin during the
winter semester of 1899-1900. These were published in 1900
as *Das Wesen des Christentums* and were translated into English
as *What Is Christianity?* As the title implies, Harnack was
interested in setting forth the essence of Christianity, and
in so doing he discussed the life and message of Jesus.

Harnack began by reminding his hearers that it is of prime
importance to remind humankind again and again that a man of
the name Jesus Christ once stood in their midst. However,
we have to begin our task by confessing that we are unable to
write a Life of Jesus. Except for the birth stories in
Matthew and Luke (which contain mythical elements), the evangelists tell us nothing about the history of Jesus' early
development; they tell us only of his public activity. Consequently, Harnack asked, "How can we write the history of "How
a man of whose development we know nothing, and with only a year
or two of whose life we are acquainted?"[131] But though the
gospels are insufficient for a "biography," they are important
for three basic reasons: (1) they offer a plain picture of
Jesus' teaching, in regard both to its main features and to
its individual application; (2) they tell us how his life
issued in the service of his vocation; (3) they describe the
impression that he made upon his disciples, which they trans-

mitted.[132] Thus, though a full biography of Jesus is impossible, there is hope for an understanding as to what his
aims were, what he was, and what he signifies for us.

Harnack believed that some things can be said negatively
about the thirty years of silence. For one, it is very unlikely
that Jesus attended a rabbinical school. He nowhere speaks
like a man who has assimilated any theological culture of a
technical kind or learned the art of scholarly exegesis. He
was at home with the sacred writings, but he was not a pro-
fessional teacher or scholar.

There is no evidence that Jesus experienced a stormy
crisis or conversion that represented any radical break with
his past. Though Jesus summoned people to repentance, he
never spoke of his own repentance. Though he manifested deep
emotion and experienced temptation and doubt, it is unimaginable
that his life could have been spent in inner conflict. "Everything seems to pour from him naturally, as though it could not
do otherwise, like a spring from the depths of the earth, clear
and unchecked in its flow."[133]

Harnack's final negative inference was that the picture
of Jesus' life and his discourses stand in no relation with
the Greek spirit. This is surprising, because there were many
Greeks in Galilee and Greek was spoken in many of its cities.
There were Greek teachers and philosophers in Galilee, and it
is highly unlikely that Jesus was unacquainted with their language. But there is no evidence that he was in any way influenced by them or was ever in touch with the thought of Plato
or the Porch.

In spite of the gospels' silence about Jesus' early life,
Harnack believed that they give us vital insights into his
person and teaching. Jesus lived his religion; and his whole
life, all his thoughts and feelings, were absorbed in the relation to God. Yet he never talked like an enthusiast or a
fanatic. "He spoke his message and looked at the world with a
fresh and clear eye for the life, great and small, that surrounded him."[134] The most astonishing and greatest fact about
him was that Jesus remained kind and sympathetic to every living
thing. He never uses any ecstatic language, and the tone of
stirring prophecy is rare. Rather, he is possessed of a quiet,
uniform, collected demeanor, with everything directed to one
goal. His parables are clear even to those whose minds are
childlike, and they exhibit an inner freedom and a cheerfulness
of soul in the midst of the greatest strain, such as no other
prophet ever possessed. In words reminiscent of Renan, Harnack
noted: "His eye rests kindly upon the flowers and the children,
on the lily of the field ... on the birds in the air and the
sparrow on the house-top."[135] The parable is Jesus' most
familiar form of speech, but he does not speak as one who has

broken with everything, or like a heroic penitent, or like an ecstatic prophet, but like a man who has rest and peace for his soul, and is able to give life and strength to others. Even though he strikes the mightiest notes, the strongest emotion comes naturally to him. "He clothes it in the language in which a mother speaks to her child."[136] Jesus' religion was characterized by his living in the continual consciousness of God's presence. He was not an ascetic who turned his back on the world, but everywhere he recognized the hand of the living God.

The predominant theme of all that Jesus taught and did is summarized in the words of Isaiah that Jesus read to those assembled in the synagogue at Nazareth. His message was an "evangel" that brought blessing and joy. Harnack believed that Jesus' teachings can be grouped under three headings: the Kingdom of God and its coming; God the Father and the infinite value of the soul; and the higher righteousness and the commandment of love.[137]

There is a dichotomy in Jesus' teaching concerning the Kingdom of God. The Kingdom is in the future and will be marked by conflict and judgment, but it is also already here. The former view Jesus shared with his contemporaries, but the latter was Jesus' own view, according to Harnack. We must distinguish between what is traditional and what is peculiar, between kernel and husk in Jesus' message of the Kingdom of God. In order to do this, we must read and study the parables. Harnack concluded:

> The Kingdom of God comes by coming to the individual, by entering into his soul and laying hold of it.... It is the rule of the holy God in the hearts of individuals.... From this point of view everything that is dramatic in the external and historical sense has vanished; and gone, too, are all the external hopes for the future.... It is not a question of angels and devils, thrones and principalities, but of God and the soul, the soul and its God.[138]

The message of Jesus, for Harnack, appears in the clearest and most direct light in connection with the idea of God the Father and the infinite value of the soul. Indeed, the whole of Jesus' message may be reduced to these two concepts. They show us that the gospel is *religion itself*. In the ideas of God the Father, Providence, the position of persons as God's children, and the infinite value of the soul, religion for the first time finds its full expression.

Harnack's third characterization of Jesus' message, as "the higher righteousness and the commandment of love," shows that the gospel is an ethical message. Jesus combined religion and

morality in the sense that religion can be called the soul
of morality, and morality the body of religion. Jesus defined
the sphere of the ethical in a way that no one before him had
ever done. He freed ethics from its connection with self-
seeking and ritual elements and reduced it to *one* root and to
one motive--love. "But should we be threatened with doubts
as to what he meant, we must steep ourselves again and again
in the Beatitudes of the Sermon on the Mount. They contain
his ethics and his religion, united at the root, and freed
from all external and particularistic elements."[139]

In addressing the question of Christology, Harnack maintained that Jesus desired no other belief in his person and
no other attachment to it than is contained in the keeping of
his commandments. His consciousness of being the Son of God
was nothing but the practical consequence of knowing God as
the Father and as *his* Father. In an oft-quoted phrase, Harnack
wrote, "The gospel, as Jesus proclaimed it, has to do with
the Father only and not with the Son."[140]

Finally, a word must be said about Harnack's view of the
gospels as a source for our knowledge of Jesus. Our authorities for the message that Jesus delivered are the first three
gospels. The Fourth Gospel cannot be taken as a historical
authority in the ordinary meaning of the word. Its author
"acted with sovereign freedom, transposed events and put them
in a strange light, drew up the discourses himself, and illustrated great thoughts by imaginary situations." Though the
Fourth Gospel cannot be considered an authority for Jesus'
history, it is an authority for answering the question, "What
vivid views of Jesus' person, what kind of light and warmth,
did the gospel disengage?"

Harnack noted that David Friedrich Strauss thought that
he had destroyed the credibility of the gospels. However,
the historical criticism of two generations succeeded in re-
storing that credibility in its main outlines. The gospels
are not historical works; they were composed for the work of
evangelization. Their purpose is to awaken a belief in Jesus
Christ's person and mission. Nevertheless, the tradition
they present is, in the main, firsthand. In terms of "agreement, inspiration, and completeness," the gospels leave a great
deal to be desired, and they suffer from imperfections. The
conviction that Old Testament prophecy was fulfilled in Jesus'
history had a disturbing effect on tradition. In addition,
the miraculous element is intensified in some of the narratives. But, argues Harnack, except for the accounts of Jesus'
childhood, Strauss' contention that the gospels contain a
great deal that is mythical has not been borne out. Harnack
concluded: "None of these disturbing elements affect the
heart of the narrative; not a few of them easily lend them-

selves to correction, partly by a comparison of the gospels one with another, partly through the sound judgment that is matured by historical study."[141]

Joseph Klausner

Joseph Klausner's *Jesus of Nazareth; His Life, Times, and Teaching* was published in Hebrew in 1922 and was intended for "Jewish Hebrew readers." It was the first appearance of a work that described what modern Jewish scholarship had to offer on the subject of the Jewish background of the gospels. Its aim was to provide for a better understanding of the Jewish mental and historical environment in which Jesus lived and worked. Klausner hoped to provide in Hebrew, for Hebrews, a book along the lines of modern criticism that would avoid the exaggerated and propagandist claims of both Judaism and Christianity. His basic objective was to give Hebrew readers a truer idea of the historic Jesus and by so doing to show how Judaism and Christianity remain distinct from each other.

The book is divided into three sections. The first is a study of the sources for the history of Jesus. In the second, the political, economic, and spiritual life of Jesus' time are described. The final section is devoted to a description of the life and the teaching of Jesus.

In his treatment of the gospels, Klausner presented a notable survey of the history of gospel criticism. He recognized the "urgent need" of giving Hebrew readers (who had no scholarly work on the subject) "a true idea of the far-reaching and difficult work carried out by hundreds of scholars of all nations in the last hundred years and more."[142]

Klausner's chief problem with the gospels as sources for a Life of Jesus concerned their lack of an orderly presentation of events. He quoted Papias, who noted that Mark wrote "accurately all that he remembered of the words and deeds of Christ, but not in order." Each of the gospels that relied on Mark reflects this lack of order. Klausner wrote: "Therefore it is difficult to give a complete Life of Jesus, not so much because of scarcity or credibility of material, but because we do not know the chronological order of his sayings or actions."[143] In addition, the chief object of the evangelists in writing was not historical or biographical, but religious. However, there is no reason whatever to cast wholesale doubt on the historicity of the synoptic gospels, because they accurately reflect the Palestine of Jesus' time and contemporary Jewish life and Pharisaic teaching.

As for the Fourth Gospel, its value is theological rather than historical or biographical. It is not a religio-historical

but a religio-philosophical book. It was the last of the gospels to be composed, and its object is to interpret Jesus as
the *Logos*, the "Word of God" in the extreme Philonic sense.
Consequently, it minimizes such details in the life and death
of Jesus as would appear too human. Though it may include a
few historical fragments, it is not a trustworthy source for
a Life of Jesus.

Before proceeding to the life of Jesus, Klausner presented
a detailed description of the political, economic, religious,
and intellectual conditions of first-century Palestine. Because of his firsthand and extensive knowledge of Judaism,
Klausner's discussion of the religious and intellectual conditions of Jesus' time is especially noteworthy. For a non-
Jewish reader, his treatment of the Messiah concept and the
various Jewish sects or parties is most informative.

Though Klausner faulted the gospels for their lack of an
orderly presentation of Jesus' life, his account follows a
carefully constructed order based on the synoptic gospels from
Jesus' childhood and youth to his crucifixion and resurrection. The fact that Klausner viewed Jesus through "Jewish
eyes" is evident throughout the section on Jesus' life and
teachings. He was in agreement with Wellhausen's bold esti-
mate that Jesus was first and foremost a Jew. That it could
be otherwise was inconceivable for Klausner. "Jesus was a Jew
and a Jew he remained till his last breath. His one idea was
to implant within his nation the idea of the coming of the
Messiah and, by repentance and good works, hasten the 'end.'"[144]
In referring to Jesus' attitude toward civil power and justice, Klausner wrote: "In all this Jesus is the most Jewish
of Jews...."[145]

As Klausner saw it, the main strength of Jesus lay in his
ethical teaching: "If we omitted the miracles and a few mys-
tical sayings which tend to deify the Son of Man, and preserved
only the moral precepts and parables, the gospels would count
as one of the most wonderful collections of ethical teaching
in the world."[146] Jesus condensed and concentrated ethical
teachings in a fashion not done previously in Judaism. "A
man like Jesus, for whom the ethical ideal was everything, was
something hitherto unheard of in the Judaism of the day."[147]
Jesus' ethical consciousness was so extreme that, unlike
Judaism, he ignored the relationship between the national
world-outlook and its ethico-religious base. He relegated
the requirements of the national life to a separate sphere and
set up only an ethico-religious system bound up with his conception of the Godhead. "Like all who have become immersed in
ethics and nothing else, he became a 'pessimist'; life, the life
as it is lived in this world, is valueless...."[148] Klausner's
main charge against Jesus' ethical teaching was that, though

it is lofty and ideal, it is divorced from political and social life. The major reason for this lies in Jesus' eschatology. His ethic was extremist and individualistic because he was convinced that the world was about to end and that God would create a "new creation." It is a morality of "the end of the world" and is necessarily gloomy and pessimistic. Moreover, these differences between the ethic of Christianity and the ethic of Judaism have persisted to the present day.

Toward the end of his work, Klausner raised the question about the character of Jesus and the secret of his influence. He pointed out that the influence of Jesus upon his followers was exceptional. As time went on, their perception of his spiritual character grew, until it reached the status of divinity. "Never has such a thing happened to any other human creature in enlightened, historic times and among a people claiming a two-thousand-years'-old civilization."[149] For Klausner, the secret of this astonishing influence lay in the complex nature of Jesus' personality and in his methods of teaching. As with other great men, Jesus is recognized not alone for his virtues but also for his defects, which in certain combinations, can be transformed into virtues. "Like every great man, Jesus was a complex of many amazing contradictions; it was these which compelled astonishment, enthusiasm, and admiration."[150]

Klausner noted that, on the one hand, Jesus was humble and lowly-minded, tender and placable, and tolerant to an unprecedented degree. But on the other hand, he possessed a belief in his mission that bordered on the extreme of self-veneration. However, Jesus' intense self-confidence was not necessarily repellent, because he "masked" it with his frequent expressions of tenderness, gentleness, and humility. The combination in Jesus' person of extreme kindliness and violent passion, of gentleness and rigorous moral demands, had the effect of influencing and attracting people.

Another paradox that Klausner discerned as accounting for Jesus' influence was that Jesus was both "a man of the world" and an unworldly visionary. By themselves, these qualities do not have a lasting impact, but when they are combined, they exert a potent influence. Klausner wrote:

> Only where mystic faith is yoked with practical prudence does there follow a strong, enduring result. And of such a nature was the influence exerted by Jesus of Nazareth upon his followers, and, through them, upon succeeding generations. Such is the secret of Jesus' influence. The contradictory traits in his character, its positive and negative aspects, his harshness and his gentleness, his clear vision combined with his cloudy visionariness--all these united to make him a

force and an influence, for which history has never yet
afforded a parallel.[151]

The second reason for Jesus' influence was his method of
teaching. Like the prophets, he spoke with authority, though
he depended little on the scriptures. He spoke in parables
and striking and pregnant proverbs. "He was a great *artist*
in parable." Even though some of his parables eluded the
simple Galileans, they instinctively felt that beneath the
attractive covering there was hidden a kernel of great value.
In Jesus' parables and proverbs, we must recognize a personality
of great magnitude. He had the ability of setting forth profound truths in language and story that can never be forgotten.

His method of teaching combined with his complex character
explains why Jesus' teaching was not forgotten and why it became the basis of a new faith. Klausner maintained, however,
that Jesus presented nothing new (i.e., not already contained
in Judaism), except in arrangement and construction. What
happened was that the personality of Jesus became mingled with
his teaching, because most of what he taught had its origin
not in theory but in a practical life situation.

Klausner concluded his discussion of Jesus' character and
influence thus:

> The tragedy of the dreadful death which came upon Jesus
> wrongly (though in accordance with the justice of the
> time) added a crown of divine glory both to the personal-
> ity and to the teaching. Later arose the legend of the
> resurrection, heightening every value, obscuring every
> defect and exalting every virtue--and Jesus the Jew be-
> came half-Jew, half-Gentile, and began to hold that
> supernatural rank which is his today among hundreds and
> millions of mankind.[152]

In a brief concluding section, Klausner responds to the
question of what Jesus is to the Jews. A few of his observations are in order, because this essay has dealt largely with
scholars related to the Christian tradition.

He observes that all of Jesus' life and teaching is "stamped
with the seal of Prophetic and Pharisaic Judaism and the Palestine of his day." Jesus was one of the prominent Jews of his
day, and though his teaching is Jewish it reflects a truth and
imagination that is remarkable.

Jesus was not a Christian, as Wellhausen said. But Klausner notes that he *became* a Christian, and as a consequence his
teaching and his history have been severed from Israel. Though
the Jews have not accepted him, and though his followers have
persecuted the Jews and Judaism, it is impossible to ignore
him in any investigation of the history of the Jews in the
time of the Second Temple.

Klausner states that for the Jews Jesus can be neither God nor the Son of God in any dogmatic or theological sense. Neither can he be regarded as the Messiah, or as a prophet, or as a lawgiver, or as the founder of a new religion. Who then is he, and what can be said about him? Klausner's answer is that for the Jewish nation Jesus is *a great teacher of morality and an artist in parable*. But his ethic is so extreme that it is "simply an ideal for the isolated few" and is no ethical code for the nations and the social order of today. Klausner's concluding statement is noteworthy:

> In his ethical code there is a sublimity, distinctiveness, and originality in form unparalleled in any other Hebrew ethical code; neither is there any parallel to the remarkable art of his parables.... If ever the day should come and this ethical code be stripped of its wrappings of miracles and mysticism, the Book of the Ethics of Jesus will be one of the choicest treasures in the literature of Israel for all time.[153]

Shirley Jackson Case

From 1908 to 1938, Shirley Jackson Case taught New Testament and early church history at the University of Chicago. He was a prime leader in the development of the "Chicago School" of theology.

In 1927, Case's *Jesus: A New Biography* was published. As the title suggests, he believed that a "new biography" was possible and sought "to depict Jesus as he actually appeared to the men of his own time in Palestine nineteen hundred years ago." Case noted that the scholarly attempt to recover the story of Jesus' career centered perhaps too exclusively upon the critical examination of the gospels. Though he was not about to ignore this critical work, he intended to give more attention to social orientation. Case's biography was written "with more than usual emphasis upon the social point of view, both in handling the early Christian literature and in reproducing the story of Jesus' life and religion."[154]

Case observed that in more recent times there has been a renewed interest in reconstructing the career of the earthly Jesus. One gathers that Case is ready to show us the real Jesus of history as he lived in Palestine among his contemporaries many centuries ago.

In the first chapter of the *New Biography*, Case refers to the gospels as "ancient biographies of Jesus." Each gospel is a separate Life of Jesus, marked by its own distinctiveness.

Mark places much emphasis upon the deeds of Jesus and pictures him preeminently as a figure in action. Furthermore,

this gospel views Jesus as the founder of a new religion, as
Christianity's heaven-appointed founder. Case concludes that
the Marcan interest in Jesus was dominantly interpretative
in character and that it reflects a pervasive apologetic
atmosphere. However, these motifs are not so pronounced that
they completely obscure the earlier outlines of an earthly
Jesus.

As for Matthew and Luke, they copy very faithfully the
Marcan account. They seemingly are at pains to preserve, and
occasionally heighten, those features which made Jesus the
object of religious devotion. As Case viewed it, by far the
most distinctive features added to the Marcan picture is
Matthew's and Luke's emphasis upon Jesus as teacher. There
is less emphasis in Matthew and Luke than in Mark upon Jesus
as the object of the disciples' faith. Case drew the familiar
liberal distinction between the religion *of* Jesus and the
religion *about* Jesus when he wrote: "Among the Christians who
passed on this tradition portraying Jesus more specifically
as the teacher, it was the religion of Jesus, religion as
taught and lived by him, not the religion of which he was the
object, that held the center of attention."[155]

In comparison with the synoptics, the Fourth Gospel's
portrayal of Jesus is characterized by omissions and supplements. It is a genuinely new and largely original product.
In spite of the prevailing critical opinion, Case did not
dismiss the Fourth Gospel as a valid source for biographical
material about Jesus. He wrote of "the daring originality of
its portraiture, The writer's conviction that a new type of
biography was necessary for the further progress of the Christian movement was sufficient justification for writing the
Gospel." Case believed that the interests of the author of
the Fourth Gospel are not very different from those of the
other three evangelists. Each is concerned primarily to
picture Jesus as the founder of a new religion. He is a great
teacher and a unique personality, supernaturally qualified to
inaugurate a new order.

Case concluded his evaluation of the Fourth Gospel thus:

> The Johannine representation certainly is no mechanical
> photograph. Nor is it a literary mosaic, such as one
> finds in Matthew and Luke. Rather, it is manifestly
> the work of an artist, who, however true to life he may
> strive to paint, at the same time has an irrepressible
> genius for interpretative decoration.[156]

If one is to return to the historical Jesus, one must
distinguish between the unhistorical and the historical features
in the documents. How are the original elements to be separated
from later accretions and additions? Case rejected the view

that canonicity or apostolic authorship are genuine criteria of historical validity. Nor are the establishment of the earliest written sources and the methodology of a new "school" of research (form criticism) satisfactory for distinguishing historical from unhistorical parts in the gospels. However, there is yet a more fundamental consideration--the social experience reflected in the tradition, whatever its age or form.

Each gospel reveals the distinctive social experience of its writer, and though the gospels are biographies of Jesus they are also treatises dealing with contemporary issues and interests. Case proceeds to give examples, showing the social context of Jesus' words and deeds. "To visualize in concrete fashion the social setting in which he did his work will carry one a long way toward a genuine understanding of the tasks that confronted him and the line of conduct he chose to adopt."[157] The problem of historical material about Jesus becomes more readily soluble when one discerns the relationship between him and the Palestinian society of his day.

The social experience of Jesus and his earliest biographers largely coincided. Their social environment was the same as his. Consequently, the earliest Christians gave a true-to-life picture of Jesus. For Case, the fundamental test for the historicity of the sources is the social experience revealed in the content of the narrative. He wrote:

> Every statement in the records is to be judged by the degree of its suitableness to the distinctive environment of Jesus, on the one hand, and to that of the framers of gospel tradition at one or another stage in the history of Christianity, on the other. When consistently applied, this test will prove our safest guide in recovering from the present gospel records dependable information regarding the life and teaching of the earthly Jesus.[158]

Elaborating further on the social situation or social experience of Jesus, Case described in considerable detail Jewish life in Palestine. It was in this Jewish setting that Jesus lived and worked. "He was a Hebrew of the Hebrews and a Palestinian of the Palestinians." The Palestinian social context supplied the environment, which was both a deterrent and a stimulus to Jesus' course of action. Case noted: "The gravest problems to engage his attention were bequeathed to him by the people of this land in which he was born, and the hope of bringing his ideals to realization lay in a successful appeal to his contemporaries."[159]

Turning to the "home life of Jesus," Case believed that the tradition that portrays Jesus as growing up in Nazareth is historically accurate. References to Bethlehem are apologetically conditioned, designed to endow Jesus with messianic credentials.

Case observed that Jesus' "silent years" at Nazareth have
often "inspired" flights of fancy. Though the gospels are of
little help in this area, apocryphal literature portrays Jesus
as superhuman and as the veritable incarnation of divine power.
He manifested power over nature, and his wisdom was transcendent. Case dismissed these portrayals as fanciful and suggested
that the only way to visualize the real home life of Jesus is
to begin our quest with the characteristic activities of a
Jewish youth at the time and in the land of Jesus' nativity.
Case described the political, social, and economic conditions
of the Nazareth of Jesus' day, and in so doing provided his
readers with insights into the probable social experience of
Jesus.

After discussing the events of Jesus' life, Case elaborated
on "the religion Jesus lived." Jesus stood in the prophetic
line, and as such his religious life transcended that which
ordinary people experienced. But Jesus' early followers were
concerned more with him as an object of devotion whan with
the quality of his piety or religious life. The New Testament
writers presented Jesus as the one chosen by God to establish
the Kingdom, as preached by him and, earlier, by John the Baptist.

Case believed that the evangelists' perception of Jesus'
state of mind was conditioned by two factors--his words and
his wonderful acts. These two types of religious interest
may be referred to as the didactic and the heroic. Case observed that both were possible in the Palestinian setting
where Jesus had lived. However, among the Jews, the didactic
was more significant for religion than the heroic. It was
among the Gentiles that the heroic or miraculous displays
were more highly esteemed. Case concludes that the "garish
display of the miraculous" in the story of Jesus' life was
the result of the demands of the Gentile mission field, where
Christianity was struggling for recognition against rival
faiths that also made claim to the miraculous. Case noted:

> Appropriate as this picture is for a Gentile audience,
> it ill accords with the realities of that Palestinian
> Jewish setting where Jesus had actually lived and
> preached. A continuous series of marvelous deeds,
> such as are spread upon the pages of the gospels, finds
> no suitable place in the manner of life becoming a
> preacher of reform in Israel.[160]

Even though Jesus may have been convinced that he was
God's chosen one, the work to which he had been summoned was
primarily didactic. The working of miracles was not his daily
routine. He identified himself with the experiences known to
his contemporaries. "He shared their feelings of storm and

stress and rose to greater heights of assurance only as he
answered more unreservedly the summons of God to greater loyalty
in personal religious living."[161]
    Case felt that the messianic consciousness of Jesus and
his awareness of divine sonship were attributed to him by his
followers. He did not identify himself with these designa-
tions. The early Christians' experience of the risen Christ
caused them to invest him with transcendent qualities. This
development was intimately related to the religious history
of the disciples and had not been a part of the personal
religion of Jesus. "Messianic self-interpretation had not
concerned him. His energies had been consecrated to the task
of preparing his fellow-Jews for membership in the Kingdom."[162]
    The outstanding feature of Jesus' religion was not the
performance of miracles by appeal to divine power but his absolute devotion to the will of God. He had a vivid awareness
of the presence of God. At the very core of Jesus' religion
was his feeling of personal relation with God, the Heavenly
Father.
    But there was not only a vertical dimension to Jesus' re-
ligion; it was also horizontal. His experience of the divine
resulted in his sense of obligation to his fellow humans.
Spirituality undergirded prophetic discourse and ethical sen-
sitivity. His consecration to God resulted in service to
humanity.
    Jesus' religion was mystical, but he did not lose himself
in God or display an "orgy of emotions." Rather, he was concerned with increasing righteousness in the world and contribu-
ting to human welfare. The end was the establishment of the
Kingdom of God. That is, Jesus' religion was essentially ex-
periential, but it eventuated in words and deeds. He was "a
living example of the individual whose piety springs forth
spontaneously from the depths of his being."
    In his concluding chapter, Case wrote of "the religion
Jesus taught." He found that both the content of Jesus' message and the portrait of him as teacher in the gospels had
been modified in accordance with Christianity's new needs
around the turn of the first century. The spontaneous prophet
of reform was transformed into the figure of the rabbi.
Gradually, he lost those characteristics of dynamic personality
which were so evident during his lifetime, and he became the
author of Christianity's new law—a second Moses with the
official stamp of divine approval, which God had placed upon
him at the beginning of his career. He was also represented
as a conventional seer who foretold the future and as a sage
whose wisdom was more profound than Solomon's. Case noted:
"After the model of Judaism the new religion now presented
its founder in the role of lawgiver, seer, and sage, but

more excellent than any who had ever before appeared among
men."¹⁶³

Thus, Case maintained that before the end of the first
century Christianity had extensively institutionalized the
figure of Jesus the teacher. This occurred in order to serve
the pragmatic interests within the expanding life of the new
society. Parables used by him to clarify his message were
transformed into esoteric teachings understood by only a
select few. His teachings became new regulations for the conduct of religious life within the church, where duties were
discharged with a punctiliousness exceeding that of the scribes
and Pharisees.

But Case believed that we can and must go behind this situation if we are to recover the message of Jesus. To do this,
we must replace the interests of early Christianity with
those that were of prime importance among the Jews of Palestine
at the time of Jesus' public career. "It is still possible,"
Case maintained, "from the gospel records and our acquaintance
with contemporary Judaism, to reconstruct with a fair degree
of certainty a picture of Jesus the preacher in his own distinctive environment delivering his forceful utterances to
those with whom he came in contact."¹⁶⁴

Though Jesus possessed clear religious opinions and though
he held strong moral convictions, he was, claims Case, neither
a dogmatic theologian nor a theoretical moralist. Rather, his
views grew out of his personal contacts and his experiences
in actual life. "His problems were how to meet existing conditions, how to shape one's course of life in view of what
might be expected in the near future, and how to make more
contagious and convincing the type of conduct and the state
of mind which Jesus himself had come to feel were necessary
for the highest attainments in righteousness."¹⁶⁵

Of first importance in Jesus' teaching was the imminence
of the Kingdom of God. His aim was to move his hearers to
action by calling them to repentance. His purpose was not to
present an eschatological apologetic or to elaborate on its
imagery but to prepare people for entrance into the Kingdom.
His dominating ambition was to impel his hearers to higher
attainments in righteousness. In the interim before the
catastrophic advent of the Kingdon, Jesus' purpose was to
motivate people to exemplify now the very same manner of life
that would characterize them in the new age.

It is clear that Case viewed Jesus' understanding of the
Kingdom of God in essentially ethical terms. Though Jesus
was an eschatologist, he did not preach an "interim" ethic,
as Schweitzer thought. Jesus did not advocate one type of
ethic appropriate for the present as a mere preparation for
the future and another appropriate for the age to come. The

requirements for the new life were the same now as in the
future.

For Case, the religion Jesus taught was not dogmatic but
profoundly ethical. It was a rigorous ethic, not only taught
to others but also deeply grounded in Jesus' life amd experience. Case concluded:

> Jesus proclaimed that the good life was the perfect life.
> He was no champion of either mediocrity or moderation
> in spiritual affairs. No limit was to be set either to
> the ideal or to the effort necessary for worthy religious
> living.... And what Jesus demanded of others he himself
> was ready to perform. His own loyalty to the ideals
> that he preached carried the prophet from his carpenter's
> home in Nazareth to Christendom's cross on the Golgotha
> hill.[166]

James Mackinnon

James Mackinnon, who was Professor of Ecclesiastical History at the University of Edinburgh, published *The Historic
Jesus* in 1931. He defended the addition of one more book on
Jesus to the multitude of books already in existence by saying
that in his office as professor he had to treat the subject
of the historic Jesus. Moreover, a thorough study of the
historic Jesus is an indispensable condition of an adequate
treatment of Christian history. Christianity was founded on
his life and teaching, and the historian of Christianity can
never get away from the historic Jesus because his person and
achievement are the fundamental problem of this history.

At the outset of his work, Mackinnon drew a sharp line
between the historic Jesus and the Jesus who in later history
became the object of Christian faith and the spiritual head
of a universal religion. His intention was "to depict Jesus
as he actually manifested himself in his life and work on
earth" and "to set forth what manner of man he was and what he
accomplished or sought to accomplish during his mission in
Palestine."[167] Mackinnon sought to portray the Jesus of the
short span of his actual life and not the Jesus of later religious experience, or the ever-expanding Christian church,
or theological evaluation.

Though Mackinnon granted that a full-blown biography of
Jesus is impossible, he was far more optimistic about the possibility than were, for example, Wrede, Wellhausen, and the
form critics. After listing the difficulties regarding a
Life of Jesus, Mackinnon concluded:

> Nevertheless, such record as we have, if critically
> treated, cautiously weighed, is of the highest value.

> If imperfect from the point of view of comprehensiveness,
> it is wonderfully informative, both in what it contains
> and what it enables us reasonably to infer. It is in
> my opinion, possible to construct, in accordance with
> scientific historic method, a fairly adequate account
> of the mission of Jesus, as far at least as it has been
> recorded in the first three gospels. It is possible by
> a critical examination of this record to attain ap-
> proximately a knowledge of the facts of his active career,
> and a reasonably realistic conception of the personality
> which the facts reveal.[168]

Mackinnon's disagreement with German criticism, as represented
by Wellhausen and the form critics, was that they were too
disposed to deal with the tradition in an arbitrary, subjective
fashion. They would have profited by being more cognizant of
psychological insights and the exercise of imagination, which
would have enabled them to visualize more truly a situation
or an incident. Mackinnon maintained that a "cautious and
judicial criticism" would lead to a fairly adequate and sub-
stantially real view of the historic Jesus.

As for the Fourth Gospel, Mackinnon granted that its historical value is more problematic than the synoptics. It reflects the conditions of the time of its origin and the theological views of the writer. It is an interpretation of the
historic Jesus and not a historic account of Jesus in the usual
understanding of the term. Even so, "It contains valuable
historic data, and may, with discrimination, be used in a source
for the actual life of Jesus.... The Fourth Gospel does undoubtedly contain historic matter with which the historian
ought to reckon."[169]

Mackinnon observed that the synoptic gospels do not give
a chronological account of Jesus' ministry. Though the Fourth
Gospel does make a chronological arrangement of the synoptic
material with a series of feasts that Jesus attended in Jerusalem, it cannot be relied upon for his Galilean mission,
because its interest is mainly in the mission in the south and
its account of the Galilean mission is fragmentary.

The synoptists evidently did not find their material arranged chronologically in their source or sources. The material
was employed by the early church for preaching and edification.
Their chief interest was not historical instruction, but propa-
ganda. The writers were not so much concerned with chronology
as with giving illustrative details of the work of Jesus as
teacher and healer, arranged in what may appear to be, but
really is not, a consecutive narrative. Mackinnon added: "We
might describe them as collections of stories, interspersed
with didactic matter and set down without any real sense of

exact chronological sequence, and without critical discrimination."[170] The gospels are incomplete accounts of Jesus' mission and are but illustrative of his activity as healer and teacher.

In reference to the apocalyptic and eschatological aspects of Jesus and his message, Mackinnon rejected Schweitzer's "one-sided presentation." "Jesus was a supremely great moral and religious teacher as well as an apocalyptic seer, and his message is concerned with the revelation and inculcation of principles of religion and conduct which have an eternal validity and significance, apart from the apocalyptic coloring of his teaching."[171] The Sermon on the Mount and the practical parables are ample evidence that Jesus was not an apocalyptic visionary who lost sight of the moral and spiritual life in the haze of apocalypse and eschatology. The Kingdom of God was a reality to be realized in the present. Jesus' overriding concern was to reveal the Father-God and to invite people to enter into a relationship with him and to serve him by doing his will in actual life here and now. The Kingdom of God is of a distinctively spiritual and ethical rather than of an eschatological character. Mackinnon concluded: "To depict him solely in the light of the impassioned eschatologist--the Son of Man who lives and moves in a visionary world of the future-- is to present us with a sublimated Jesus that we do not recognize in the Jesus of the parables of the Good Samaritan and the Prodigal Son, the Jesus of the Sermon on the Mount, who is an essential part of the Jesus of the gospels."[172]

It must be admitted, says Mackinnon, that Jesus viewed the Kingdom of God in a twofold sense--in the present, ethical sense and in the future, eschatological sense. Both were in Jesus' mind from the beginning, though the eschatological became more prominent toward the close of his mission. The Kingdom has begun with Jesus' advent, and it will be climaxed in the full and final establishment of the rule of God, when the Son of Man will reappear to inaugurate the new order in all its fullness. As Mackinnon saw it, it is the present, ethical dimension of the Kingdom that is Jesus' basic concern. His teaching is concerned with the actual as well as the future order, and his moral ideal is meant to be exemplified in the concrete life of his followers, although it is also envisioned in the light of a higher destiny. To the end, Jesus is concerned with both ethics and eschatology, but to make him an apocalyptic only is to misread the gospels and to offer a one-sided conception both of him and his teaching.[172]

Near the close of *The Historic Jesus*, the section "Jesus as Historic Personality" summarizes Mackinnon's views on what we can know about Jesus and who he was.

It is difficult to discern exactly how Jesus conceived of himself in relation to the Father-God and of his messianic function and destiny. However, in the synoptic record, Mackinnon believed, we have genuine accounts of what Jesus thought and spoke and did. These records present an arresting and marvelous personality--one that attracted a growing band of disciples who saw in him the unique Master and later elevated him to the risen and glorified Christ. A new religious community emerged, of which he was the focus and the inspiration. Though the belief in the resurrection is central to the veneration of Jesus, it would not have been possible apart from the historic personality that underlay it. Jesus made a profound impression on the hearts and minds of those who knew him. Many surrendered themselves to his teaching because of the authoritative personality of the teacher and the arresting character of his teaching. The note of authority is his most impressive quality. He is sure of himself and never hesitates because he views himself as God's envoy and representative, and he speaks and acts accordingly. With him begins the new age that the prophets had envisioned. Moreover, his authority and preeminence rest on a solid basis of reality, inasmuch as he is the embodiment of the highest moral and spiritual ideal, which is for all time and for every class and race. He exhibits an exalted self-consciousness in that he is sent by God to accomplish human salvation, and our destiny depends upon our attitude toward and acceptance of him. What he specifically demands is faith in God as made known by him, his emissary and revealer.

Jesus manifested an authority and an imperiousness that may savor of egoism and intolerance to the modern reader. But it is not so, because his all-consuming passion was for God and the things of God. Yet he was not deranged or mentally unbalanced; the most striking feature of his character and his life was his marvelous self-possession and mastery. His assumption of the messianic function involved an indescribable sense of responsibility that only the supremely strong man could have borne. He was a superlatively strong personality, because his faith in God and his self-mastery kept the upper hand throughout. Jesus accomplished the hardest of all achievements--absolute self-dominion in devotion to the highest moral ideal.

Mackinnon observed that Jesus' imperiousness and idealism are permeated with a deep compassion for erring and suffering persons. His passion for God is combined with a magnificent love for others. Jesus manifests an admirable fusion of idealist and realist in thought and life. Though his life reflects solitariness and asceticism, it is supremely characterized by service. He understands his mission not as ruling, but as serving suffering, sinning people. He stands with the poor, the outcasts, those most in need of grace and love. He embodies an innate simplicity that intuitively knows God in his inner life and in the beauty and goodness of the divine handiwork on nature. Jesus is a great mystic, and yet his religion is singularly simple and human.

The human Jesus that Mackinnon depicted is a real, finite being. Though there is a mystery about him, and though the evangelists undoubtedly regard him as a unique personality, there is no theophany. He undergoes physical, mental, and spiritual development and is subject to the limitations of human nature. His knowledge is limited and contingent, and he confesses ignorance. He shares current beliefs, superstitions, and the faulty cosmogony of his time. The science and philosophy of the Greco-Roman world are unknown to Jesus. He reveals the senses and the emotions of every human person, in that he hungers, thirsts, is weary, and becomes angry at the unbelief of his opponents and even at times by the disciples' lack of insight. He rejoices at success, is exposed to temptation to the end, and constantly feels the need of prayer for strength and guidance. And, like others, he experiences a natural shrinking from pain and death.[174]

Mackinnon concluded his work with a discussion of how Jesus conceived of his relation to God, the Father. He noted that later dogmatic views about him tended to blur or ignore the picture of the historic Jesus. With the resurrection, Jesus entered upon a higher existence. However, Mackinnon maintained that prior to this transition it was the man Jesus of Nazareth that the primitive tradition preserved with a notable fidelity.

Jesus' relationship as Son to the Father should not be construed metaphysically or dogmatically. Jesus conceived of himself as the fulfiller of God's will and purpose in his divinely appointed vocation. But to put this in trinitarian or metaphysical terms is "to enter the realm of speculation." The relation should be understood religiously and ethically, not metaphysically. Mackinnon wrote:

> That Jesus stood in unique nearness to God in virtue of his Godlike character and profound communion with him, that he possessed in a superlative degree the vision of God that accrues from the perfection of the spiritual life, that he realized, as the fruit of this personal experience, a compelling supremacy over the hearts and minds of men, that he rose to the conception of a destiny, in the providence of God, unique in human history-- this is amply borne out by what we know of his life and mission.... The relation is religious and ethical, not

metaphysical. Jesus is not yet touched by philosophy,
and his conception of God and himself is the religious,
not the metaphysical one.[175]

Father and Son are distinct in person as well as function.
From first to last, Jesus distinguishes between himself and
God. Jesus should be viewed as the highest manifestation of
the divine in the human, rather than as a divine being becoming human. "The assumption that Father and Son embody a
divine duality, and the attempt to reduce this duality into an
absolute unity on later trinitarian lines is not warranted by
his own authentic teaching or the primitive apostolic preaching...."[176]

For Mackinnon, the greatness and uniqueness of Jesus re-
side in his spiritual and ethical life. The secret of the
power of Christianity is in the moral elevation, the enthusiasm
in well-doing, the spiritual dynamic of the New Testament ethic.
"The real Jesus needs no apologetic. His life and his influence are their own all-sufficient attestation. Here assuredly
is the supreme life on earth, the most compelling personality,
the king of us all, the greatest inspiration to the highest
things in the whole range of religious history."[177] Mackinnon
added:

> The wonderful power of his personality is not circum-
> scribed by the short span of his actual existence on
> earth. It has made itself felt in the hearts and lives
> of successive generations of his followers, appealing
> to the souls of men with a perennial force, inspiring,
> uplifting, illuminating, and directing them in their
> aspiration after God and the highest good, and verifying
> itself in the moral and spiritual progress of humanity....
> In this upward evolutionary process Jesus has been, and
> is, the greatest factor. In this respect the greatest
> of idealists has approved himself as the greatest of
> realists.[178]

Maurice Goguel

La Vie de Jésus, by Maurice Goguel, appeared in 1932, with
an English translation (*The Life of Jesus*) in 1933. It differed from most Lives of Jesus in that about half of the book
was given to preliminary critical problems, such as non-Christian
sources of the gospel story, the Pauline evidence, the gospels
and the gospel tradition, problems and method, the chronology
of the gospel narrative, and the length and setting of the
ministry of Jesus. The opening section consists of an overview
of the history of Life of Jesus research.

Like the preceding liberal scholars, Goguel maintained
that the bearers of the gospel tradition had no interest in
history or biography in the usual sense of the words. Their
orientation was dogmatic and apologetic, so that they were
indifferent to historical accuracy and indeed were very little
able to judge on this point. What concerned them primarily
were not facts but the transcendent reality revealed in Christ.
What should surprise us is not that the material was altered
but that the Christian tradition did not subject it to a more
thorough transformation by replacing the gospel history with
a myth. This certainly would have been an interpretation and
an explanation of the Christian faith more homogeneous, more
direct, and more integral.[179]

Primitive Christianity did not feel that it was directly
connected with the earthly life of Jesus. The object of its
faith and worship was not Jesus but the Christ. The early
Christians were indifferent to the facts about Jesus' life.
The center of their faith was the resurrection, through which
the messianic nature of Jesus was manifested. Moreover, their
attention was not directed to a figure in the past but toward
the immediate future when the Lord of glory would appear and
consummate his Kingdom. This explains why the early church
was satisfied to preserve fragmentary recollections of Jesus.
It was when the eschatological hope began to weaken that more
and more importance began to be attached to the messianic
element in the life of Jesus.

It was out of this milieu that Mark, the first gospel,
appeared. A transformation from the hope in the imminent
parousia to the needs of an ongoing community had taken place.
Consequently, the Christian community felt "the need to gather
the traditions which related to the earthly life of Jesus into
a unity, within a fixed framework, and to give to them both
the coherence of a connected story and the character of a systematic exploration of the messiahship of Jesus, and thus,
indirectly, of Christianity itself. But this explanation was
regarded from the transcendental point of view, not merely as
imminent in history."[180]

Goguel observed that the development of the tradition was
neither casual nor accidental but was due to forces inherent
in the tradition itself, which were operative long before the
earliest gospel had been compiled. From the time of Jesus'
death, people were convinced that he had been a miracle worker
and that he was no ordinary man, but rather a divine being.

Goguel, while admitting that the methodology of form criticism is legitimate and necessary, judged it to be inadequate
by itself. He held that it is impossible to reconstruct the
most ancient form of the gospel tradition because the causes
that determined the changes in the tradition were not those

that determined its genesis. "The creation and the transformation of a tradition are two quite different things, and we have
no proof that the development of the tradition has always taken
place in the same direction." Thus, Goguel concluded that it
will never be possible to resolve the problem of the life of
Jesus, except in a fragmentary and conjectural manner.[181]

It is clear that we cannot find, directly, a Life of Jesus
in the gospels. We should not expect the story of Jesus to
give us absolute certainty, because such certainty lies more
in the realm of religious intuition and faith, says Goguel.
The person of Jesus raises two problems, because he belongs
to the realms of both history and religious faith--to both
humanity and transcendent reality. This dual situation poses
a serious problem for anyone attempting to reconstruct the life
of Jesus. "All that can be done is to construct something as
well as one can. Is it possible thus to reconstruct the story
without falling into the error of being arbitrary?... We will
not demand an absolute certitude from a Life of Jesus. Our
ambition will be more modest. All we ask is this: is it possible to attain, in all that concerns the life of Jesus, that
degree of certitude comparable to that which we are able to
attain in other spheres of ancient history?"[182]

In reviewing the Life of Jesus research, Goguel noted
that though the critical method can furnish "some isolated
fragments of material" it cannot produce a Life of Jesus.
The critic's work must be supplemented by that of the historian, whose aim it is "to set in order the facts which have
been accepted as reliable, from the threefold point of view
of chronology, geography, and psychology, to link them together, and to explain one set of facts in the light of
another."[183]

Life of Jesus research has been dominated by the critical
sense and the work of the historian reduced to something secondary. Goguel felt that the time had come for a renewal of the
historical method. "It is time to attack, in a more broadly
historical spirit, the problem of the arrangement of the
material of the life of Jesus which can be retained as authentic." This can be accomplished by seeing the significance
of the internal relation of the facts to each other and trying
to understand them from the inside, "by entering into the
psychology of those who have been the actors in the story,
by an attempt to revive their state of mind through an effort
of intelligent sympathy and understanding." There is need
for psychology and intuition rather than a simple record of
facts set down in succession.[184]

Goguel's methodology was characterized more by historicism
and psychology than by higher criticism. Consequently, the
setting of the life of Jesus is in the context of crises. The

principal effort of the historian should be directed toward
the three crises of the gospel story: Jesus' return to Galilee,
his journey to Judea, and the passion. Though external circumstances were influential in these crises, they were chiefly
due to psychological causes. "They were occasioned by the
reaction caused by his preaching and the development of his
thought, under the influence of his own experiences, and by
the deepening of his religious life."[185] For Goguel, the
way to Jesus is through an understanding of his thought and
his religious experience. He noted: "The thought of Jesus is
peculiarly simple and coherent in character; it is in direct
relation with a religious experience which doubtless we are
not in a position to understand in its depth, but of which we
are able to perceive the dominant features."[186]

A Life of Jesus must of necessity be fragmentary and incomplete because the sources do not provide us with the detailed account we would so much like to possess, There will
always be large gaps because nothing is known about his
youth, and there is a lack of detailed chronological information that would provide a coherent framework for the
story. It is impossible to determine the total length of
Jesus' ministry and of its various periods. Approaching Jesus'
life from the critical or exterior point of view will always
be inadequate. The basic approach must be psychological.
Goguel wrote: "As in the case of all historical reconstruction, in the last resort every attempt to understand the life
of Jesus must be based upon psychology."[187] Goguel believed
that it is possible to outline some features in Jesus' personality and to perceive some elements in his history, even
though one can neither make a complete portrait of him nor
compose a detailed biography.

Goguel arranged his Life of Jesus around the three crises
mentioned above. The crisis in Galilee is precipitated by
Herod's decision to kill Jesus and causes Jesus to leave
Galilee to engage in the "Jerusalem ministry." Goguel discerned a development in the tradition here. Originally,
people thought that Jesus left Galilee because of the hos-
tility of Herod. However, the early Christians felt uneasy
at the suggestion that Jesus yielded to the threats of Herod.
So they concluded that Jesus went to a more important area
(Jerusalem) in order to continue his ministry or to manifest
his messiahship.

After discussing the ministry of Jesus in Galilee and in
Jerusalem, where Jesus was crucified, Goguel concluded his
book with a section entitled "The Gospel." This discusses
Jesus' relationship to Judaism, his conception of God, and his
teachings regarding eschatology and ethics. Let us consider
briefly one of these--Jesus' understanding of God.

The God whom Jesus knew was not merely a reality in the
past or just an abstract idea. He was a living, present
reality. God was in him and was experienced, felt, known.
"The unique originality of Jesus consists in his sense of
the presence of God, in that conscious and living communion
with God in which he lives."[188] Though Jesus believed in a
God characterized by such abstract categories as omnipotence,
omniscience, transcendence, and holiness, he was a God who
was very near to persons and was known best as "Father."
God is just and righteous, but in Jesus' own experience God
had not revealed himself as an inflexible Judge or a strict
Master but as a Father.

As for Judaism, Jesus did not condemn it, and thus he did
not feel that he had founded a new religion. Goguel noted
that Jesus became detached from empirical Judaism through
fidelity to the ideal Judaism. A religion grew out of the
work of Jesus, in that the founders of the new movement developed the feelings and experiences that directly or indirectly had been implanted in them through the impression made on
them by Jesus' person and teaching.

The Gospel of John records that when he was crucified
Jesus said: "It is finished." Goguel stated that the evan-
gelist, perhaps without knowing it, expressed a great truth.
He concluded *The Life of Jesus* as follows:

> The work of Jesus was finished. The faith which he had
> been able to plant in the hearts of a few men, feeble
> and hesitating as it was, had roots which were too deep
> to be ever eradicated. Nothing was finished; in reality,
> everything had just begun. The faith in the Resurrec-
> tion was about to be born, and with it that Christianity
> which was destined to conquer the ancient world and to
> march through the centuries.[189]

Form Criticism

Albert Schweitzer, while paying tribute to the devoted
labors of the nineteenth-century critics, argued that their
combined efforts had led simply to failure. He maintained
that it was impossible to reconstruct the life of Jesus from
the historical point of view. From different perspectives,
Wrede and Wellhausen had come to the same conclusion.

Just after the close of World War I, a new school arose
that renewed the contention that it was impossible to construct
a Life of Jesus. This movement came to be called *Formgeschichte*,
"form criticism," or more literally "form history." It found
antecedents in Wrede and Wellhausen, and though its methodology
and presuppositions differed from Schweitzer's it came to the

same negative conclusion regarding the possibility of writing
a Life of Jesus.

Within two years, from 1919 to 1921, four German scholars--
Martin Dibelius, Karl Ludwig Schmidt, Martin Albertz, and
Rudolf Bultmann--independently produced original studies of
the various forms of the pre-literary traditions regarding
the gospel accounts.[190] The movement provoked considerable
discussion and controversy in Germany, and it came to super-
sede the former interest in research on the synoptic problem
that had dominated for the greater part of the nineteenth
century. Form criticism has been accepted in Germany,
and its methods and presuppositions are central in contemporary
German New Testament study. In England, the situation has
been otherwise, and many of England's New Testament scholars
have been critical of the methods and conclusions of form
criticism.[191]

The beginnings of form criticism antedate the period
1919-1921. The form critics were not the first to arrive at
the conclusions that form criticism holds. Rather, they
brought to the surface and put into concrete form concepts
that had been abroad for many years prior to this time.

Dibelius mentioned the following precursors of form criticism: Eduard Norden, Johann Gottfried Herder, Franz Overbeck,
Hermann Gunkel, and Adolf Deissmann. Bultmann, in dealing
with the background of form criticism, referred to Wrede's
Das Messiasgeheimnis in den Evangelien, calling it "undoubtedly the most important work in the field of gospel research in
the generation now past." In addition to Wrede, Bultmann
singled out Wellhausen as one who, like Wrede, came to the
same general conclusion.

At first, the form critics applied their methods of investigation principally to the synoptic gospels. They worked
in the belief that the evangelists were not primarily authors
but rather editors, whose gospels consisted of collections
of material that at first circulated in oral form. The form
critics were interested in trying to determine the nature of
the tradition before the evangelists took it and fixed it in
its present form as we have it in the gospels. Thus, they
attempted to get behind the traditions that were used in the
"editing" of the gospels. By so doing, the form critics believed that they could throw light on the life and faith of
the early Christian community, through which the gospels came
into being. Dibelius in describing the objectives of form
criticism wrote:

> The method of *Formgeschichte* has a twofold objective.
> In the first place, by reconstruction and analysis, it
> seeks to explain the origin of the tradition about
> Jesus, and thus to penetrate into a period previous to

that in which our gospels and their written sources
were recorded. But it has a further purpose. It seeks
to make clear the intention and real interest of the
earliest tradition. We must show with what objective
the first churches recounted stories about Jesus, or
copied them from papyrus. In the same manner we must
examine the sayings of Jesus and ask with what intention
these churches collected them, learned them by heart,
and wrote them down. The present-day reader should
learn to read the individual passages of the early
tradition in the way they were meant, before the time
when, more or less edited, they were included in the
gospels.

The method of *Formgeschichte* seeks to help in answering the historical questions as to the nature and
trustworthiness of our knowledge of Jesus, and also in
solving a theological problem properly so-called. It
shows in what way the earliest testimony about Jesus
was interwoven with the earliest testimony about the
salvation which had appeared in Jesus Christ. Thereby
it attempts to emphasize and illuminate the chief elements of the message upon which Christianity was founded.[192]

Bultmann reflects the same basic concerns:

The purpose of form criticism is to study the history
of the oral tradition behind the gospels.... Form criticism begins with the realization that the tradition contained in the synoptic gospels originally consisted of
separate units, which were joined together editorially
by the evangelists. Form criticism is therefore concerned to distinguish these units of tradition, and to
discover their earliest form and origin in the life of
the early Christian community. It views the gospels
as essentially compilations of this older material. But
it also studies them as finished works, in order to
evaluate the literary activity of the evangelists, and
to discover the theological motives that guided them.[193]

The form-critical investigations, which were marked by the
most careful and thorough examination of the synoptic gospels,
came to the unanimous conclusion that the oldest tradition
about Jesus was in the form of *pericopes*—i.e., the tradition
was made up of single actions, sayings, and parables. Each
of these "forms" was an independent entity in itself and was
formed in accordance with certain rules or practical needs
of the primitive Christian community. The resulting framework
of these forms was largely the work of the evangelists. They
were the "editors" who set up the framework, who established

the "order of events," and who provided almost all the details
of place and time. The only exception to this pattern is the
passion narrative, which conveyed the events of the last days
of Jesus' life in an orderly fashion from a very early
stage of the tradition.

The laws governing the shaping of the tradition and the
motivation behind this process must be seen in the context
of the life and faith of the community. This is one of the
decisive insights of the form-critical method. The principal
occasion and purpose of the shaping of the tradition was
preaching. The term "preaching" is used in its widest context
here. It includes everything that pertains to the proclamation
of the primitive Christian community regarding their faith in
Jesus. The gospels are "church books," and they have been
shaped, if not produced, by the needs and interests of the
early Christians.

The basic question regarding form criticism is not methodo-
logical but theological, although the two are closely related.
One of the first and foremost insights of form criticism is
that the tradition about Jesus arose and was preserved from
considerations not of history but of faith. There was a
Christology behind the tradition from the beginning. There
never was a picture of Jesus apart from faith. So Dibelius
writes:

> The first understanding afforded by the standpoint of
> *Formgeschichte* is that there never was a "purely" his-
> torical witness to Jesus. Whatever was told of Jesus'
> words and deeds was always a testimony of faith as formu-
> lated for preaching and exhortation in order to convert
> unbelievers and confirm the faithful. What founded
> Christianity was not knowledge about a historical pro-
> cess, but the confidence that the content of the story
> was salvation: the decisive beginning of the end.[194]

The historical entity that we confront in the tradition is not
the historical Jesus but the faith of the community in him.
For form criticism, the "quest" leads not to the historical
Jesus but to the primitive Christian community. We come to
the historical Jesus and see him only through the eyes of the
community, and their picture of him is governed by their belief that he is the Christ. As the writer of the Fourth Gospel
states: "Now Jesus did many other signs in the presence of his
disciples, which are not written in this book; but these are
written that you may believe that Jesus is the Christ, the
Son of God, and that believing you may have life in his name"
(John 20:30-31).

In many cases, it is the community that may have created
stories about Jesus, and put words into his mouth that he had

never spoken, and credited to him deeds that he may never
have done. This process did not happen only after a later
time before which there was "objective" material about Jesus.
Rather, it was the primitive community that originally began
and transmitted the tradition about Jesus.

The gospels, unlike other types of ancient historical
writing, are unique in this respect. They are not biographical
or historical documents but statements of faith. Their intent
is not to picture Jesus "as he once was" but to proclaim him
as he now is--the risen and living Lord. The gospels are
written not to portray history accurately or to present
authentic biographical material about Jesus but to confront
people with him who is the Christ, so "that believing they
might have life in his name."

To put the matter in other terms, we always confront Jesus
in the kerygma--i.e., in the faith and proclamation of the
community. The history is in the kerygma, and the kerygma
is in the history. Thus, Hans Conzelmann says, the historical-
critical study of the history of Jesus has reached "a higher
stage of historical reflection."[195] The concern is no longer,
as with the earlier study of the life of Jesus, to reconstruct
a Life of Jesus from a historical evaluation of the sources.
The concern is now to interpret the evidences of faith--the
texts that were meant as kerygma. James M. Robinson characterizes the contemporary situation:

> The basic reorientation is to the effect that *all* the
> tradition about Jesus survived only in so far as it
> served some function in the life and worship of the
> primitive church. History survived only as kerygma.
> It is this insight which reversed our understanding of
> the scholar's situation with regard to the relation of
> factual detail and theological interpretation in the
> gospels. If the nineteenth century presupposed the de-
> tailed historicity of the synoptic gospels except where
> "doctrinal tampering" was so obvious as to be inescapable
> (they had in mind such things as "Paulinisms" and the
> miraculous), the twentieth century presupposes the keryg-
> matic nature of the gospels and feels *really* confident
> in asserting the historicity of its details only where
> their origin cannot be explained in terms of the life
> of the church. In the nineteenth century the burden
> of proof lay upon the scholar who saw theological inter-
> pretations in historical sources; in the twentieth cen-
> tury the burden of proof lies upon the scholar who sees
> objective factual source material in the primitive
> church's book of common worship.[196]

It is quite obvious from the foregoing discussion that
form criticism has greatly accentuated the difficulties of

constructing a Life of Jesus. If Jesus is only to be discerned
in the kerygma of the community, what is still left of the
"real Jesus"? It would appear that form criticism has once
and for all obliterated from our view Jesus "as he really was."
Bultmann has gone so far as to suggest that "I do indeed think
we can now know almost nothing concerning the life and personality of Jesus, since the early Christian sources show no
interest in either, are moreover fragmentary and often legendary; and other sources about Jesus do not exist."[197]

Rudolf Bultmann

Since Bultmann is generally regarded as the leading New
Testament scholar of the twentieth century, let us pursue
further his interpretation of Jesus.

Bultmann's view of Jesus is influenced primarily by two
considerations--form criticism and the existentialist interpretation of history. Form criticism leads him to the position
that the New Testament writers had no interest in the personality
of Jesus, that they were primarily interested in the work of
Jesus. The existentialist interpretation of history leads
Bultmann to speak of Jesus as the eschatological event that
calls people to decision now.

Bultmann is primarily indebted to three thinkers in his
understanding of history: Wilhelm Dilthey, Martin Heidegger,
and R.G. Collingwood. They reflect an "existentialist" approach to history in that each sees a definite relationship
between history and the historical existence of the historian
himself. John Macquarrie has set forth four basic proposi-
tions that characterize this existentialist approach to history: (1) Historical reflection has for its subject-matter
human existence in the world. (2) In historical reflection,
the reflecting subject participates in a peculiar way in the
object of his reflection. (3) The function of historical reflection is to provide a self-understanding. (4) Historical
reflection is concerned primarily with possibility.[198]

It is such an understanding of history or "viewpoint"
that underlies Bultmann's *Jesus and the Word*: "Thus I would
lead the reader not to any 'view' of history, but to a highly
personal *encounter* with history.... Attention is entirely
limited to what Jesus *purposed*, and hence to what in his purpose
as a part of history makes a present demand on us."[199] For
Bultmann, consequently, Jesus Christ is the eschatological
event, the action of God by which God has set an end to the
old world. Moreover, it is in the act of the preaching of
the church that the eschatological event becomes present and
also will become present again and again in faith. "It becomes an event repeatedly in preaching and faith. Jesus Christ

is the eschatological event not as an established fact of
past time but as repeatedly present, as addressing you and
me here and now in preaching."[200]
    Bultmann's interest is not in the historical Jesus but in
Jesus Christ as an ever-present event. In his introduction
to *Jesus and the Word*, Bultmann says that his book "lacks all
the phraseology which speaks of Jesus as great man, genius,
or hero; he appears neither as inspired nor as inspiring, his
sayings are not called profound, nor his faith mighty, nor
his nature child-like. There is also no consideration of the
eternal value of his message, of his discovery of the infinite
depths of the human soul, or the like."[201]
    It is the teaching or the message of Jesus that is central
for Bultmann. The message of Jesus is an eschatological one
that lends a new understanding of existence. It is the proclamation that now the fulfillment of the promise is at hand,
that now the Kingdom of God begins. Jesus' message calls us
to decision now and puts us in a crisis of decision before God.
It is precisely this aspect of crisis that is characteristic
of our humanity. Every hour is the last hour. Jesus pressed
the whole contemporary mythology into this picture of human
existence. Thus, he understood and proclaimed his hour as
the last hour.
    Bultmann's proposal that the New Testament must be demyth-
ologized has this same intent. The mythology that provides
the framework for the kerygma is to be interpreted anthropo-
logically or, better still, existentially. The important point
is that the essence of myth is not in its imagery but in the
understanding of human existence that is expressed through the
imagery.
    One can rightly conclude that Bultmann, with his form-
critical, demythologizing, and existential-historical methodology, has dehistorized and reduced the kerygma, at least insofar as its relation to the historical Jesus is concerned.
It appears that Bultmann is ready to attribute to the church
creative powers and imaginative genius that he is unwilling to
attribute to Jesus. He writes:

> But Christian faith did not exist until there was a
> Christian kerygma; i.e. a kerygma proclaiming Jesus
> Christ--specifically Jesus Christ the Crucified and
> Risen One--to be God's eschatological act of salvation.
> He was first so proclaimed in the kerygma of the earliest
> church, not in the message of the historical Jesus, even
> though that church frequently introduced into its ac-
> count of Jesus' message, motifs of its own proclamation.
> Thus, theological thinking--the theology of the New
> Testament--begins with the kerygma of the earliest church
> and not before. But the fact that Jesus had appeared

and the message which he had proclaimed were, of course, among its historical presuppositions; and for this reason Jesus' message cannot be omitted from the delineation of New Testament theology.[202]

The relationship between the kerygma and history is a fundamental question for Bultmann's critics. Bultmann never denies that there is a relation between the two, but he insists that the truth of the kerygma cannot be proven from history. He says: "I still deny that historical research can ever encounter any traces of the epiphany of God in Christ; all it can do is to confront us with the Jesus of history. Only the church's proclamation can bring us face to face with Kyrios Christos."[203]

Martin Dibelius

Like Bultmann, Dibelius has written a book on Jesus.[204] In keeping with the conclusions of form criticism, Dibelius notes that we cannot describe the events of Jesus' life except during the last days. The communities that collected his sayings and the stories about him were interested neither in evolution nor in psychology. They were concerned with preserving the words and deeds of Jesus.

The narrative sections of the synoptic gospels are not the creation of the evangelists but have been taken over from the already-existing oral, and eventually also written, tradition. Except for the passion and Easter stories, the material consists of completely self-contained units whose positions can be interchanged without affecting the picture of Jesus' activity. Thus, we cannot establish the chronological order or reconstruct the psychological development of Jesus. A "biography" of Jesus in this sense cannot be written. All we know is individual incidents, not interconnected events. The evangelists merely framed and combined these materials. The original material consisted always of the single unit of narrative, the single saying--not the connected text, the transitions, or the editorial notes that provide the continuity.

At the center of Jesus' message is the Kingdom of God. Though he never specifically interpreted or defined the expression "Kingdom of God," he gave it both a future and a present reference. The Kingdom had not yet appeared, but its signs were visible. Dibelius maintains that one can understand Jesus' mission only if one keeps in view these two poles between which lies everything that he said and did. On the one hand, the Kingdom of God is in the future and opposed to this world. On the other hand, it is already in process of coming and has already put itself in motion. "This existence

between 'not yet having arrived' and 'having arrived' one must
understand if one is to comprehend the historical position of
the gospel."[205]

For Jesus, the *one* sign of the Kingdom was his own person,
his preaching, his movement. The miracle stories point to and
attest to the one who is the exalted Lord of the community.
Dibelius notes: "God himself is drawing near to the world,
and his nearness is perceived in the fact that through Jesus
he speaks, through him he acts, through him he heals."[206]

Dibelius' intention in his book on Jesus is to describe
the public activity of Jesus as far as it can be ascertained
by historical science. The tradition is fragmentary and reflects the "faith needs" of the early Christian communities.
It insists that Jesus' mighty deeds, his words, even the fact
of his appearing in the course of human history, are all
"signs" of the Kingdom of God. However, these signs cannot
finally be proved or authenticated by historical research,
but a genuine decision of faith or of unfaith is required.
The eschatology of faith implies that the actuality of God's
Reign exists but that it has not yet fully come to pass. "Faith
must content itself with the historical sign of the revelation
in Jesus the Christ."

Dibelius says that this sign is historical—a piece of
human history. This fact makes it possible to doubt and also
to investigate critically the story that is told. He summarizes
the relationship between the tradition and faith thus:

> As human accounts of human events they are of course
> proper subjects of research; but research cannot answer
> any of the questions involving decision—only faith can
> provide their answer. Yet since faith discovers, in a
> piece of history, God's own testimony and guarantee,
> necessity is accordingly laid upon it to set forth this
> bit of history as clearly and accurately as possible.
> Moreover, since through faith this bit of history has
> itself now become a historical factor of undreamed
> range of influence, everyone who reflects at all upon
> the history and the destiny of mankind must be concerned
> with it.[207]

New Quest of the Historical Jesus

The seeming discontinuity between history and the kerygma,
between the earthly Jesus and the risen Lord, and Bultmann's
insistence that we confront Jesus Christ as the eschatological
event in the preaching of the church, has led to a "new quest"
of the historical Jesus. Richard R. Niebuhr states the problem
concisely:

Unless somehow it can be shown that the Jesus of history, whose historical acts of crucifixion and resurrection are the origin of the church, transcends the existential Christ of our interpretations, we have lost the
basis of our community and our common history and have
become isolated from one another. Without a historical
basis in memory, the existential "Christ of faith" is
an ineffable experience of religiousness.[208]

The new quest of the historical Jesus arose as a protest
or an attempted corrective to Bultmann in regard to the relation of the kerygma to history. It is significant that the
leaders of the movement were well-known pupils of Bultmann and
thus were quite familiar with his methodology and his theology.
The new quest was associated particularly with Ernst Käsemann,
Günther Bornkamm, Gerhard Ebeling, Ernst Fuchs, and Hans
Conzelmann. In the United States, the most prominent spokesman was James M. Robinson.

The classical Bultmannian position against which these
scholars are reacting is found in the following quotation:

So one may not go behind the kerygma, using it as a
"source," in order to reconstruct a "historical Jesus"
with his "messianic consciousness," his "inwardness"
or his "heroism." That would be precisely the Christ
according to the flesh, who is gone. Not the historical
Jesus, but Jesus Christ, the proclaimed, is the Lord.[209]

The new quest, concerned with Bultmann's unsatisfactory
dealing with the historical question, attempted to arrive at
a more tenable solution. Those who pursued the new quest
discerned in Bultmann a discontinuity between the historical
Jesus and the risen Christ who comes to us through the kerygma.
There is no sufficient continuity between Jesus' preaching
and the preaching of the early church. There is no continuity
between Jesus' self-understanding and the church's understanding
of Jesus.

But if the old quest ended in failure, why should a new
one fare any better? How does the situation differ so that
more positive results will accrue? There are two possibili-
ties--new sources and new methods.[210] It is the second al-
ternative that the new quest followed. Those who led the new
quest rejected the Life of Jesus movement as radically as did
Bultmann. They worked with form-critical methods. They
acknowledged that historicism cannot become the key to New
Testament interpretation. One cannot recover the historical
Jesus merely by poring over the old sources, even if more
diligently than before.

Though there are no new sources, there are "new methods"
or "new views." The existentialist understanding of the self

and of history offers new possibilities for the new quest.
Statements by James M. Robinson describe the new situation:

> The possibility of resuming the quest of the historical
> Jesus *has* been latent in the radically different under-
> standing of history and of human existence distinguish-
> ing the present quest from the one which ended in
> failure....
>   The effect of this modern view of history and human
> existence upon New Testament study has been primarily
> to focus attention upon the kerygma as the New Testament
> statement of Jesus' history and selfhood.... Jesus'
> understanding of his existence, his selfhood, and thus
> in the higher sense his life, is a possible subject of
> historical research.[211]

> The quest is now possible not because our view of the
> sources has changed, but rather because our view of his-
> tory has changed. An understanding of history does not
> consist essentially in the still impossible reconstruc-
> tion of chronology, psychological development, and causal
> relationships, but rather in an encounter with "history
> as occurrence and event".... The message reveals the
> historical intention (i.e. the historical reality in
> the actions), which in turn reveals the view of existence
> constituting the self; i.e through the message one en-
> counters the person.[212]

Thus, the spirit of the new quest was characterized by an
openness to existential encounter with the being of Jesus in
the immediacy of his presence in his words and deeds. The
purpose of the new quest was not to establish the factuality
of this or that word or deed of Jesus, this or that miracle,
this or that sequence of events in his life. Rather, its purpose was to elucidate the nature of the gospel tradition so
that we might encounter Jesus in the immediacy of his power
and presence. Günther Bornkamm states it concisely: "In every
layer, therefore, and in each individual part, the tradition
is witness of the reality of his history and the reality of
his resurrection. Our task, then, is to seek the history in
the kerygma of the gospels, and in this history to seek the
kerygma."[213]

The new quest of the historical Jesus was launched in 1953
by Ernst Käsemann in an address to a meeting of "old Marburgers"
(i.e., Bultmannians) on "The Problem of the Historical Jesus."[214]

Käsemann began his address by saying that the question
concerning the historical Jesus had receded almost completely
into the background in German New Testament scholarship in
the last generation. This had led to the point (at least in

Bultmann) where "Christian faith is understood as faith in
the exalted Kyrios, a Lord for whom the historical Jesus as
such no longer possesses fundamental meaning."[215] He adds:

> Bultmann's radical approach practically shouts for a
> reaction. More than that, the question of a suitable
> understanding of history and historicity is a question
> which today concerns every one of us without exception;
> and, in the case of the theologian, it must, of necessity,
> take concrete form in the problem of the historical Jesus
> and of his significance for faith.[216]

Thus, the question of the historical Jesus cannot be by-
passed, and, since something (even though slight) can be known
about Jesus, it is our task to concern ourselves with working
it out. Moreover, it is the New Testament itself that gives
us the right because the gospels assign their kerygma to the
earthly Jesus. Primitive Christianity was not willing to
put a myth in the place of history or a heavenly being in
the place of the Nazarene.

Käsemann concluded that it is impossible to construct a
detailed history of Jesus from the sources. This, however,
dare not lead us to skepticism and lack of interest in the
earthly Jesus. The historian must recognize that there actually are authentic pieces of the synoptic tradition having
to do with Jesus' deeds and preaching.

In spite of Käsemann's criticisms of Bultmann, and his
urgent claim that we must address ourselves anew to the question of the historical Jesus, one must conclude that he does
not move significantly beyond Bultmann. For Käsemann finally
throws the decisive question back into the lap of faith, and
that is precisely where Bultmann had placed it all along.
Käsemann's concluding statements make this clear:

> The gospel is attached to him who revealed himself to
> his disciples before and after Easter as Lord by
> placing them before the God who is close at hand and
> by therewith placing them into the sphere where both
> the freedom and the responsibility of faith are opera-
> tive.... The problem of the historical Jesus is in so
> far not our discovery, but the puzzle which he himself
> places before us as our task. The historian may estab-
> lish the fact of this puzzle; he does not solve it. It
> is only solved by those who since the cross and the
> resurrection confess him as the one whom he in his
> earthly life did not claim to be and whom he became,
> namely, as their Lord and as the bringer of the freedom
> of the children of God which is the correlate of divine
> rulership. For corresponding to this contingency of
> faith, for which the story of Jesus happens anew, now

as the story of the exalted and preached Lord and
still, as once upon a time, as the earthly history in
which the gospel's promise and its claim meet.[217]

Among those who have taken up the challenge of Käsemann
to reopen the long-neglected concern with the historical
Jesus is Günther Bornkamm. Of all the "Bultmänner," he appears the "boldest" because he has written a book about
Jesus.[218] But from the outset it becomes clear that Bornkamm
stands squarely in the Bultmannian, form-critical tradition.
He begins with the bold announcement that no one is any longer
in the position to write a Life of Jesus. "We possess no
single word of Jesus and no single story of Jesus, no matter
how incontestably genuine they may be, which do not contain
at the same time the confession of the believing congregation
or at least are embedded therein."[219]

But in spite of all his reservations, Bornkamm believes
that we must not be discouraged from raising the question
of the historical Jesus. Though faith is not finally dependent upon historical research, the latter still has significance for the believer. Bornkamm notes:

> Nevertheless, the gospels justify neither resignation
> nor skepticism. Rather they bring before our eyes, in
> very different fashion from what is customary in
> chronicles and presentations of history, the historical
> person of Jesus with the utmost vividness. Quite clear-
> ly what the gospels report concerning the message, the
> deeds and the history of Jesus is still distinguished
> by an authenticity, a freshness, and a distinctiveness
> not in any way effaced by the church's Easter faith.
> These features point us directly to the earthly figure
> of Jesus.[220]

For Bornkamm, the reality of the historical Jesus becomes
an unmediated presence in and through his message. Jesus is
present in his words, and he is completely one with his words.
Behind the words, even the interpreted words, there is a real
person--the historical Jesus--who confronts us. At the close
of his discussion on the messianic question, Bornkamm speaks
in a manner consistent with the above interpretation:

> The result of these deliberations is in no way merely
> negative, but is preeminently positive as well. They
> recall us to the recognition which has governed our
> whole treatment of the message and history of Jesus,
> namely, that the messianic character of his being is
> contained in his words and deeds and *in* the un-
> mediatedness of his historic appearance.[221]

Even though Bornkamm announces that no one is in a position to write a Life of Jesus, he nevertheless includes chapters in his *Jesus of Nazareth* on Jesus' disciples (Chapter 6)
and his final journey to Jerusalem (Chapter 7). In Chapter 3,
he collects whatever general biographical information is
available about Jesus, giving a kind of personality sketch.
The significance of this third chapter is that Bornkamm seeks
to show the impact that Jesus made on other people. But it
is clear that for Bornkamm this impression is within the context of faith, and the suggestion emerges that a human contact
with Jesus was also potentially a contact with the kerygma.[222]
One must conclude that Bornkamm places more emphasis upon the
connection between the historical Jesus and the church's
kerygma than Bultmann has done.

Ernst Fuchs is more ambitious than either Käsemann or
Bornkamm in trying to establish historically the continuity
between the historical Jesus and faith. Christian faith is
not a timeless idea or universal truth but is historical.
The importance of the historical Jesus for faith can be seen
in the following passage by Fuchs:

> Faith knows that in the announcement of the resurrection
> the historical Jesus approaches us. The so-called Christ
> of faith is in fact none other than the historical
> Jesus. But more important is the assertion that God
> himself encounters us in the historical Jesus. The
> question of the historical Jesus turns now properly
> into the actuality of the encounter with God in *preach-
> ing*.... The dogmatic continuation of exegetical analy-
> sis must not lose sight of the historical Jesus as a
> pattern of the Word of God.[223]

Fuchs centers his attention on the conduct (*Verhalten*) of
Jesus as the real context of his preaching. What did Jesus
do? Taking as an example Jesus' gracious act in eating with
publicans and sinners, we have a preview of the eschatological
age. In this act of Jesus, the redeeming activity of the
Reign of God is already making itself felt in advance. It is
just this that is Jesus' real deed. What is here said in
reference to the eschatological meals is then generalized as
an interpretation of Jesus' conduct as a whole. "This attitude is neither that of a prophet nor that of a sage; it is
rather that of a man who dares to act in God's place, by
drawing to himself sinners who without him would have to flee
before God."[224]

In speaking of Jesus' message, Fuchs says that it is dependent upon Jesus' action. To support this claim, he refers
to Jesus' parables, many of which are spoken in the setting
of the eschatological meals. The interpretation of the

parables for the disciples was supplied by Jesus by an act of
goodness. Thus, the parable does not clarify Jesus' conduct,
although he does at times appeal to parables to defend his
actions or sayings. Rather, it is the other way around.
Jesus' conduct explains the will of God with a parable that
can be read out of his conduct. The parables that Jesus
speaks are a witness to himself, and they apply to our relationship with him.[225] This kind of analysis is then projected
to all of Jesus' teaching. This means that Jesus' words
generally reflect his conduct historically. It is in Jesus'
teaching, which is based upon his conduct, that we confront
the historical Jesus. Or, as James M. Robinson puts it in
summarizing Fuchs' position: "In the message and action of
Jesus is implicit an eschatological understanding of his person which becomes explicit in the kerygma of the primitive
church."[226]

Fuchs has further elaborated this basic understanding of
our confrontation of the historical Jesus with his concept
of the proclamation of Jesus being a "speech event" (*Sprach-
ereignis*). Fuchs believes that the synoptic gospels still
preserve some insight for us into Jesus' own proclamation:

> Jesus' proclamation shows us that he understands
> himself as the one "who brought to speech" the call of
> God in the final hour.
> I understand Jesus' proclamation as "speech event."
> This is not to say that Jesus created new concepts.
> It is his parables which are typical of Jesus....
> In the parables Jesus' understanding of his situa-
> tion "comes to speech" in a special way....
> That is the decisive achievement of the parables
> of Jesus: whoever understands and goes this way moves
> already in a new context, in being before God.... Thus
> Jesus intends to "bring God to speech"....
> The concept of the situation, which is understood
> as the essence of the "speech event," is able to reveal
> that Jesus' person belongs to the context of his procla-
> mation.[227]

It is clear that the early Christian proclamation intended
to bring God "to speech." Therefore, it was decisive that
Jesus' own person moved into the center of the proclamation.
Jesus became the text of the proclamation. Now faith in God
speaks out of that same self-understanding to which Jesus
once summoned his hearers. The time of the parable has now
been superseded by the time of confession to Jesus. "The
being which Jesus revealed is fulfilled as being before God,
by means of the Word which, in the name of Jesus, is spoken
as our word of faith.... Therefore the confession of faith is

the principal motif of Christology, and Christology is the
correct answer to the question concerning the historical
Jesus."[228]

In the United States, James M. Robinson was the most influential figure in the new quest. His *A New Quest of the
Historical Jesus* provided English-speaking readers with a good
background and summation of its status. But it also represented Robinson's own contribution to the quest.

As Robinson views the situation, the possibility of a new
quest does not lie in the kerygma, in new sources, or in a
new view of the gospels but in a new concept of history and
of the self. The new quest is necessary because of the nature
of the situation in which we find ourselves. The kerygma
locates the saving event in a historical person. Our situation is such that we now have a second avenue of access to the
historical person, thanks to the rise of scientific historiography since the Enlightenment. Robinson goes so far as to
declare: "These two avenues of access to the same person create
a situation which has not existed in the church since the time
of the original disciples, who had both their Easter faith
and their factual memory of Jesus."[229] It is in the concern
of the kerygma for the historicity of Jesus, and in the new
view of history that gives us a "second avenue" to Jesus, that
the necessity for the new quest resides.

The scientific historiography about which Robinson speaks
is not the nineteenth-century kind, because the kerygma is
largely uninterested in a positivistic historiography that
tries to ascertain the objectively verifiable facts. The new
historiography, unlike the old, is concerned with the *meaning*
of events, and since the kerygma consists in the meaning of a
certain historical event, there is a convergence of the goals
of both the kerygma and of twentieth-century historiography.
Or to put it another way, as Robinson does: "It is because
modern historiography mediates an existential encounter with
Jesus, an encounter also mediated by the kerygma, that modern
historiography is of great importance to Christian faith."[230]

The upshot of Robinson's new quest is the recognition,
along with the form critics, that historiography cannot and
should not prove the kerygma because the kerygma proclaims
Jesus as eschatological event calling for existential commitment. But a new quest must be undertaken because we now have
a second access to an existential encounter with Jesus--modern
historiography. If one asks, "What can finally be expected
of the new quest?," Robinson answers:

> And if in this encounter with Jesus one is confronted
> with the *skandalon* of recognizing in this all-too-human
> eschatological message the eternal word of God, and

consequently of breaking with the present evil aeon so
as to live now out of the grace of God, i.e. if in en-
countering Jesus one is confronted with the same existential decision as that posed by the kerygma, one has
proved all that can be proved by a new quest of the historical Jesus: not that the kerygma is true, but rather
that the existential decision with regard to the kerygma
is an existential decision with regard to Jesus.[231]

In evaluating the new quest, one must conclude that, in
spite of its claims that there is a relationship between the
historical Jesus and the kerygma, it provides a meager picture
of Jesus. Moreover, there is the tendency to hold a preconceived portrait of what Jesus said and did. Jesus' message
is subjected to preconceived dogmatic or philosophical principles. One can sympathize with Oscar Cullmann's observation:
"Albert Schweitzer's *Quest of the Historical Jesus* was written
in vain if the 'liberal' portrait of Jesus, which corresponds
to the idealistic philosophy of the nineteenth century, dis-
appeared only in order to make room for the existentialist
philosophy of the twentieth century."[232] Cullmann contends
that the Bultmann school's exegesis is subjected to the principle of "self-understanding of existence." This has become a
principle of exegesis and a presupposition for them.

Between the poles of historicism and a symbolic Christology dependent upon existentialist presuppositions, there is
a more moderate position, represented by Joachim Jeremias and
by such British scholars as C.H. Dodd, T.W. Manson, William
Manson, Vincent Taylor, D.M. Baillie, Edwyn Hoskyns, and Noel
Davey. They hold a common conviction that the gospels and even
the Pauline writings present a more authentic picture of Jesus
than those under the influence of form criticism will acknowledge.[233] A quotation from William Manson must suffice as
representative of this view:

The faith of the Christian society penetrates and suf-
fuses the matter of the tradition: we see Jesus in the
light of the community's faith and love. But this glow
or aureole in which the glory of the risen Lord blends
to some extent with the lineaments of the Jesus of history does not mean that the image of Jesus as he was on
earth is so refracted as no longer to appear in its
reality. It does not mean that because Jesus is Lord
we have no credible glimpse of him as teacher, as healer,
as man of God wrestling with the demonic powers of evil
and darkness, as evangelist seeking the lost, as the
friend of sinners and of little children, as the terrible
judge of injustice and hypocrisy.... The tradition may,
as we have suggested, be a function of the church's faith

and life, but this does not mean that it has not taken
up history into itself and preserved it.[234]

Redaction Criticism

Following World War II, another type of New Testament
criticism developed, known as redaction criticism. Redaction
criticism is the English equivalent of *Redaktionsgeschichte*,
which Willi Marxsen proposed as the designation for this new
discipline.[235] Like form criticism, to which it is closely
related, redaction criticism posed further negative implications for the possibility of constructing a Life of Jesus.
Three German scholars working independently were its origina-
tors: Günther Bornkamm worked on Matthew, Hans Conzelmann
on Luke, and Willi Marxsen on Mark.[236]

Redaction criticism can be seen as a second phase of form
criticism. The latter held that the gospels consist of collections of material that were selected and arranged by the individual evangelists. The gospel material had a previous
history in the early church and circulated in individual units
or small collections. It was transmitted orally before it
was written down. Its basic purpose was not historical or
biographical; rather, its function related to worship, preaching, teaching, and apology. These units of the tradition have
specific forms that served definite functions in the life of
the early church. Form criticism is interested in analyzing
the forms and going behind them to their *Sitz im Leben*--their
concrete situation in the early church.

Norman Perrin has written a concise and illuminating study
of redaction criticism. He defines it as follows: "It is
concerned with studying the theological motivation of an author
as this is revealed in the collection, arrangement, editing,
and modification of traditional material, and in the composition of new material or the creation of new forms within the
traditions of early Christianity."[237] Thus, according to
redaction critics, the evangelists were not only editors who
selected and arranged their material, they were also "theologians." The gospels reflect the theological stances and
biases of the individual evangelists. It is this theological
orientation with which the redaction critics are basically
concerned.

Among the precursors of redaction criticism, perhaps none
is more significant than William Wrede. As noted earlier,
prior to Wrede the priority of Mark as a source for the life
of Jesus was widely recognized. Wrede, however, seriously
challenged this view. Through his thorough and painstaking
analysis of Mark, he concluded that Mark's basic intention was

not historical but dogmatic and theological. Mark, as the
gospel of the "messianic secret," was an unreliable source for
an objective view of Jesus. In a fundamental sense, Wrede
can be regarded as the first "redaction critic."
    Norman Perrin believes that R.H. Lightfoot's Bampton Lec-
tures for 1934 contained elements that anticipated redaction
criticism.[238] More than most British New Testament scholars,
Lightfoot has been strongly influenced by form criticism. He
finds in the Gospel of Mark "interpretation continually present
in a book most of us were taught to regard as almost exclusively historical." He argues further that the introduction to
Mark (1:1-13) reveals the evangelist's theological purposes
and that the presentation of John the Baptist--designed as it
is by the evangelist to explain who Jesus is--has a Christological purpose. Lightfoot believes that the main purpose of
Mark is clearly theological. "We have found reason to believe
that, rightly regarded, it may be called the book of the (secret)
Messiahship of Jesus."[239]
    Of the three redaction critics mentioned above, Hans Con-
zelmann is the most important and has had the widest impact.
Norman Perrin characterizes his *Theology of Luke* as "one of
the few truly seminal works of our time in the field of New
Testament research." After Conzelmann, "neither the discipline
of New Testament theology as a whole nor the understanding of
Luke in particular will ever be the same again."[240]
    Luke has been widely regarded by New Testament scholars as
the historian of early Christianity. Conzelmann, however,
sees Luke as less a historian than a theologian. The composition of Luke reflects a distinct theological motivation.
Conzelmann's intention is to go beyond form criticism to a
second phase, "in which the kerygma is not simply transmitted
and received, but itself becomes the subject of reflection."[240]
    Perrin notes that the Lucan theology represents Luke's
response to the central theological problem of his day, namely,
the delay of the parousia and the subsequent necessity for the
church to come to terms with its continued and continuing
existence in the world. Whereas at first the period of the
church's existence was considered as a brief interim before
the parousia, for Luke the time of the church in the world had
to be regarded as indefinite. This created the problem to
which his theological enterprise is a proposed solution, a solution reflected in the details of his theology and affecting
every aspect of his presentation of the ministry of Jesus and
of the early church. Perrin concludes: "One of the remarkable
aspects of Conzelmann's work is not only that he shows how
great the Lucan theological enterprise is in its conception,
but also that he shows how detailed it is in its execution."[242]

The implications of redaction criticism for Life of Jesus research is obvious. It continues the "erosion of the sources" that began with Wrede and Wellhausen and proceeded with Schweitzer and form criticism. With its emphasis upon the theological presuppositions and orientation of the evangelists, it seriously questions the historical trustworthiness of the gospels. If, as the redaction critics suggest, the intention of the evangelists was primarily theological, then their interest in historical objectivity and in a biography of Jesus was inconsequential. Consequently, critical scholars will have to establish the authenticity of the gospel material with the most careful stringency.

But, as Norman Perrin views the situation, the most crucial problem is not that redaction criticism makes Life of Jesus research more difficult, but that it raises the question as to whether the view of the historical Jesus as the locus of revelation and the central concern of Christian faith is in fact justifiable.

The historiographical presuppositions of the Life of Jesus movement were based on the belief that one could discover the "real Jesus," "Jesus as he actually was." For these scholars, "historical" implied "factual data" or description of a situation as it "actually was." Perrin observes that the ancients did not think in these terms: "... the early church, not having our sense of the word 'historical' and being motivated by an intense religious experience, saw no reason to distinguish between words originally spoken by the historical Jesus and words ascribed to him in the tradition of the church." In addition to this, one must take into account the sense of the presence of the risen Christ in the experience of the believer or the church. This Jesus who speaks *is* the Jesus who once spoke. Here is where redaction criticism makes its impact, for it reveals to us how very much of the material ascribed to the Jesus who spoke in Galilee or Judea must in fact be ascribed to the Jesus who spoke through a prophet or evangelist in the early church.[243]

That Perrin is under the influence of redaction criticism and has moderated his former position regarding the historicity of the gospels is evident from his concluding remarks concerning the significance of redaction criticism for Life of Jesus research and theology:

> It [redaction criticism] makes clear the fact that the voice of the Jesus of the gospels is the voice of living Christian experience, and that the evangelists and the tradition they represent are indifferent as to whether this experience is ultimately related to anything said or done in Galilee or Judea before the crucifixion. In

light of this fact it seems very hard indeed to justify
a Life of Jesus theology. If the Jesus of the Gospel of
Mark is the Jesus of Mark's own Christian experience and
that of the church before him, then the claim that the
"historical" Jesus is the center and source of Christian
faith would seem to have no necessary basis in the New
Testament. It has always been clear that neither Paul,
John, nor the Catholic epistles have the kind of attitude toward the earthly Jesus that would justify a central place for the historical Jesus in Christian theology.
It is no accident that the rise of a Life of Jesus
theology was closely connected with an acceptance of the
Marcan hypothesis. In destroying the Marcan hypothesis
redaction criticism would seem to have cut the ground
from under the feet of that theology.[244]

Concluding Reflections

As evidenced by the preceding essay, the attempt to write
Lives of Jesus or to find the real or historical Jesus, has
had a long and fascinating history. Before the rise of critical scholarship in the eighteenth century, it was generally
assumed that the gospel sources were adequate for the purpose
of constructing a biography of Jesus. They were historical
accounts that described who Jesus was, what he did, and what
he said. They portrayed the situation as it really is or was
(*wie es eigentlich gewesen ist*). The advent of biblical criticism radically altered the picture so that contemporary critics
are much more skeptical about the possibility of recovering
the historical Jesus. But as the bibliography that follows
reveals, the great majority of works on the life of Jesus are
not critical but are based on pre-critical presuppositions.
Piety, devotion, and literal interpretation are the prevailing
motifs regarding interpretation of Jesus' life and message.
I think that it is correct to say that the vast majority
of Christians read the gospels "historically" and are oblivious
to the nuances and conclusions of critical scholarship. The
"average" Christian, when reading the gospels, "hears" the
words of the real Jesus and gets a fairly vivid picture of the
kind of person he was. Thus, for most Christians it is as if
the period from the eighteenth century to the present never
existed insofar as their understanding of Jesus is concerned.
The reason for this is that the methods and results of biblical
criticism have largely been the prerogative of a small and
elite group of scholars whose work has never affected the faith
of most Christians. And with the conservative trend that pre-
vails today, this situation is all the more evident.

But this devotion to the historical Jesus and the un-
examined belief that the gospels portray the real Jesus are
reflective of one of the most central issues in gospel re-
search--the relationship between history and the kerygma.
Popular piety cannot conceive of or tolerate a mythical or
non-historical Jesus. Though conservative apologetics insists upon the divinity of Christ, it also presupposes a human
Jesus through whom God revealed his nature and purpose. Jesus
is Savior and Lord, but he is also elder brother, example, and
one whose teachings and commands are to be obeyed and followed
because they are the "word of God." And so the "naïveté" of
popular piety and devotion underscores the fact that has remained central for critical scholarship--the relationship between faith and history. What Joachim Jeremias said about New
Testament scholarship is applicable to all Christians whether
or not they have ever heard about the "historical Jesus,"
kerygma, demythologizing, the new hermeneutic, form criticism,
redaction criticism, or existentialism. "Study of the historical Jesus and his message is no peripheral task of New
Testament scholarship, a study of one particular historical
problem among many others. It is *the* central task of New
Testament scholarship."[245]
It appears so often that there is a glaring dichotomy between the scholarly world of New Testament research and the
piety and faith of most Christians. The activities and pro-
grams of local churches and the priorities of most pastors
seem far removed from the vital problems of biblical scholarship. It is like two parallel paths, each marked by commitment
and ultimate concern, but never quite intersecting and becoming
interrelated. In a wider context, it is the problem of the
relationship between biblical theology and practical theology,
between seminary and church, between love of God with mind as
well as heart, between Jesus as an academic problem and Jesus
as the one who "walks with me and talks with me and tells me
I am his own."
This situation has led some observers to declare the bank-
ruptcy of biblical criticism. To be sure, fundamentalists and
conservatives have always looked upon higher criticism as a
serious threat to biblical authority and inspiration and to
orthodoxy--to the "faith once and for all delivered to the
saints."
Within the last decade, Walter Wink has written a brief
volume on a new paradigm for biblical study. He begins with
a criticism of higher criticism, saying that it has run its
course and has become bankrupt. It should be noted that Wink
is a spokesman from within the liberal, critical tradition.
He acknowledges the remarkable achievements of higher criticism
but charges that it is incapable of achieving what most of its

practitioners considered its purpose to be: "so to interpret
the Scriptures that the past becomes alive and illuminates
our present with new possibilities for personal and social
transformation."[246]
    Wink lists a number of reasons for his charge that biblical
criticism is bankrupt. Its methodology was marked by an "objective neutrality" that was incommensurate with the intention
of the texts that were written "from faith to faith." Biblical criticism fell prey to a form of technologism that regards as legitimate only those questions that its methods
can answer. Furthermore, Wink charges that biblical criticism
became cut off from any community for whose life its results
might be significant. A "guild of biblical scholars" developed
who became accountable not to the church but to themselves.
This separation was disastrous for critical scholarship, because the questions asked about the biblical texts were seldom
ones on which human lives hinged but rather were those most
likely to win a hearing from the "guild." Wink notes:

> Historical criticism sought to free itself from the com-
> munity in order to pursue its work untrammeled by
> censorship and interference. With that hard-won freedom
> it also won isolation from any conceivable significance.
> For since truth is not absolute, but only approximate
> and relational, its relevance can only emerge in the
> particularity of a given community's struggle for in-
> tegrity and freedom.[247]

    Whether or not one judges Wink's charges as being too ex-
treme, he has raised legitimate concerns. For Christian
faith, Jesus cannot be objectified. Schweitzer and Bultmann,
who were among the most "radical" critics of the historical
Jesus, nevertheless saw Jesus as the one who calls us to commitment and decision. Schweitzer's Jesus called people to
follow him and to discern his spirit operative in their lives
and in the world. For Bultmann, the preaching of the kerygma
confronts one with the necessity to choose for or against
authentic existence. There is an existential dimension here
that is an exception to the false objectivity and neutrality
that Wink criticized and that he rightly saw as characteristic
of much biblical criticism.
    In his recent book *The New Biblical Theorists*, George A.
Kelly notes that the historical-critical method of biblical
study has become the object of widening, sometimes strident
controversy in the Catholic church. He surveys the uncertain
status of the new biblical theories, both as a scholar and a
pastor. Kelly believes that the reason for the oftentimes
subjective, fragmentary, and unreliable results of biblical
criticism is that the critics exclude tradition and neglect

the role of faith in their study. Some would like to erect
another authority in place of the authority of scripture and
the church's pastors--the authority of biblical scholarship.[248]
Reginald H. Fuller has cogently described the relationship
between historical criticism and faith as follows:

> Historical investigation therefore has an important,
> though subordinate, role to play in connection with
> Christian faith. It is important since faith makes a
> claim with respect to a figure of history, and his-
> torical investigation is necessary to show that that
> figure can support the claims made for him. But it is
> subordinate, since historical investigation cannot in
> the nature of the case validate the claim that kerygma
> and faith make for him.... The Christian believer does
> not therefore have to wait for the professors to tell
> him what he has to believe, nor need he fear because
> the professors are always changing their minds or dis-
> agreeing among themselves. He can only look to them to
> clarify the issues involved in the historical aspects of
> faith which, though historical, nevertheless transcends
> history.[249]

There is little doubt that the life of Jesus will continue
to captivate the most erudite scholar as well as the unlettered
devotee. As long as the Christian faith endures, he who was
the proclaimer and subsequently became the proclaimed, will
both "stretch" our minds and "strangely warm our hearts."

NOTES

1. Adolf Harnack, *What Is Christianity?*, trans. Thomas
Bailey Saunders (New York: Harper, 1957), p. 19.

2. Harvey K. McArthur, *The Quest Through the Centuries*
(Philadelphia: Fortress, 1966), p. 44. See also A.A. Hobson,
The Diatessaron of Tatian and the Synoptic Problem (Chicago:
University of Chicago Press, 1904). This work deals with
numerous critical problems about the *Diatessaron*, with special
emphasis upon its relation to the four gospels and whether
this relation supports or discredits the documentary theory
on the origin of the synoptic gospels.

3. McArthur, p. 51.

4. *The Works of Aurelius Augustine*, Vol. 8, *The Sermon on
the Mount* and *The Harmony of the Evangelists*, Marcus Dods, ed.
(Edinburgh: Clark, 1873), p. 138.

5. See *Corpus Scriptorum Ecclesiasticorum Latinorum*, Vol. 25, Johannes Huemer, ed. (Vienna, 1891).

6. Gerard Cormac Cappon in a Yale University dissertation, "The Gospels as Epic," presents a detailed analysis of Juvencus' poetic version of the gospels considered from the standpoint of his appropriation and reworking of Vergilian material.

7. See *Corpus Scriptorum Ecclesiasticorum Latinorum*, Vol. 16, C. Schenkl, ed. (Vienna, 1888), pp. 569-609.

8. See Ibid., Vol. 10, Johannes Huemer, ed. (Vienna, 1885), pp. 14-146.

9. The manuscript contains nearly 200 illustrations, which are produced in the Ragusa volume. Spaces (and instructions for filling them) were left for an additional 100 illustrations. Consequently, the manuscript as originally conceived must have been prepared for about 400 illustrations.

10. *Meditations on the Life of Christ*, trans. Isa Ragusa (Princeton: Princeton University Press, 1961), p. 2.

11. Ibid., p. 5.

12. Ibid., p. 133.

13. Ibid., p. 152.

14. McArthur, p. 72.

15. For an extended discussion of Fidati's biography, see Sister Mary Germaine McNeil, *Simone Fidati and His De gestis Domini Salvatoris* (Washington, D.C.: Catholic University of America Press, 1950), pp. 1-38. See also Nicola Matliola, *Il Beato Fidati de Cascia* (Rome: Antologia Agostiniana, 2, 1898).

16. McNeil, p. 69.

17. Ibid., p. 209.

18. For a listing of the manuscripts of the *De gestis*, see McNeil, pp. 211-24.

19. Ibid., p. 210.

20. For a discussion and listing of the sources of the *Vita Christi*, see Sister Mary Immaculate Bodestedt, *The Vita Christi of Ludolphus the Carthusian* (Washington, D.C.: Catholic University of America Press, 1944), pp. 24-52.

21. Ibid., p. 17; see pp. 18-23 for a discussion of the manuscripts.

22. Ibid., p. 101.

23. Ibid., p. 31.

24. McArthur, p. 86.

25. Ibid., p. 89.

26. Ibid., p. 97; for a detailed discussion of the Osiander and non-Osiander patterns in sixteenth-century gospel harmonies, see pp. 93-101.

27. Albert Schweitzer, *The Quest of the Historical Jesus*, trans. W. Montgomery (New York: Macmillan, 1960), p. 14.

28. Joseph Klausner, *Jesus of Nazareth*, trans. Herbert Danby (New York: Macmillan, 1925), pp. 75-76.

29. For a recent English translation, see *Reimarus: Fragments*, Charles H. Talbert, ed., trans. Ralph S. Fraser (Philadelphia: Fortress, 1970).

30. Ibid., pp. 71, 123.

31. Ibid., pp. 249-50.

32. Ibid., pp. 230, 232-34, 239, 262.

33. Ibid., pp. 236-37.

34. Schweitzer, pp. 22-23.

35. Ibid., p. 26.

36. Ibid., pp. 27-67.

37. Ibid., p. 28.

38. Klausner, pp. 80-81.

39. Schweitzer, p. 38.

40. Ibid., pp. 38-47.

41. Ibid., p. 50.

42. Ibid., pp. 50-51.

43. Ibid., pp. 52-55.

44. Ibid., p. 58.

45. Ibid., pp. 59, 61.

46. Friedrich Schleiermacher, *The Life of Jesus*, Jack C. Verheyden, ed., trans. S. Maclean Gilmour (Philadelphia: Fortress, 1975), p. 34.

47. Ibid., p. 43.

48. Ibid., pp. 45-481.

49. Ibid., especially pp. 263-69.

50. For Schleiermacher's discussion of Jesus' miracle-working activity, see pp. 190-229.

51. Schweitzer, p. 67.

52. David Friedrich Strauss, *The Life of Jesus Critically Examined*, Peter C. Hodgson, ed., trans. George Eliot (Philadelphia: Fortress, 1972), p. li.

53. Ibid., p. 80.

54. Ibid., pp. 86-87.

55. Ibid., p. 91.

56. Ibid., p. lii.

57. See pp. 413-534, for Strauss' discussion of Jesus' miracles.

58. For Strauss' discussion of Jesus' messianic understanding, see pp. 281-308, 563-98.

59. Ibid., pp. 381-86, 387-91.

60. For a detailed discussion of the views of Wilke and Weisse, see Schweitzer, pp. 121-36.

61. For Schweitzer's portrait of Bauer, see pp. 137-60. See also Klausner, p. 86.

62. Maurice Goguel, *The Life of Jesus*, trans. Olive Wyon (New York: Macmillan, 1949), p. 50.

63. Ibid., p. 50.

64. Ibid., p. 51.

65. Klausner, p. 87.

66. For Renan's discussion of the sources for his *Vie de Jésus*, see Ernest Renan, *The Life of Jesus* (New York: Modern Library, 1927), pp. 25-65.

67. Ibid., pp. 118, 120.

68. Ibid., p. 375.

69. Goguel, p. 52.

70. Schweitzer, pp. 191-92.

71. Renan, pp. 392-93.

72. Klausner, p. 88.

73. Schweitzer, p. 221; for a detailed discussion of the liberal lives of Jesus, see pp. 193-222, and Klausner, pp. 88-90.

74. Daniel L. Pals, *The Victorian "Lives" of Jesus* (San Antonio: Trinity University Press, 1982), p. 10; for further discussion of German and British scholarship on the Lives of Jesus, see pp. 125-55.

75. Ibid., p. 40.

76. Ibid., p. 40.

77. Ibid., pp. 48-50.

78. Ibid., p. 77.

79. Ibid., p. 85.

80. Ibid., pp. 94-97.

81. For Pals' discussion of Stalker, Fairbairn, and Nicoll, see pp. 98-103.

82. For Pals' discussion of Edersheim, see pp. 104-08.

83. Ibid., p. 155.

84. Schweitzer, pp. 1, 399.

85. Hugh Ross Makintosh, *Types of Modern Theology* (London: Nisbet, 1952), pp. 182-83.

86. Heinz Zahrnt, *The Historical Jesus*, trans. J.S. Bowden (New York: Harper, 1963), pp. 56-57.

87. Quoted by Zahrnt, p. 58.

88. Ibid., p. 59.

89. Ibid., pp. 60-61.

90. Martin Kähler, *The So-Called Historical Jesus and the Historic Biblical Christ*, trans. Carl E. Braaten (Philadelphia: Fortress, 1964), p. 43.

91. Ibid., pp. 44-45.

92. Ibid., p. 53.

93. Ibid., p. 55.

94. Ibid., pp. 21-22.

95. Ibid., pp. 65, 66.

96. Ibid., p. 73.

97. Ibid., p. 80.

98. Ibid., p. 92.

99. For a fairly detailed description and criticism of Kähler's views, see Charles C. Anderson, *Critical Quests of*

Jesus (Grand Rapids: Eerdmans, 1969), pp. 75–86. See also Zahrnt, pp. 82–84.

100. Johannes Weiss, *Jesus' Proclamation of the Kingdom of God*, trans. Richard Hyde Hiers and David Larrimore Holland (Philadelphia: Fortress, 1971), pp. 59–60.

101. Ibid., p. 114.

102. Ibid., p. 132.

103. William Wrede, *The Messianic Secret*, trans. J.C.G. Grieg (Cambridge and London: Clarke, 1971), p. 67.

104. Ibid., p. 68.

105. Ibid., pp. 113–14.

106. Ibid., pp. 130–31.

107. Richard R. Niebuhr, *Resurrection and Historical Reason* (New York: Scribner, 1957), p. 132.

108. Albert Schweitzer, *Out of My Life and Thought*, trans. C.T. Campion (New York: Holt, 1933), p. 20.

109. Albert Schweitzer, *The Mystery of the Kingdom of God*, trans. Walter Lowrie (New York: Macmillan, 1950), pp. 48, 51.

110. Ibid., p. 56.

111. Ibid., p. 148.

112. Ibid., pp. 152–53.

113. Ibid., p. 156.

114. Schweitzer, *The Quest*, pp. 370–71.

115. Schweitzer, *Out of My Life and Thought*, p. 58.

116. Schweitzer, *The Quest*, p. 350.

117. Ibid., p. 398.

118. Ibid., pp. 399, 401, 403.

119. Ibid., pp. 399, 401.

120. Cited by Werner Georg Kümmel, *The New Testament: The History of the Investigation of Its Problems*, trans. S. McLean Gilmour and Howard C. Kee (Nashville: Abingdon, 1972), pp. 282–83.

121. Ibid., p. 284.

122. See Goguel, pp. 61–62.

123. Ibid., pp. 63–64. Also Maurice Goguel, *Jesus the Nazarene; Myth or History?*, trans. Frederick Stephens (New York: Appleton, 1926), p. 15.

124. For a discussion of the twentieth-century non-historical theories, see Goguel, *Jesus the Nazarene*, pp. 15-25; Goguel, *The Life of Jesus*, pp. 65-69; Fred C. Conybeare, *The Historical Christ* (Chicago: Open Court, 1914); Johannes Weiss, *Jesus von Nazareth; Mythos oder Geschichte* (Tübingen: Mohr [Paul Siebeck], 1910). Conybeare concentrates on J.M. Robertson, A. Drews, and W.B. Smith; Weiss on A. Kalthoff, A. Drews, and P. Jensen.

125. Arthur Drews, *The Witness to the Historicity of Jesus*, trans. Joseph McCabe (Chicago: Open Court, 1912), p. xi.

126. Ibid., p. 235.

127. Ibid., pp. 296, 297.

128. Ibid., p. 306.

129. Ibid., p. 306.

130. Ibid., p. 308.

131. Harnack, pp. 30-31.

132. Ibid., p. 31.

133. Ibid., p. 33.

134. Ibid., p. 35.

135. Ibid., p. 36.

136. Ibid., p. 37.

137. Ibid., p. 51.

138. Ibid., p. 56.

139. Ibid., p. 74.

140. Ibid., p. 144.

141. Ibid., p. 24.

142. Klausner, p. 125.

143. Ibid., p. 126.

144. Ibid., p. 368.

145. Ibid., p. 374.

146. Ibid., p. 381.

147. Ibid., p. 389.

148. Ibid., p. 391.

149. Ibid., p. 408.

150. Ibid., p. 408.

151. Ibid., p. 411.

152. Ibid., p. 412.

153. Ibid., p. 414.

154. Shirley Jackson Case, *Jesus: A New Biography* (Chicago: University of Chicago Press, 1927), p. vi.

155. Ibid., pp. 33-34.

156. Ibid., p. 45.

157. Ibid., p. 110.

158. Ibid., p. 115.

159. Ibid., p. 159.

160. Ibid., pp. 356-57.

161. Ibid., p. 360.

162. Ibid., pp. 377-78.

163. Ibid., pp. 409-10.

164. Ibid., p. 414.

165. Ibid., p. 418.

166. Ibid., p. 441.

167. James Mackinnon, *The Historic Jesus* (London: Longmans, Green, 1931), p. vii.

168. Ibid., pp. viii, x.

169. Ibid., p. xiv.

170. Ibid., p. 87.

171. Ibid., p. 204.

172. Ibid., p. 206.

173. Ibid., pp. 311-14.

174. Ibid., pp. 379-86.

175. Ibid., pp. 389-90.

176. Ibid., p. 393.

177. Ibid., pp. 395-96.

178. Ibid., p. 397.

179. Goguel, *The Life of Jesus*, p. 180.

180. Ibid., p. 181.

181. Ibid., pp. 182-83.

182. Ibid., pp. 201, 203-04.

183. Ibid., pp. 208-09.

184. Ibid., p. 210.

185. Ibid., p. 211.

186. Ibid., p. 212.

187. Ibid., p. 214.

188. Ibid., p. 558.

189. Ibid., p. 586.

190. These studies were the following: M. Dibelius, *Die Formgeschichte des Evangeliums*, 1919, 1933; K.L. Schmidt, *Der Rahmen der Geschichte Jesu*, 1919; M. Albertz, *Die synoptischen Streitgespräche*, 1921; R. Bultmann, *Geschichte der synoptischen Tradition*, 1921, 1931.

191. E.g., F.C. Burkitt, F.W. Howard, A.H. McNeile, C.H. Dodd, and T.W. Manson. A number of English-speaking scholars have accepted the basic tenets of form criticism but with generally less radical conclusions than their German colleagues. See, e.g., B.S. Easton, *The Gospel Before the Gospels* (New York: Scribner, 1928); V. Taylor, *The Formation of the Gospel Tradition* (London: Macmillan, 1933); R.H. Lightfoot, *History and Interpretation of the Gospels* (London: Hodder and Stoughton, 1935); F.C. Grant, *The Gospels: Their Origin and Growth* (New York: Harper, 1957).

192. Martin Dibelius, *From Tradition to Gospel*, trans. Bertram Lee Wolf (New York: Scribner, 1935), pp. v-vi.

193. Rudolf Bultmann and Karl Kundsin, *Form Criticism: Two Essays on New Testament Research*, trans. Frederick C. Grant (New York: Harper, 1962), pp. 3-4.

194. Dibelius, *From Tradition to Gospel*, p. 295.

195. Hans Conzelmann, "Zur Methode der Leben-Jesu-Forschung," *Zeitschrift für Theologie und Kirche*, LVI (1959): 3.

196. James M. Robinson, *A New Quest of the Historical Jesus* (London: SCM, 1959), pp. 37-38.

197. Rudolf Bultmann, *Jesus and the Word*, trans. Louise Pettibone Smith and Erminie Huntress Lantero (New York: Scribner, 1958), p. 8.

198. John Macquarrie, *The Scope of Demythologizing: Bultmann and His Critics* (London: SCM, 1960), pp. 81ff.

199. Bultmann, *Jesus and the Word*, pp. 6, 8.

200. Rudolf Bultmann, *History and Eschatology* (Edinburgh: University Press, 1957), pp. 151-52.

201. Bultmann, *Jesus and the Word*, p. 8.

202. Rudolf Bultmann, *Theology of the New Testament* I, trans. Kendrick Grobel (New York: Scribner, 1955), p. 3.

203. Hans Werner Bartsch, ed., *Kerygma and Myth* I, trans. Reginald H. Fuller (New York: Macmillan, 1955), pp. 117-18.

204. Martin Dibelius, *Jesus*, trans. Charles B. Hedrick and Frederick C. Grant (Philadelphia: Westminster, 1959).

205. Ibid., p. 69.

206. Ibid., p. 83.

207. Ibid., p. 146.

208. Niebuhr, p. 146.

209. Rudolf Bultmann, *Glauben und Verstehen* I (Tübingen: Mohr, 1933). Quoted in Robinson, *A New Quest of the Historical Jesus*, p. 19.

210. In reaction to Bultmann's position, Ethelbert Stauffer suggests a fresh way to approach the historical Jesus. His intent is to produce a "history of Jesus" using chronology as a guide and making use of "indirect" sources on Jesus. The indirect sources are the Jewish and Greco-Roman references to the period of the New Testament. These consist of historians, apocalyptics, books of ritual, legal treatises, inscriptions, papyri, coins, and topographical monuments. Stauffer states that a systematic evaluation of these contemporary sources will lead us out of the intellectual impasse in which we have found ourselves and will enable us to go beyond Lives of Jesus based solely on the Bible or on imaginative techniques and arrive at a pragmatic history of Jesus. See Ethelbert Stauffer, *Jesus and His Story*, trans. Richard and Clara Winston (New York: Knopf, 1960), pp. vii, viii, xiii, 5-6.

211. James M. Robinson, "The Quest of the Historical Jesus Today," *Theology Today*, XV, 2 (1958): 187, 188, 189.

212. James M. Robinson, Review of *Jesus von Nazareth*, by Günther Bornkamm, *Journal of Biblical Literature*, LXXVI, 4 (1957): 311, 312.

213. Günther Bornkamm, *Jesus of Nazareth*, trans. Irene and Fraser McLuskey and James M. Robinson (New York: Harper, 1960), p. 21. The original German edition, *Jesus von Nazareth*, was published in 1956.

214. Ernst Käsemann, "Das Problem des historischen Jesus," *Zeitschrift für Theologie und Kirche*, LI (1954): 125-53. Subsequent quotations from this essay will be based on an unpublished English translation by Ralph Gehrke.

215. Ibid., p. 126.

216. Ibid., p. 127.

217. Ibid., pp. 152-53.

218. Bornkamm, p. 21.

219. Ibid., p. 14.

220. Ibid., p. 24.

221. Ibid., p. 178.

222. Ibid., especially pp. 58-63.

223. Ernst Fuchs, *Zur Frage nach dem historisches Jesus* (Tübingen: Mohr, 1960), pp. 166-67.

224. Ernst Fuchs, "Die Frage nach dem historischen Jesus," *Zeitschrift für Theologie und Kirche*, LIII (1956): 229. Quoted in Zahrnt, p. 115.

225. For a further discussion of Fuchs' interpretation of the parables, see Warren S. Kissinger, *The Parables of Jesus: A History of Interpretation and Bibliography* (Metuchen, N.J.: Scarecrow, 1979), pp. 180-87.

226. Robinson, *A New Quest*, p. 16.

227. Ernst Fuchs, "Proclamation and Speech-Event," *Theology Today*, XIX, 3 (1962): 347, 348, 350.

228. Ibid., p. 354.

229. Robinson, *A New Quest*, p. 86.

230. Ibid., p. 90.

231. Ibid., p. 92.

232. Oscar Cullmann, "Out of Season Remarks on the 'Historical Jesus' of the Bultmann School," *Union Seminary Quarterly Review*, XVI, 2 (1961), 132.

233. See especially Joachim Jeremias, *The Parables of Jesus*, trans. S.H. Hooke (New York: Scribner, 1955, 1963); "The Present Position in the Controversy Concerning the Problem of the Historical Jesus," *Expository Times*, LXIX, 11 (August 1958). C.H. Dodd, *The Apostolic Preaching and Its Development* (New York: Harper, 1962); "The Gospels as History: A Reconsideration," *Bulletin of the John Rylands Library*, 22 (1938); *History*

110 *Historical Overview*

and the *Gospel* (New York: Scribner, 1938); *New Testament Studies* (Manchester: Manchester University Press, 1953). T.W. Manson, "The Life of Jesus: A Study of the Available Materials," *Bulletin of the John Rylands Library*, XXVII (1942-43) and XXVIII (1944); *The Servant Messiah* (Cambridge: Cambridge University Press, 1953). William Manson, *Jesus the Messiah* (London: Hodder and Stoughton, 1943). Donald M. Baillie, *God Was in Christ* (New York: Scribner, 1948). Vincent Taylor, *The Life and Ministry of Jesus* (Nashville: Abingdon, 1955). Edwin Hoskyns and Noel Davey, *The Riddle of the New Testament* (London: Faber, 1931).

234. William Manson, p. 32.

235. Willi Marxsen, *Mark the Evangelist*, trans. James Boyce et al. (New York and Nashville: Abingdon, 1969), p. 21.

236. Günther Bornkamm, *Tradition and Interpretation in Matthew*, trans. Percy Scott (London: SCM, 1963; Philadelphia: Westminster, 1963) (this is an article first published in the journal of the theological school of Bethel in 1948 by Bornkamm and two of his students, G. Barth and H.J. Held). Willi Marxsen, *Der Evangelist Markus; Studien zur Redaktionsgeschichte des Evangeliums* (Göttingen: Vanderhoeck and Ruprecht, 1956, 1959; *Mark the Evangelist*. Hans Conzelmann, *Die Mitte der Zeit; Studien zur Theologie des Lukas* (Tübingen: Mohr, 1954); *The Theology of St. Luke*, trans. Geoffrey Buswell (London: Faber, 1960; New York: Harper, 1960).

237. Norman Perrin, *What Is Redaction Criticism?* (London: SPCK, 1970), p. 1.

238. R.H. Lightfoot, *History and Interpretation in the Gospels* (London: Hodder and Stoughton, 1935).

239. Cited by Perrin, p. 23.

240. Ibid., p. 39.

241. Hans Conzelmann, *The Theology of St. Luke*, trans. Geoffrey Buswell (New York: Harper, 1960), p. 12. Cited by Perrin, p. 30.

242. Perrin, p. 32.

243. Ibid., p. 73.

244. Ibid., p. 74.

245. Joachim Jeremias, *The Problem of the Historical Jesus*, trans. Norman Perrin (Philadelphia: Fortress, 1964), p. 21.

246. Walter Wink, *The Bible in Human Transformation* (Philadelphia: Fortress, 1973), p. 2.

247. Ibid., pp. 10-11.

248. See George A. Kelly, *The New Biblical Theorists: Raymond E. Brown and Beyond* (Ann Arbor, Mich.: Servant, 1983).

249. Reginald H. Fuller, *The New Testament in Current Study* (New York: Scribner, 1962), p. 142.

PART II
THE BIBLIOGRAPHY

Abbott, Lyman, and J.R. Gilmore. *The Gospel History; Complete Connected Account of the Life of Our Lord.* New York: 1881.

————. *Jesus of Nazareth.* New York: Harper and Brothers, 1869, 522p.; *A Life of Christ.* New York: Harper and Brothers, 1882 (1896), 534p.

————. *The Life of Christ.* Boston: Bible Study Pub. Co., 1895, 179p.

Abrams, Richard Irwin. *An Illustrated Life of Jesus: From the National Gallery of Art Collection.* Nashville: Abingdon, 1982, 159p.

The Activities of Jesus (Filmstrip). Society for Visual Education, 1943. Made by Thomas Nelson and Sons, 50 fr.

Acton, Alexander Archibald. *Thou Art the Christ; Studies on the Life and Work of Jesus Christ.* New York: Fleming H. Revell Co., 1936, 150p.

Adams, Ambrose. *The Story of Jesus Christ.* Boston: Marlier and Co., 1903, 271p.

Adams, Charles Coffin. *Life of Our Lord Jesus.* New York: C.F. Roper, 1878, 407p.

Adams, Charlotte Hannah. *The Mind of the Messiah.* New York: National Board of the Young Women's Christian Associations of the United States of America, 1914. 204p.

Adams, David Ernest. *Man of God.* New York: Harper and Brothers, 1941, 210p.

Adams, Frank Durwood. *Glimpses of Grandeur.* New York: Harper and Brothers, 1930, 234p.

Adams, Katherine Carter (Smith). *We Learn How the Boy Jesus Lived.* New York: National Council, Protestant Episcopal Church, 1941, 48p.

Albright, Leland Sanford. *Turning Points in the Life of Jesus.* New York: Pageant Press International Corp., 1969, 133p.

Alden, Isabella (Macdonald). *The Prince of Peace; or, The
Beautiful Life of Jesus*. Philadelphia: John Y. Huber Co.;
St. Louis: Riverside Pub. Co., 1890, 605p.; Boston: Lothrop
Pub. Co., 1898, 561p.

Alexander, Gross. *The Son of Man; Studies in His Life and
Teachings*. Nashville; Dallas: Publishing House of the M.E.
Church South, 1900, 380p.

Allard, Abraham. *De groote herschepper der waereld, ofte De
monarch des levens, nederig gebooren, onschuldig gedood, en
eeuwig verheerlykt*. Amsterdam: C. Allard, 1710?, 32p.

Allard, Daniel. *War against War; or, The Joys of Peace*.
Boston: Stratford Co., 1926, 156p.

Allen, Beatrice Elizabeth. *The Life of Our Lord Jesus Christ*.
New York: Morehouse-Gorham Co., 1940, 109p.

Allen, Bernard Meredith. *The Story behind the Gospels*.
London: Methuen and Co., 1926, 122p.

Allen, Marion Campbell. *A Voice not Our Own*. Valley Forge,
Pa.: Judson Press, 1963, 174p.

Allen, R. Earl. *Trials, Tragedies, and Triumphs*. Westwood,
N.J.: Revell, 1965, 160p.

Allison, Ronald. *Look Back in Wonder: The Story of Jesus of
Nazareth Covered by a Radio and Television Journalist*.
London: Hodder and Stoughton, 1968, 94p.

Almazán Domingo, Manuel. *Jesucristo, Hijo de Dios, Redentor*.
Managua: Editorial Artes Gráficas, 1964, 410p.

Alonso, Daniel J. *El hombre que vino de arriba*. Buenos Aires:
Ediciones Verbo y Vida de America Latina, 1970, 224p.

Alvarez de Paz, Diego. *The Life of Our Lord, Jesus Christ,
in Meditations*. Trans. Sister M. Emmanuel. St. Louis:
B. Herder Book Co., 1933, 265p.

Ambruzzi, Aloysius. *Gesù "ieri: oggi: in eterno" (Ebrei 13, 8)*.
Vincenza: L. Favero, 1960, 722p.

————. *Jesus: "Yesterday and Today, and Forever" (Heb. 13:8)*.
Trans. Gilda dal Corso. Westminster, Md.: Newman Press,
1962, 687p.

Ammon, Christoph Friedrich von. *Die Geschichte des Lebens
Jesu mit steter Rücksicht auf die vorhandenen Quellen*. 3
vols. Leipzig: Vogel, 1842-47.

Amoretti, Aquiles R. *Y Jesús entró al Evangelio*. Montevideo:
Editorial Alfa, 1968, 786p.

Anderson, John. *The Life of Christ from the Cradle to the Cross.* London: W.R. M'Phun, 1862, (1871), (1874), 640p.

Andrews, David Peter. *Bhagavāna Yeśū Khrista.* Puṇe: Śrī Lekhana Vācana Bhaṇḍāra, 1965. 154p.

Andrews, Samuel James. *The Life of Our Lord upon the Earth Considered in its Historical, Chronological, and Geographical Relations.* New York: Charles Scribner's Sons, 1864, (1868), (1891), 624p.; *The Bible Student's Life of Our Lord.* London: 1895.

Angus, Joseph. *Christ Our Life: In Its Origin, Law, and End.* Philadelphia: American Baptist Publication Society, 1853, 336p.

Anthony, Alfred Williams. *An Introduction to the Life of Jesus.* Boston: Silver, Burdett and Co., 1896, (1899), 206p.

Antonio Maria de Montevideo, Padre. *Hacia El. Introducción a la vida de Cristo; conferencias radiadas por C X 8 Radio Jackson de Montevideo.* Monteviedo: Escuela tipográfica Talleres Don Bosco, 1934, 115p.

Arai, Sasagu. *Iesu to sono jidai.* Tokyo: Iwanami Shoten, 1974, 208p.

Aretino, Pietro. *L'umanità di Cristo.* Roma: Colombo, 1945, 247p.

Armstrong, Garner Ted. *The Real Jesus.* Kansas City, Mo.: Sheed Andrews and McMeel, 1977, 280p.

Arnaboldi, Paolo M. *Incontri vivi con Gesù vivo.* Velate/ Varese: FAC, 1968, 387p.

Arumainathan, Aruldoss. *Cilampu kanta ciluval.* Cennai: Perumpūr Pāri Kalai Maṉram, 1971, 94p.

Ārumukam, Cōma. *Ēcunātar.* Kōvai: Kalā Papḷikēṣans, 1971, 99p.

Atlanta's Behold the Man (Filmstrip). A M D Studios, 1969.

Atwater, John Birdseye. *The Real Jesus of the Four Gospels.* Minneapolis: Review Pub. Co., 1921, 162p.

Aula, Olavi. *Jeesuksen testamentti.* Helsinki: Kirjanelio, 1972, 134p.

Auslegung des Lebens Jesu Christi. Ulm: Johann Zainer, not before 1478.

Austin, Mary (Hunter). *The Man Jesus; Being a Brief Account of the Life and Teaching of the Prophet of Nazareth.* New York: Harper and Brothers, 1915, 214p.

————. *A Small Town Man*. New York: Harper and Brothers, 1925, 230p.

Avancini, Nicolaus. *The Life and Teaching of Our Lord Jesus Christ*. Trans. Kenneth Mackenzie. London: Society for Promoting Christian Knowledge; New York: Macmillan, 1937, 499p.

————. *The Life and Teaching of Our Lord Jesus Christ. Taken from the Gospels and Arranged for Daily Meditations*. Trans. B.E. Kenworthy-Browne. New York: P.J. Kenedy, 1962, 554p.

————. *Meditations on the Life and Doctrine of Jesus Christ*. Trans. E.E. Bazalgette. London: Burns, 1875. 2 vols.

————. *Vita et doctrina Jesu Christi*. 2 vols. Bononiæ: Typis C. Pisarii, 1705.

Babb, Clement Edwin. *Talks about Jesus: His Birth, His Life, His Parables*. Cincinnati: Western Trust and Book Society, 1868, 109p.

Badano, Nino. *E abito tra noi*. Roma: G. Volpe, 1980, 226p.

Baigorri y Azanza, Luis. *Caminos de lus; meditaciones para adolescentes*. Madrid: Ediciones Studium de Cultura, 1953, 528p.

Baily, Caleb. *The Life of Jesus*. London: The Author, 1726, (1732), 362p.

Baker, Septina. *Life of Our Master, Christ Jesus*. San Francisco: California Press, 1925, 260p.

Baldwin, Louis. *Jesus of Galilee: His Story in Everyday Language*. Valley Forge, Pa.: Judson Press, 1979, 142p.

Balfern, William Poole. *Glimpses of Jesus*. 3rd ed. London: 1857; New York: 1858.

Ball, Charles Otis. *The Christ and His Message with a Short Bible Dictionary*. Siloam Springs, Ark.: The University Press, 1937, 211p.

Ballantine, William Gay. *The Young Man from Jerusalem*. Boston; New York: Houghton Mifflin Co., 1921, 73p.

Ballweg, Irmgard, and Marie Luise Schwarze. *Christus im Wort*. Düsseldorf: Haus der katholischen Frauen, 1967, 63p.

Ban, Joseph D. *Jesus Confronts Life's Issues*. Valley Forge, Pa.: Judson Press, 1972, 128p.

Bapst, Edmond. *La vie historique de N.-S. Jesus-Christ*. 2 vols. Paris: Lahune, 1924.

Barage, Friedrich. *Jesus obimadisiwin ajonda aking.* Paris:
E.J. Bailly ogimisinakisan manda misinaigan, 1837, 211p.

Barbieri, Antonio María. *En la tarde, comentarios al tercer
año de la vida pública de Cristo.* Montevideo: Editorial
Mosca Hermanos, 1942, 268p.

————. *Siembra, segundo año de la vida pública de Cristo.*
2. ed. Monteviedo: Editorial Mosca Hermanos, 1947, 221p.

Barclay, William. *Crucified and Crowned.* London: SCM Press,
1961, 192p.

————. *Jesus of Nazareth.* London; Cleveland: Collins, 1977;
Nashville: T. Nelson, 1981, 285p.

————. *The Life of Jesus for Everyman.* New York: Harper
and Row, 1966, 96p.

————. *The Mind of Jesus.* London: SCM Press, 1960, 190p.

————. *A New People's Life of Jesus.* London: SCM Press,
1965, 96p.

Bargellini, Piero. *Figlio dell'uomo-figlio di Dio.* Vol. II.
Brescia: Morcelliana, 1936, 267p.

————. *Lui. Racconti della vita di Gesù.* 7. ed. Firenze:
Vallecchi, 1969, 189p.

Barker, Joseph. *Jesus, a Portrait.* Philadelphia: Methodist
Episcopal Book Room, 1873, 264p.

Barnett, Walter. *Jesus, the Story of His Life: A Modern Retelling Based on the Gospels.* Chicago: Nelson-Hall, 1975,
273p.

Bartholomew, Christopher Churchill. *Life and Doctrines of Our
Lord and Saviour Jesus Christ.* London: 1880.

Barton, Bruce. *The Man of Galilee.* New York: Cosmopolitan
Book Corp., 1928, 137p.

————. *A Young Man's Jesus.* Boston: Pilgrim Press, 1914,
233p.

Barton, Charles M. *The Teacher of Galilee, an Inductive Study
of the Teaching of Jesus in the First Three Gospels.* Chicago: Epworth League of the Methodist Episcopal Church,
1916, 176p.

Barton, George Aaron. *Jesus of Nazareth; a Biography.* New
York: Macmillan, 1922, 396p.

Barton, William Eleazar. *Jesus of Nazareth; the Story of His
Life and the Scenes of His Ministry.* Boston: Pilgrim Press,

1903, 558p.; *The Sweetest Story ever Told: The Story of Jesus and His Love*. Chicago: The Bible House, 1906, 572p.

Battenhouse, Henry Martin. *Christ in the Gospels; an Introduction to His Life and its Meaning*. New York: Ronald Press Co., 1952, 339p.

Baubil, François Hippolyte. *Vive Jésus! Appel au peuple du manifeste déicide de m. Renan*. Paris: E. Dentu, 1864, 160p.

Bauer, Bruno. *Kritik der evangelischen Geschichte der Synoptiker*. 3 vols. Leipzig: O. Wigand, 1841-42, (1846); Hildesheim; New York: Olms, 1974.

Bauman, Edward W. *The Life and Teaching of Jesus*. Philadelphia: Westminster Press, 1960, 240p.

Bayerle, Bernard Gustav. *Die Erlösung der Welt*. 2 vols. New York: Debitert durch S. Zickel, 1862.

Beardslee, Clark Smith. *Jesus, the King of Truth; a Series of Lessons for Sunday Schools*. Hartford, Conn.: Hartford Seminary Press, 1904, 130p.

Beasley, Norman. *This Is the Promise*. New York: Duell, Sloan, and Pearce, 1957, 103p.

Beaudenom, Chanoine. *Meditaciones afectivas y prácticas*. 3 vols. Barcelona: E. Subirana, 1930-31.

Beaufays, Ignace. *L'Homme-Dieu*. 2. éd. Paris: S. François; Gembloux: J. Duculot, 1934, 460p.

Beck, Dwight Marion. *Through the Gospels to Jesus*. New York: Harper, 1954, 468p.

Becker, Thomas Aloysius. *The Public Life of Christ*. New York: Apostleship of Prayer, 1939, 273p.

Bedcher, Henry Ward. *The Life of Jesus the Christ*. New York: J.B. Ford; Edinburgh: T. Nelson and Sons, 1871, 387p.; New York: Bromfield and Co.; London: R.D. Dickinson, 1891, 2 vols.

Beginning of Christ's Public Life (Filmstrip). J.S. van den Nieuwendijk, Zeist, Netherlands. Released in the U.S. by Encyclopedia Britannica Films, 1958, 25 fr.

Beiler, Irwin Ross. *Studies in the Life of Jesus*. Ann Arbor, Mich.: Edwards Brothers, 1931; Nashville: Cokesbury Press, 1936, 319p.

Beilner, Wolfgang. *Jesus ohne Retuschen*. Graz; Wien; Köln: Verlag Styria, 1974, 332p.

Bennett, Ella Kellum. *My Pilot*. New York: Pegasus Pub. Co., 1940, 152p.

Bennett, James. *Lectures on the History of Jesus Christ*. 2 vols., 2nd ed. London: F. Westley and A.H. Davis, 1828.

Bennett, Leo. *The Prophet of Love; an Appreciation of Jesus*. San Antonio: Naylor Co., 1940, 616p.

Berg, Emil P. *The Spiritual Biography of Jesus Christ, According to the Saintly Essenes*. 2 vols. London: A.H. Stockwell, 1911.

Bergsma, Jan. *De levens van Jezus in het middelnederlandsch*. Groningen: J.B. Wolters, 1895-98, 288p.

Berkemeyer, William C. *Diary of a Disciple; a Contemporary's Portrait of Jesus; Devotional Reading for Forty Days*. Philadelphia: Muhlenburg Press, 1954, 219p.

Berthe, Augustine. *Jesus Christ, His Life, His Passion, His Triumph*. Trans. Ferreol Girardey. St. Louis: B. Herder, 1914, 514p.

Bertolaso Stella, Jorge. *A vida de Jesus Cristo*. São Paulo: Imprensa Metodista, 1972, 86p.

Beyschlag, Willibald. *Das Leben Jesu*. 2 Bde. Halle: E. Strein, 1885-86, (1887-88), (1893), (1901-02), (1912).

Bhave, Vinoba. *Khrista-dharma-sāra*. Vārāṇasī: Sarva Sevā Saṅkha Prakāśana, 1970, 162p.

Bichlmair, Georg. *Der Mann Jesus*. 2. Aufl. Wien: Herder, 1946, 270p.

Binns, William. *Life of Jesus*. London: 1875, 32p.

Biography of the Saviour, and His Apostles, with a Portrait of Each. New York: Taylor and Dodd, 1840, (1847), 108p.

Bird, Robert. *Jesus, the Carpenter of Nazareth*. 2nd ed. New York: Charles Scribner's Sons, 1891 (1905) (1907) (1910) (1912) (1921), 498p.; London: Kegan Paul, 1890 (1892) (1900), 458p.; London: Nelson, 1933, 512p.

Birth, Life, and Death of the Redeemer. Manchester: 1840.

Bishop, Eric Francis Fox. *Jesus of Palestine; the Local Background to the Gospel Documents*. London: Lutterworth Press, 1955; Fair Lawn, N.J.: Essential Books, 328p.

Bishop, John. *Seeing Jesus Today; a Portrait of Jesus the Man*. Valley Forge, Pa.: Judson Press, 1973, 158p.

Black, James Macdougall. *The Dilemmas of Jesus*. New York: Revell, 1925, 213p.

Blackburn, Kate Eubank. *The Kingdom of Love*. Jacksonville, Fla.: Drew Press, 1936, 208p.

Bliedner, Karl Ernst. *Vom Heiland*. Wolgast: P. Christiansen, 1934, 44p.

Blomfield, E. *Life of Christ with a History of the First Propagation of the Christian Religion, and the Lives of the Most Eminent Persons Mentioned in the New Testament*. Bungay: Printed by C. Brightly, for himself and T. Kinnersley, 1809, 636p.; Bungay: Brightly and Childs, 1813; London: George Virtue, 1809, 859p.

Blunt, Henry. *Lectures upon the History of Our Lord and Saviour Jesus Christ*. Philadelphia: Hooker and Claxton, 1839; Philadelphia: H. Hooker, 1840; Philadelphia: 1848 (1857), 462p.; London: 1835.

Bo, Dino del. *Il Dio della felicità: una storia di Gesù*. Milano: Rizzoli, 1975, 268p.

Boddy, Alexander A. *Christ in His Holy Land; a Life of Our Lord*. London: Society for Promoting Christian Knowledge, 1897, 320p.

Bodington, Charles. *Jesus the Christ*. London: SPCK, 1892, 80p.

Bogoliûbov, Andreĭ. *Syn chelovecheskiĭ*. Bruxelles: Life with God, 1968?, 335p.

Bolles, William. *The Complete Evangelist; Comprising a History of the Life of Jesus Christ*. New London: 1845, 226p.

Bonaventura, Saint, supposed author. *Das Leben Christi*. 3. Ausgabe. Wien: Verlag der Mechitharisten-Congregations-Buchhandlung, 1856.

————. *Das Leben Jesu Christi*. München: Katholischen Büchervereins, 1890, 378p.

————. *The Life of Christ*. Trans. and ed. W.H. Hutchins. London: Rivingtons, 1881, 337p.; Dublin: 1845; London: 1844, Trans. F. Oakeley.

————. *The Life of Our Lord and Saviour Jesus Christ*. London: 1739, 364p.; London: J. Toovey, 1866, 282p., Trans. Frederick Oakeley; Baltimore: 1868; New York: P.J. Kenedy, 1887, 407p.

————. *Meditatione de la vita di Nostro Signore*. Paris: 1929.

————. *Méditationes sur la vie Jésus-Christ*. 2 éd. Trans. Lemaire-Esmangard. Paris: Putois-Cretté, 1860, 541p.

————. *Meditationes vitae Christi.* Augustae Vindelicorum,
Gintherus Zainer, 1468, 72 l.; Westminster: William Caxton,
ca. 1490, 148 l.; Venice: Barnardinus Benalius and Matteo
Capcase, before 8 May 1491, (1492), 34 l.; Florence: Antonio
di Bartolommeo Miscomini, ca. 1493; London: R. Pynson, 1494;
Westminster: W. de Worde, 1494; Strassburg: Johann Grüninger,
ca. 1496; Florence: Laurentius de Morgianis and Johannes
Petri, ca. 1496; Paris: Pierre Levet, for Denis Roce, 1497;
Venice: Lazarus de Soardis, 1497; Venice: Manfredus de Bonel-
lis, de Monteferrato, 1497; Pavia: Jacobus de Pasis Drapis
Burgofrancho, 1499; Montserrat: Johanez Luschner, 1499.

————. *Les méditations dela vie du Christ.* 6 éd. Trans. H.
de Riancey. Paris: Poussielque, 1880, (1914), 608p.

————. *Meditations of the Life of Christ.* Trans. Sister
M. Emmanuel. St. Louis; London: B. Herder Book Co., 1934,
441p.

————. *Meditazioni della vita di Gesù Cristo.* Milano: S.
Brambilla, 1823, 265p.

————. *The Miroure of the Blessed Life of Our Lorde and
Savioure Iesus Christe.* Douai?: 1590?

————. *The Mirror of the Blessed Life of Jesu Christ.* London: Burns, Oates, Washbourne, 1926, 322p.

————. *The Mirroure of the Blessyd Lyfe of Jesu Cryst.*
England: 15th cent., 123 l.; London; Edinburgh: H. Frowde,
1908, 330p.

————. *St. Bonaventure's Life of Our Lord and Saviour Jesus
Christ.* New York: J. Doyle, 1839, 308p.; Baltimore: John
Murphy, 1860; New York: P.J. Kenedy, Excelsior Catholic
Publishing House, 1894, 407p.

————. *Smaointe beatha Chriost.* Baile Átha Cliath: Insti-
tiúid árd-léighinn Bhaile Átha Cliath, 1944. 400p.

Bonforte, John. *The Rebellious Galilean.* New York: Philosophical Library, 1982, 319p.

Booth, Edwin Prince. *One Sovereign Life; Thoughts on the Life
of Christ.* New York: Abingdon Press, 1965, 144p.

Booth, Henry Kendall. *The World of Jesus; a Survey of the Background of the Gospels.* New York: Charles Scribner's Sons,
1933, 242p.

Borden, Lucille (Papin). *Once--in Palestine.* New York: Macmillan, 1938, 177p.

Bordet, Charles. *Kajottersgedachten bij het evangelie.* 3.
uitg. Trans. C. Van den Bliek. Brussels: K.A.J. Uitgaven,
1943, 280p.

————. *Regards jocistes sur l'évangile.* 5 éd. Paris: Editions ouvrières, 1945, 125p.

Borer, Wilbur J. *Book of the Lord: Reflections on the Life of Christ.* Huntington, Ind.: Our Sunday Visitor, 1978, 493p.

Borning, Walther. *Die Botschaft Jesu von Nazareth.* Frankfurt am Main: Englert und Scholsser, 1930, 310p.

Bornkamm, Günther. *Jesus of Nazareth.* Trans. Irene and Fraser McLuskey with James M. Robinson. New York: Harper, 1960; London: Hodder and Stoughton, 1960, 239p.

————. *Jesus von Nazareth.* Stuttgart: Kohlhammer, 1956, (1957), (1959), 214p.

Bosley, Harold Augustus. *The Mind of Christ.* Nashville: Abingdon Press, 1966, 143p.

Bosworth, Edward Increase. *Christ in Everyday Life.* New York: Young Men's Christian Association Press, 1910, 215p.

————. *The Life and Teaching of Jesus According to the First Three Gospels.* New York: Macmillan, 1924, (1928), 424p.

————. *Studies in the Life of Jesus Christ.* New York: International Committee of Young Men's Christian Associations, 1904, (1906), 259p.

————. *Thirty Studies about Jesus.* New York: Association Press, 1917, 180p.

Bouhuys, Mies, and Piet Worm. *De man van Nazareth. Gezinsboek over leven, land en volk van Jezus.* Amsterdam: Van Kampen, 1970, 172p.

Bourne, Henry H. *Gleanings from the Life and Teachings of Christ.* London: 1880.

Bousset, Wilhelm. *Jesus.* Halle: Gebauer-Schwetschke, 1904, 103p.; Tübingen: Mohr, 1907, 100p., 3 Aufl.

————. *Jesus.* Trans. Janet Penrose Trevelyan. New York: G.P. Putnam's Sons; London: Williams and Norgate, 1906, 211p.

Bowie, Walter Russell. *The Master; a Life of Jesus Christ.* New York: Scribner, 1928, (1930), (1958), 331p.

Boyall, Charles Spurgeon. *The Man for Others.* Sydney: Alpha Books, 1973, 145p.

Braden, Charles Samuel. *Jesus Compared; a Study of Jesus and Other Great Founders of Religions.* Englewood Cliffs, N.J.: Prentice-Hall, 1957, 230p.

Bradley, Samuel Carlyle. *Jesus of Nazareth; a Life*. Boston: Sherman, French, and Co., 1908, 575p.

Brennan, Richard. *The Life of Our Lord and Saviour Jesus Christ, and His Blessed Mother*. New York: 1879; New York: Benziger Brothers, 1907.

Brett, Robert. *Reflections, Meditations, and Prayers, with Gospel Harmony on the Most Holy Life and Sacred Person of Our Lord Jesus Christ*. London: 1849, (1852), 402p.

Briggs, Charles Augustus. *New Light on the Life of Jesus*. New York: Charles Scribner's Sons, 1904, 196p.

Brock, Erich. *Die Grundlagen des Christentums*. Bern; München: Francke, 1970, 370p.

Bromley, Samuel. *The Life of Christ*. London: Milner and Sowerby, 1840?, (1865), 331p.

Bronx, Humberto. *Historia de Jesús*. Medellín, Colombia: Editorial Bedout, 1961, 605p.

Brooks, Arthur. *The Life of Christ in the World*. New York: T. Whittaker, 1887, 360p.

Brough, W. *Memory Pictures of the Life of Christ*. London: 1870.

Brown, Charles Reynolds. *The Master's Way; a Study in the Synoptic Gospels*. Boston; Chicago: Pilgrim Press, 1917, 553p.

Brown, Parker B. *He Came from Galilee*. New York: Hawthorn Books, 1974, 164p.

Browne, Edith. *Readings on the Life of Our Lord*. London: G. Bell and Sons, 1900, 125p.

Bruce, Alexander Balmain. *With Open Face; or, Jesus Mirrored in Matthew, Mark, and Luke*. New York: Charles Scribner's Sons, 1896, 257p.

Bruckberger, Raymond Léopold. *L'histoire de Jésus-Christ*. Paris: B. Grasset, 1965, 626p.; Paris: Le Livre de Poche, 1971, 635p.

————. *The History of Jesus Christ*. Trans. Denver Lindley. New York: Viking Press, 462p.

Brumback, Robert H. *Where Jesus Walked*. St. Louis: Mission Messenger, 1959, 157p.

Bruner, Benjamin Harrison. *Evenings with the Master*. St. Louis: Christian Board of Publishing, 1920, 143p.

Brunet, Manuel. *Pàgines de la vida de Jesucrist*. Barcelona: Ediciones Destino, 1961, 600p.

Buck, Florence. *The Story of Jesus*. Boston: Beacon Press, 1917, (1932), 317p.

Bullock, James George. *The Track of the Light; or, Christ's Footsteps Followed*. London: W. Hunt and Co., 1873, 109p.

Bultmann, Rudolf Karl. *Jesus*. Berlin: Deutsche Bibliothek, 1926, 204p.

————. *Jesus and the Word*. Trans. Louise Pettibone Smith and Erminie Huntress Lantero. New York: Charles Scribner's Sons, 1934, (1958), 226p.

Burgh, William. *Discourses on the Life of Christ; or, The Personal Events in the Personal History of the Redeemer*. London: F. and J. Rivington, 1849, 276p.

Burkitt, Francis Crawford. *Jesus Christ; an Historical Outline*. London and Glasgow: Blackie and Son, 1932, 90p.

Burman, Axel. *I Jesu sällskap*. Stockholm: Filadelfia; Solna: Seelig, 1969, 207p.

Burnham, Anna F. *A Study of the Life of Jesus the Christ, in Fifty-two Lessons for Little Folks*. Boston; Chicago: Congregational Sunday-School and Publishing Society, 1892, 172p.

Burnham, Benjamin Franklin, and Celeste Shute. *The Life of Lives, Being the Records of Jesus Reviewed by a Throng of Recent Biblical Scholars, Teachers, and Thinkers*. Boston: Cleaves, Macdonald and Co., 1885, 378p.

Burnham, Sarah M. *The Roman's Story in the Time of Claudius I*. Boston: A.I. Bradley and Co., 1898, 311p.

Burt, Nathaniel Clark. *Hours among the Gospels; or, Wayside Truths from the Life of Our Lord*. Philadelphia: J.B. Lippincott and Co., 1865, 215p.

Burton, Ernest DeWitt, and Shailer Matthews. *Constructive Studies in the Life of Christ*. Chicago: University of Chicago Press, 1900, (1901); London: 1901, 302p.

————. *Jesus of Nazareth, How He Thought, Loved, Worked, and Achieved*. Chicago: University of Chicago Press, 1920, 81p.

————. *The Life of Christ*. Chicago: University of Chicago Press, 1908, (1917), (1921), (1927), (1930), 282p.

Bushell, Gerard. *Jesus: Where It All Began*. New York: Abelard-Schuman, 1975, 223p.

Businger, Lucas Caspar. *The Life of Christ.* New York; Cincinnati: Benziger Brothers, 1913, 439p.

————. *The Life of Our Lord and Saviour Jesus Christ and of His Virgin Mother Mary.* New York; Cincinnati: Benziger Brothers, 1907, 876p.

Byers, Samuel Hawkins Marshall. *A Layman's Life of Jesus.* New York: Neale Pub. Co., 1912, 108p.

Byrum, Enoch Edwin. *The Man of Galilee.* Anderson, Ind.: Gospel Trumpet Co., 1907, 173p.

Cable, John Henry. *Christ in the Four Gospels.* New York: Christian Alliance Pub. Co., 1926, 375p.

Cabodevilla, José Maria. *Cristo vivo; vida de Cristo y vida cristiana.* Madrid: Editorial Católica, 1963, 919p.

Cachutt Morales, Manuel. *Este es Jesús.* Caracas: 197-?

Caine, Hall. *Life of Christ.* New York: Doubleday, Doran, and Co., 1938, 1310p.

————. *Vita di Gesù Cristo.* 2 vols. Trans. Elio Vittorini. Milano: Mondadori, 1946.

Campanella, Tommaso. *Vita Christi.* 2 vols. Trans. Romano Amerio. Roma: Centro internazionale di studi umanistici, 1962-63.

Campbell, G. *The Life of Our Lord and Saviour Jesus Christ.*

Campbell, Reginald John. *The Life of Christ.* New York: D. Appleton and Co., 1921, 437p.

Campbell, William M. *Foot-prints of Christ.* New York; London: Funk and Wagnalls, 1889, 375p.

Campelo, Moisés María. *Dios bajó al llano.* Barcelona: Ediciones Eler, 1964, 230p.

Cappe, Catherine Harrison. *A Connected History of the Life and Divine Mission of Jesus Christ as Recorded in the Narratives of the Four Evangelists.* York: 1809; York: Printed by Thomas Wilson, 1819, 545p.

Cardwell-Hill, Henry. *The-me; an Imaginary Auto-biography of Jesus Christ.* London: Regency P., 1966, 84p.

Carey, Samuel Pearce. *Jesus.* London: The Book Club, 1940, 256p.

Carpenter, William Boyd. *The Son of Man among the Sons of Men.* New York: T. Whittaker, 1894, (1896), (1897), (1901); London: Isbester, 1893, 307p.

Carrington, Philip. *Our Lord and Saviour, His Life and Teachings*. Greenwich, Conn.: Seabury Press, 1958, 138p.

————. *The Road to Jerusalem*. London: Society for Promoting Christian Knowledge; New York: Macmillan, 1933, 131p.

Carroll, Patrick Joseph. *The Man-God; a Life of Jesus*. Chicago; New York: Scott, Foresman, and Co., 1927, 345p.

Carter, Sarah Maud. *The Life of Christ*. Devils Lake, N.D.: Printed and bound at the North Dakota School for the Deaf, 1931, 105p.

Carter, Thomas Thellusson. *The Devout Christian's Help to Meditation on the Life of Our Lord Jesus Christ*. 2 vols. London: 1866, (1869).

Case, Carl Delos. *My Christ*. Philadelphia; Boston: Griffith and Rowland Press, 1915, 169p.

Case, Shirley Jackson. *Jesus; a New Biography*. Chicago: University of Chicago Press, 1927, (1934); New York: Greenwood Press, 1968; New York: AMS Press, 1969, 452p.

Caspers, A. *Christi Fusstapfen in vier Büchern*. 2 Aufl. Leipzig: Teubner, 1863, 820p.

————. *The Footsteps of Christ*. Trans. A.E. Rodman. Edinburgh: T. and T. Clark, 1871. 434p.

Cassels, Louis. *The Real Jesus, How He Lived and What He Taught*. Garden City, N.Y.: Doubleday, 1968, 131p.

Cassidy, James Francis. *Christ and Littleness*. New York; Chicago: Benziger Brothers, 1937, 150p.

Catholic Truth Society of Ireland. *Beatha ár dTighearna Íosa Criost*. Dublin: Office of Solatair, 1943, 99p.

Cell, Charles W. *Jesus the Divine Layman; God's Gift to Humanity*. Riverside, Calif.; Rahway, N.J.: Quinn and Boden Co., 1941, 179p.

Center for Hermeneutical Studies in Hellenistic and Modern Culture. *The Hero Pattern and the Life of Jesus: Protocol of the Twentieth Colloquy, 12 December 1976*. Berkeley: The Center, 1977, 98p.

Ceresi, Vincenzo. *Gesù il maestro*. 3. ed. Roma: Coletti, 1945, 375p.

Cesari, Antonio. *La vita di Gesù Cristo e la sua religione*. 5 vols. Verona: L'erede Merlo, 1817.

Chadwick, John White. *The Man Jesus: A Course of Lectures*. Boston: Roberts Brothers, 1881, 258p.

Chalet, François. *Flashes sur Jésus-Christ*. Paris: Éditions ouvrières, 1965, 147p.

Chalmers, Robert Scott. *Lessons on the Life of Our Lord
Jesus Christ.* Milwaukee: Morehouse Pub. Co., 1933, 211p.

Chapman, Edwin. *The Life of Our Lord and Saviour Jesus
Christ.* London: Green, 1840, 134p.; Boston: 1844.

Chatham, Josiah George. *In the Midst Stands Jesus.* Staten
Island, N.Y.: Alba House, 1972, 220p.

Cheney, Harriet Vaughan. *Sketches from the Life of Christ.*
Boston: Crosby, 1844, 147p.

Chhabra, Bahadur Chand. *ABC of Christianity.* Pondicherry:
Ashoka Maurya and Pallava Historical Trust, 1977, 174p.

Chirayath, Francis. *Kristuvinṟe jīvacaṟitram.* Cochin:
Universal Book House, 1963, 337p.

Christmas, Henry. *Scenes in the Life of Christ: A Course of
Lectures.* 2nd ed. London: 1820, (1853).

*Christus natus est, Christ Is Born. The History of Christ;
His Life and Death.* London: 1680.

*Christus Redivivus; or, the History of the Life and Death of
Our Blessed Lord and Saviour.* London: 1680.

Clark, Dennis E. *Jesus Christ: His Life and Teaching.* Elgin,
Ill.: Dove Publications, 1977, 324p.

Clark, Horace. *Life of Jesus Christ as by the Apostles Matthew,
Mark, Luke, and John.* Hartford, Conn.: Case, Lockwood and
Brainard Co., 1906, 195p.

Clark, M.B. Sterling. *The Scripture History of Our Blessed
Lord and Saviour, Jesus Christ.* New York: D. Dana, 1860,
135p.

Clark, Mary Latham. *The Story of Jesus. A Question-Book
for Children.* Dover, N.H.: Freewill Baptist Printing Establishment, 1867, 85p.

Clark, Rufus Wheelwright. *Life Scenes of the Messiah.* New
York: Sheldon, Lamport, and Blakeman, 1855, 330p.; *The True
Prince of the Tribe of Judah; or, Life Scenes of the Messiah.*
Boston: A. Colby and Co., 1859, 355p.; *Life of Christ and
His Apostles.* Baltimore: A. Colby, 1867, 355p.; *The Life
of Our Lord and Saviour Jesus Christ.* Lowell: A. Colby,
1871, 355p.

Clarke, James Freeman. *The Legend of Thomas Didymus, the
Jewish Sceptic.* Boston: Lee and Shepard; New York: C.T.
Dillingham, 1881, 448p.; *Life and Times of Jesus as Related
by Thomas Didymus.* Boston: Lee and Shepard; New York: C.T.
Dillingham, 1887, (1891).

Clarke, Samuel. *The Blessed Life and Meritorious Death of Our Lord and Saviour Jesus Christ*. London: Printed for W. Miller, 1664, (1665), 54p.

Cleveland, Philip Jerome. *Beauty's Pilgrim, a Portrait of Jesus*. Brooklyn, Conn.: Ingland Co., 1937, 356p.

Cliff, Judity. *Jesus, a Gospel Guide to His Life*. Jerusalem: Franciscan Print. Press; Fulton, Calif.: Cliff House, 1976, 263p.

Clifford, Philip Henry. *Bible Studies on Jesus, the King*. New York: C.C. Cook, 1914, 96p.

Clodd, Edward. *Jesus of Nazareth: Embracing, a Sketch of Jewish History to the Time of His Birth*. London: K. Paul Trench and Co., 1880, (1886), (1889), 386p.; London: Watts and Co., 1905, 119p.

Coburn, David. *Agape; the Story of Jesus as Portrayed in the New Testament*. London: A.H. Stockwell, 1936, 206p.

Coburn, John B. *Christ's Life, Our Life*. New York: Seabury Press, 1978, 101p.

Cochem, Martin von. *Das grosse Leben Christi*. 2 vols. München: 1716; München: Druckts und verlegts Heinrich Theodor von Cöllin, 1721, 2 vols.; Mayntz; Franckfurt: Häffrerischen Erben, 1752, 1382p.; Landshut: Joh. Nep. Attenhofer, 1841. 879p.; Baltimore: Verlag von Johann Murphy, 1847, 2 vols.

————. *Leben Christi oder autzuführliche andächtige und-bewegliche Beschreibung des Lebens und Leidens unsers Herrn Jesus Christi und seiner glorwürdigsten Mutter Maria*. Franckfurt: Johann Peter Zuprodt, 1680, 1182p.

————. *Leben Jesu Christi*. 1707, 1590p.

————. *Das Leben und Leiden Christi*. Harrisburg, Pa.: Gedrucht, nach dem Original, bei Bigler und Weeber, 1838, 760p.

————. *Leben und Leiden unsers lieben Herrn und Heilandes Jesu Christi und seiner göttlichen jungfräulichen Mutter Maria*. 12 Aufl. Regensburg: Friedrich Pustet, 1881, 1582p.

————. *Das Leben unsers lieben Herrn und Heilandes Jesus Christus und seiner jungfräulichen Mutter Maria*. Einsiedeln; New York; Cincinnati: C. and N. Benziger, 1873, 1031p.

————. *Leben und Leiden unseres Herrn und Heilandes Jesu Christi und seiner gebennedeiten jungfräulichen Mutter Maria*. 2 vols. 6. Aufl. Münster: Aschendorff, 1864 (1893).

————. *Des Lebens Christi und seiner Lieben Mutter Maria*. 3 vols. Maynz; Franckfurt: 1718.

————. *The Life and Sufferings of Christ; together with a Full and Accurate Account of those of his Mother, the Blessed Virgin Mary.* Philadelphia: T.K. and P.G. Collins, 1840, 802p.

————. *The Life of Christ.* New York: Benziger Brothers, 1897 (1913), 314p.

————. *Welký žiwot Pána a Spasiltele nasseho Krista Ježisse a jeho nejswětějssí a nejmilejssí Matky Marie Panny, jakož i wssech jiných krewnich přátel Syna Božiho.* Wyd 8. W. Uh Skalici, J. Teslík, 1901, 942p.; W. Uh. Skalici, Jozefa Skarnicle, 1867; V. Praze, 1698, 1134p.

Coffin, Henry Sloane. *The Portraits of Jesus Christ in the New Testament.* New York: Macmillan, 1926, 96p.

Colaw, Emerson S. *The Way of the Master.* New York: Abingdon Press, 1965, 128p.

Coleridge, S.J. *The Life of Our Lord.* 2 vols. London: 1876.

————. *The Public Life of Our Lord.* 5 vols. London: 1875.

Colman, Benjamin. *Some of the Glories of Our Lord and Saviour Jesus Christ, Exhibited in Twenty Sacramental Discourses Preached at Boston in New England.* London: Printed by S. Palmer, for Thomas Hancock, 1728, 304p., (1979).

Colton, Ann Ree. *The Jesus Story.* Glendale, Calif.: ARC Pub. Co., 1969, 396p.

Combrink, Charles E. *What Manner of Man?* Boston: R.G. Badger, 1928, 174p.

The Coming of Christ (Motion picture). National Broadcasting Co. Released by Encyclopedia Britannica Education Corp., 1966, 33 min.

Compans, Jean. *Storia della vita de Gesù Cristo dedotta dai quattro Evangelj.* 2 vols. Trans. Francesco Pertusati. Milano: Stamperia di G. Pirotta, 1812.

Comstock, Jim F. *Good News: The Life of Jesus Reported in Newspaper Style.* McLean, Va.: EPM Publications, 1974, 48p.

Conaty, Thomas James. *New Testament Studies. The Principal Events in the Life of Our Lord.* New York; Cincinnati: Benziger Brothers, 1898, 252p.

Conder, Eustace Rogers. *Outlines of the Life of Christ.* London: Religious Tract Society, 1881, (1886), 211p.

Cone, Jessica. *Scenes from the Life of Christ, Pictured in Holy Word and Sacred Art*. New York: G.P. Putnam's Sons, 1892, 142p.

Connick, C. Mille. *Jesus: The Man, the Mission, and the Message*. Englewood Cliffs, N.J.: Prentice-Hall, 1963, (1974), 462p.

Contemplations and Meditations on the Passion and Death, and on the Glorious Life of Jesus Christ According to the Method of St. Ignatius. Trans. by a Sister of Mercy. Revised by a priest. London: 1867, (1881).

Converse, Gordon N. *Come See the Place: The Holy Land Jesus Knew*. Englewood Cliffs, N.J.: Prentice-Hall, 1978, 144p.

Cook, Peter. *The Genuine Words of Jesus According to the Older Documents Underlying the New Testament Gospels, Including a Sketch of the Life and Times of Jesus*. Alhambra, Los Angeles, Calif.: Weimar Press, 1923, 103p.

————. *Jesus of Nazareth, the Annointed of God; or, The Inner History of a Consecrated Life*. Chicago; New York: Revell, 1904, 136p.

Cook, Richard Briscoe. *The Story of Jesus. Being an Account of the Life and Work, the Walks and Talks of Christ*. Baltimore: R.H. Woodward and Co., 1889, 542p.

Cook, Walter L. *Youth Devotions on the Jesus Who Was Different*. Nashville: Abingdon Press, 1973, 96p.

Cook, Greville. *The Light of the World; a Reconstruction and Interpretation of the Life of Christ*. Indianapolis: Bobbs-Merrill, 1950, 470p.; London: Hodder and Stoughton, 1949, 455p.

Cookson, Richard. *The Life of Our Lord in Sermons*. New York: J.F. Wagner, 1925, 295p.

Cooley, William Forbes. *Emmanuel; the Story of Jesus the Messiah*. New York: Dodd, Mead, 1889, 546p.

Cornell, George W. *Behold the Man; People, Politics, and Events Surrounding the Life of Jesus*. Waco, Tex.: Word Books, 1974, 206p.

Cottrell, James J. *We Have Found the Christ; the Wonderful Meaning of the Life, Ministry, Death, and Resurrection of Our Redeeming Lord*. New York: Greenwich Book Publishers, 1959, 138p.

Counts, Bill. *Once a Carpenter*. Irvine, Calif.: Harvest House Publishers, 1975, 255p.

Coursey, Oscar William. *That Lonely Jew.* Mitchell, S.D.: Educator Supply Co., 1929, 112p.

Cowgill, Frank Brooks. *Jesus the Patriot.* Boston: Christopher Publishing House, 1928, 116p.

Cowley-Brown, George James. *Daily Lessons on the Life of Our Lord on Earth, in the Words of the Evangelists.* 2 vols. London: G. Bell and Sons, 1880.

Coyle, John Patterson. *The Imperial Christ.* Boston: Houghton Mifflin, 1896, 249p.

Crabtre, Addison Darre. *The Journeys of Jesus.* Boston: Palestine Pub. Co., 1883, 703p.; Elkhart, Ind.: Palestine Pub. Co., 1890, 703p.

Cragin, Louisa T. *Pictures in Palestine. The Story of Jesus, a Book for the Home.* New York: Fords, Howard, and Hulbert, 1886, 610p.

Cragin, Louisa T., and Edward Eggleston. *Life Studies in the Story of Jesus; together with the Words and Acts of the Master.* 4 vols. New York: Fords, Howard, and Holbert, 1900.

Craig, William. *An Essay on the Life of Jesus Christ.* Glasgow: Robert and Andrew Foulis, 1769, 177p.

Craveri, Marcello. *The Life of Jesus.* Trans. Charles Lam Markmann. London: Secker and Warburg, 1967; New York: Grove Press, 1967; Ann Arbor, Mich.: Reprinted for Grove Press by University Microfilms International, 1979, 520p.

————. *La vita de Gesù.* Milano: Feltrinelli, 1966, 466p.

Cribb, William Harris. *The Life of Christ.* Springfield, Ill.: W.H. Cribb, 1928, 530p.

Cristiani, Léon. *Jésus-Christ, Fils de Dieu, Sauveur.* 3 vols. 3. éd. Lyon: Comité catholique d'apostolat par l'évangile, 1934.

————. *Our Divine Model; the Gospel Life of Christ.* Trans. Canon L. Cristiani. Milwaukee: Bruce Pub. Co., 1940, 308p.

Crookall, Lawrence. *Topics in the Tropics; or, Short Studies in the Life of Christ.* London: Elliott Stock, 1894, 239p.

Crosby, Howard. *Jesus: His Life and Work as Narrated by the Four Evangelists.* New York; Baltimore: University Pub. Co., 1871, 551p.

Croscup, George Edward. *The Gospel History of Our Lord Made Visible.* Philadelphia: Sunday School Times Co., 1912, 50p.

Cross, Colin. *Who Was Jesus?* New York: Atheneum, 1970, 230p.

Crosse, Sarah. *The Source of the Christ Ideal; a Series of Lessons for the Children.* Boston: Society for the Expression of the Christ Ideal for its Children, 1904, 108p.

Crowe, Charles M. *The Years of Our Lord.* Nashville: Abingdon Press, 1955, 155p.

Crowell, Grace (Noll). *Come See a Man.* New York: Abingdon Press, 1956, 125p.

Cullen, John. *Pen Pictures from the Life of Christ.* London: R.D. Dickinson, 1889, 360p.

Culross, James. *Emmanuel, or, The Father Revealed in Jesus.* London: James Nisbet, 1868, 144p.

Culver, Robert Duncan. *The Life of Christ.* Grand Rapids: Baker Book House, 1976, 304p.

Cumming, John. *Life and Lessons of Our Lord Unfolded and Illustrated.* London: 1870; London: Shaw, n.d., 616p.

Curry, Albert Bruce. *Practical Lessons from the Early Ministry of Jesus.* Richmond, Va.: Presbyterian Committee of Publication, 1935, 214p.

————. *Practical Lessons from the Later Ministry of Jesus.* Richmond, Va.: Presbyterian Committee of Publication, 1938, 247p.

Cutts, Edward Lewes. *A Devotional Life of Our Lord and Saviour Jesus Christ.* New York: 1882; New York: E. and J.B. Young and Co., 1894, 536p.

Dale, Alan T. *Portrait of Jesus.* Oxford; New York: Oxford University Press, 1979, 149p.

Dana, Malcolm. *Christ of the Countryside.* Nashville: Cokesbury Press, 1937, 128p.

Daniel-Rops, Henry. *Histoire du Christ Jésus.* Liege; Thone; Paris: Club du livre sélectionné, 1965, 339p.

————. *Jesus and His Times.* Trans. Ruby Millar. New York: Dutton, 1956, (1954), 615p.

————. *Jésus en son temps.* Paris: Fayard, 1965, 503p.; (1945), 638p.; (1947), 100p.

————. *The Life of Our Lord.* Trans. J.R. Foster. New York: Hawthorn Books, 1964, 175p.; (1965), 191p.

David, Milton C. *Vida de Jesucristo.* Mexico, D.F.: Casa unida de publicaciones, 1944, 177p.

David, Noah Knowles. *The Story of the Nazarene, in Annotated Paraphrase.* New York; London: Revell, 1903, 428p.

David, William Henry. *Outline History of the Life of Christ for Boys' Bible Classes.* New York: International Committee of Young Men's Christian Associations, 1900, 24p.

Davies, Arthur Powell. *The Man from Nazareth.* Summit, N.J.: The Community Church, 1937, 28p.

Davis, Horace. *The Public Ministry of Jesus.* Boston: American Unitarian Association, 1911, 36p.

Dawson, Joseph. *Pictures of Christ Framed in Prayers. A Devotional Life of Jesus.* London: Charles H. Kelly, 1903, 232p.

Dawson, Thomas. *The New and Complete History of the Life of Our Blessed Lord and Saviour Jesus Christ.* London: A. Hogg, 1793, 495p.

Dawson, William James. *The Life of Christ.* Philadelphia: G.W. Jacobs and Co., 1901, (1904), 452p.; *The Man Christ Jesus; a Life of Christ.* New York; London: Century Co., 1925, 452p.

Day, Bertram. *The Prince of Peace.* Boston: Christopher Pub. House, 1948, 210p.

Deane, Anthony Charles. *Jesus Christ.* Garden City, N.Y.: Doubleday, Doran, and Co., 1928, 226p.

————. *The World Christ Knew; the Social, Personal, and Political Conditions of His Time.* East Lansing, Mich.: Michigan State College Press, 1953, 119p.

De Burgh, David J. *Christ Is My Life; Practical Mediations.* Boston: St. Paul Editions, 1977, 365p.

Deedes, Emily E. *Lessons on the Life of Christ.* London: Church of England Sunday School Institute, 1880, 111p.

Deems, Charles Force. *Jesus.* New York: United States Pub. Co., 1871, (1868), 756p.; *Who Was Jesus?* New York: J.H. Brown; London: R.D. Dickinson, 1880?; *The Light of the Nations.* New York: Gay Brothers and Co., 1884?

Delamarter, Arthur R. *Jesus: Achievement and Challenge.* Almons, N.Y.: New Day Pub. Co., 1930, 96p.

De Lamotte, Roy C. *The Alien Christ.* Washington, D.C.: University Press of America, 1980, 264p.

Delbare, François Thomas. *Jésus-Christ et ses apôtres.* Paris: L. Janet, 1820, 226p.

Delitzsch, Franz. *A Day in Capernaum.* Trans. George H. Schodde. New York: Funk and Wagnalls, 1887, 166p.

————. *Ein Tag in Capernaum.* Leipzig: F. Naumann, 1873; 8 Aufl., 1886, 152p.

De Ment, Byron Hoover. *The Bible Readers' Life of Christ.* New York; Chicago: Revell, 1928, 332p.

Denny, Walter Bell. *The Career and Significance of Jesus.* New York: Ronald Press Co., 1953, (1933), 466p.

De Rosa, Peter. *Jesus Who Became Christ.* London: Collins, 1975, 287p.

Deshler, G. Byron. *Finding the Truth about God; a Personal Study of Christ's Revelation of God as Portrayed in the Four Gospels.* Nashville: Tidings, 1964, 192p.

Desjardin, P.A. *Jésus de Nazareth, au point de vue historique, scientifique et social.* Paris: E. Flammarion, 1901?, 404p.

The Devout Christian's Exemplar: Or, The Sacred History of the Incarnation and Birth, Life and Death, Resurrection and Ascention of Our Lord and Saviour Jesus Christ. London: T. Worrall, 1727, 518p.

Deyhle, Arthur Adolf Wilhelm. *Christ, in Prose and Verse.* Louisville, Ky.: Pentecostal Pub. Co., 1913, 299p.

Dibelius, Martin. *Jesus.* Berlin: W. de Gruyter & Co., 1939, 134p.

————. *Jesus.* Trans. Charles B. Hedrick and Frederick C. Grant. Philadelphia: Westminster Press, 1949, 160p.

Dickson, Alexander. *All about Jesus.* New York: R. Carter and Brothers, 1875, (1878), 5th ed., 404p.

Didon, Henri Louis. *Gesù Cristo.* 2 tom. Trans. Manfredo Tarchi. Siena: 1893.

————. *Jesus Christ.* 2 vols. London: Kegan Paul, Trench, Trübner and Co., 1891, (1893), (1895), (1908); New York: Appleton, 1891, (1893); St. Louis: Herder, 1920?

————. *Jésus-Christ.* Montreal: Bearchemin, n.d.

————. *Jésus Christ.* 2 tom. Paris: E. Plon, Nourrit et Cie, 1891, (1902), (1913).

————. *Jesus Christus.* 2 vols. Trans. Geslaus M. Schneider. Regensburg: 1892; Regensburg: G.J. Manz, 1895 (1899), (1905).

————. *The Life of Jesus Christ.* 6th ed. London: K. Paul, Trench, Trübner, and Co., 1928, 399p.

————. *The Life of Our Lord Jesus Christ.* 2 vols. New York: Appleton, 1891.

————. *Vita di Gesù Cristò.* Firenze: A. Quattrini, 1928, 302p.

Dietz, Friedrich. *Jesus Christus.* Wurzburg: Echter, 1976, 204p.

Diffendorfer, Ralph Eugene. *Junior Studies in the Life of Christ.* Cincinnati: Jennings and Pye; New York: Eaton and Mains, 1903, 221p.

DiGiacomo, James. *Meet the Lord: Encounters with Jesus.* Minneapolis: Winston Press, 1977, 97p.

Dillingham, Fred Augustine. *Sunday School Text-book on the Life of Jesus.* North Attleboro?: 1893, 106p.

Dionysius. *A Clear and Learned History of Our Blessed Saviour Jesus.* London: n.d.

Dirksen, Aloys Herman. *A Life of Christ.* New York: Dryden Press, 1952, 338p.; New York: Holt, Rinehart, and Winston, 1962, 378p.

Discipleship (Motion picture). Cathedral Films, 1955, 30 min.

Discussions on the Life of Jesus Christ. Chicago: Inter-Varsity Press, 1967, (1962), 54p.

The Divine Master. 7th ed. London: 1871, 158p.

The Divine Miracle (Motion picture). Daina Krumins, 1973, 6 min.

The Divine Traveller: or, A Journal of the Peregrination of Jesus Christ, the Son of God. London: Printed by and for B. Ward, 1740, 82p.

Dix, William Chatterton. *Lessons for Children.* London: Griffith, Farran and Co., 1885, 718p.

————. *The Pattern Life; or, Lessons from the Life of Our Lord.* New York: 1886.

Dobraczyński, Jan. *Jezus Chrystus i Jego apostołowie.* Wyd 4. Warszawa: Pax, 1963, 350p.

Dodd, Charles Hastings. *Beautiful Story of the Life of Christ.* Cincinnati: n.d.

Dodd, Ira Seymour. *The Pictorial Life of Christ; Eighty Sculptural Reliefs by Dominici Mastroianni.* New York: Christian Herald, 1912, 202p.

Dole, Charles Fletcher. *Jesus and the Men about Him.* Boston: G.H. Ellis, 1888, 82p.

Dole, George Henry. *The Life and Teachings of Jesus.* Philadelphia: Dorrance, 1940, 398p.

Donovan, Marcus. *Gospel Sermons.* London: Society for Promoting Christian Knowledge, 1943, 137p.

Dougherty, Robert Lee. *Jesus the Pioneer; the Christ of the Gospels.* Boston: Christopher Pub. House, 1952, 136p.

D'Oyly, Catherine. *The History of the Life and Death of Our Blessed Saviour.* Southampton: 1794, 711p.; London: J.N. Gilpin, 1801.

Drane, John William. *Jesus and the Four Gospels.* San Francisco: Harper and Row, 1978, 191p.

Drew, George Smith. *The Human Life of Christ Revealing the Order of the Universe.* London: Longmans, 1878, 194p.

————. *The Son of Man; His Life and Ministry.* London: Henry S. King and Co., 1875, 258p.

De Buit, Michel. *En tous les temps Jésus-Christ.* Mulhouse: Éditions Salvator, 1974- .

Dudley, Dean. *Life of Jesus of Nazareth.* Montrose, Mass.: The Author, 1900, 57p.

Duggan, James. *The Life of Christ.* London: K. Paul, Trench, Trübner, and Co., 1897, 243p.

Dungan, David Roberts. *Outline Studies in the Life of Christ.* Des Moines: 1909, 94p.

Dunin-Borkowski, Stanislaus. *Jesus als Erzieher; Betrachtungen für Theologen.* Hildesheim: F. Borgmeyer, 1933.

Dunlap, Knight, and Robert Sutherland Gill. *The Dramatic Personality of Jesus.* Baltimore: Williams and Wilkins Co., 1933, 186p.

Dupanloup, Félix Antoine Philibert. *Histoire de Notre-Seigneur Jésus-Christ.* Paris: H. Plon, 1870, 422p.

Dupin, M. *The Evangelical History, or the Life of Our Blessed Saviour Jesus.* London: 1696.

Dushaw, Amos Isaac. *The Man Called Jesus.* New York: Revell, 1939, 379p.

Dwight, Charles Abbott Schneider. *The Carpenter.* New York: E.B. Treat and Co., 1900, 122p.

Eastburg, Frederick Emmanuel. *Man of the Hour.* Chicago: 1936, 107p.

Easton, Burton Scott. *Christ and His Teaching.* New York: E.S. Gorham, 1922, 118p.

Ecce Homo--Behold the Man (Motion picture). Paulist Productions, 1965?, 28 min.

Eddy, George Sherwood. *A Portrait of Jesus, a Twentieth-Century Interpretation of Christ.* New York; London: Harper and Brothers, 1943, 231p.

Eddy, Zachary. *Immanuel; or, the Life of Jesus Christ Our Lord, from his Incarnation to His Ascension.* Springfield, Mass.: W.J. Holland and Co., 1868, (1871), 752p.

Edersheim, Alfred. *Jesus the Messiah, Being an Abridged Edition of The Life and Times of Jesus the Messiah.* London: Longmans, Green, and Co., 1890. New York: A.D.F. Randolph and Co., 1890, 645p.; New York: Longmans, Green and Co., 1898, (1906), (1914), (1925); Grand Rapids: Eerdmans, 1954.

————. *The Life and Times of Jesus the Messiah.* 2 vols. New York: A.D.F. Randolph and Co.; London: Longmans, Green, and Co., 1883, (1884), (1886), (1887), (1888), (1890), (1894), (1896), (1900), (1901), (1903), (1904), (1905), (1907), (1910), (1912), (1923), (1947); New York: E.R. Herrick, 1886, (1896); Grand Rapids: Eerdmans, 1943.

Edwards, Francis Henry. *Life and Ministry of Jesus.* Independence, Mo.: Herald Pub. House, 1982, 403p.

Eikamp, Arthur R. *Jesus Christ; a Study of the Gospels.* Anderson, Ind.: Warner Press, 1963, 176p.

Elias, H. *U Nongpynim jong nga: ki saw Gospel ba la pynlong tang kawei ka jingiathuhkhana kat kum ki jingjia terter.* Shillong: Don Bosco Technical School, 1963, 357p.

Eliot, Charles J. *The Christian Warfare and Lessons from the Life of Jesus.* London: 1868.

Ellicott, Charles John. *Historical Lectures on the Life of Our Lord Jesus Christ.* Boston: Gould and Lincoln; New York: Sheldon and Co., 1862, (1863), (1864), (1866), (1867), (1868), (1872), 382p.; Andover, Mass.: W.F. Draper, 1872; London: 1860, 424p.; London: Parker, Son, and Bourn, 1862; London: Longman, 1865, (1869), (1873), (1876).

Elliott, Andrew. *A Geordie Life of Jesus.* New Castle upon Tyne: Graham, 1974, 32p.

Elliott, Walter. *The Life of Jesus Christ.* New York: Catholic Book Exchange, 1903, 763p.; *The Life of Christ.* New York: Paulist Press, 1939, (1915), 525p.

Elliott-Bins, Leonard Elliott. *Galilean Christianity.* London: SCM Press, 1956, 80p.

Elwood, Douglas J. *Christ in Philippine Context.* Quezon City: New Day Publishers, 1971, 373p.

Ely, Virginia. *Your Hand in His.* Westwood, N.J.: Revell, 1966, 126p.

Emerson, William A. *The Jesus Story.* New York: Harper and Row, 1971, 132p.

Emmerich, Anna Katharina. *Das arme Leben und bittere Leiden unseres Herrn Jesu Christi und seiner Mutter Maria.* Regensburg: Frederick Pustet, 1881, 1148p.

————. *Emmerick-Visionen. Das arme Leben und bittere Leiden unseres Herrn Jesus Christus und seiner heiligsten Mutter Maria.* 5 vols. Reussbühl/Luzern: Immaculata-Verlag, 1970-73.

————. *Jesus mutten unter den Seinen.* Kevelaer: Butzon & Bercker, 1981, 320p.

————. *Das Leben unseres Herrn ind Heilandes Jesu Christi.* 3 vols. Regensburg: Friedrich Pustet, 1858-59 (1864), 504p.

————. *The Life of Our Lord and Saviour Jesus Christ.* 4 vols. Fresno, Calif.: Academy Library Guild, 1954.

————. *Vie de N.S. Jésus-Christ.* 6 vols. Paris: P. Lethielleux; Tournai: H. Casterman, 1860.

————. *A Life of Jesus.* Trans. Richard A. Schuchert. New York: Paulist Press, 1978, 179p.

Endō, Shūsaku. *Iesu no shogai.* Tokyo: Shinchōsha, 1975, 256p.

————. *Watakushi no Iesu.* Tokyo: Shōdensha, 1976, 232p.

Enslin, Morton Scott. *The Prophet from Nazareth.* New York: Schocken Books, 1968, (1961).

An Epitome of History, Containing the Life and Death of Jesus Christ. London: 1705.

Erdman, Charles Rosenbury. *The Lord We Love; Devotional Studies in the Life of Christ.* New York: George H. Doran Co., 1924, 138p.

Erhard, Caspar. *Christlisches Hausbuch, oder Das grosse Leben Christi.* 2 vols. 20. Aufl. Augsburg: Matth. Rieger, 1858.

Erskine, John. *The Human Life of Jesus.* New York: W. Morrow and Co., 1945, 248p.

Esquereda Bifet, Juan. *Sereis mis testigos.* Artesa de Lerida: Ediciones Pisando Fuerte, 1969, 427p.

Esquiros, Alphonse. *L'Évanglile du people.* Paris: Le Gallois, 1840, 353p.

Eternal Thoughts from Christ the Teacher. 2 vols. Richard Cardinal Cushing, ed. Boston: St. Paul Editions, 1961.

Evans, William. *Epochs in the Life of Christ.* New York; Chicago: Revell, 1916, 185p.

Everett, John Nicholas. *Behold the Man: The Life and Teaching of Jesus Christ.* London: Edward Arnold, 1969, 227p.

Ewald, Heinrich. *Geschichte Christus und seiner Zeit.* Göttingen: Dietrich, 1855, 450p.

————. *Life of Jesus Christ.* Trans. and edited Octavius Glover. London: 1875; Cambridge: Deighton, Bell and Co., 1865, 364p.

Ewing, Upton Clary. *The Martyred Jew; an Expository Treatise on the Life and the Death of the Historical Jesus.* Coral Gables, Fla.: Library of Humane Literature, 1967, 95p.

The Exodus of Jesus (Filmstrip). Alpha Film Productions, 1965, 56 fr.

The Face of Jesus (Motion picture). Jenga Productions, Made by John D. Jennings, 1961, 21 min.

Fairbairn, Andrew Martin. *Studies in the Life of Christ.* Chicago: W.P. Blessing, 1880, 359p. (192-); London: Hodder and Stoughton, 1881, (1885), (1889), (1896), (1889), (1907); New York: Appleton and Co., 1882, (1895), (1900), (1902), (1905), (1908), (1912).

Faivre, Nazaire Prosper. *Jésus-lumière armour.* 8 vols. Bourg-la-Reine (Seine): Auteur, 1946-55.

Fallani, Giovanni. *Chi dite ch'io sia?* Milano: Rusconi, 1982, 267p.

Farmer, James Leonard. *John and Jesus in Their Day and Ours; Social Studies in the Gospels.* New York: Psycho-medical Library, 1956, 304p.

Farrar, Frederic William. *Beautiful Stories about Jesus.* Chicago: Cuneo Binding Co., 1913, 723p.

————. *Das Leben Jesu.* Trans. Joh. Walther. Dresden: Otto Brandner, 1893, 768p.

————. *The Life of Christ.* 2 vols. London; New York: Cassell, Petter, and Galpin, 1874; New York: E.P. Dutton, 1875, 2 vols. (1883), 472p., (1875?), (1894?), 712p.; Albany, N.Y.: R. Wendell, 1875, 744p., (1878); New York: Cassell Pub. Co., 1888?, 2 vols.; New York; London: Macmillan, 1900,

507p.; London; New York: Cassell and Co., 1903, 776p.; Cleveland: World Pub. Co., 1965, (1913), 427p.; Grand Rapids: Zondervan, 1949, 236p.

—————. *The Life of Lives.* New York: Dodd, Mead, and Co., 1900, 425p. (1900), 444p.

—————. *The Story of a Beautiful Life Illustrated.* 1900, 524p.

—————. *The Story of Jesus.* New York; Philadelphia: Commonwealth Pub. Co., 1890?, 530p.

Farrell, Melvin L. *Getting to Know Christ.* Milwaukee: Bruce Pub. Co., 1965, 221p.

Farrell, Walter. *Only Son.* New York: Sheed and Ward, 1953, 244p.

Faye, Elliott. *The Fifth Gospel.* Englewood Cliffs, N.J.: Prentice-Hall, 1972, 247p.

Feely, Joseph Martin. *Yeshu and the Essenes.* Rochester, N.Y.: 1955, 19p.

Ferguson, Fergus. *A Popular Life of Christ.* Glasgow: 1878.

Ferlita, Ernest. *Gospel Journey; Forty Meditations Drawn from the Life of Christ.* Minneapolis: Winston Press, 1983, 103p.

Fernández Truyols, Andrés. *The Life of Christ.* Trans. Paul Barrett. Westminster, Md.: Newman Press, 1958, 817p.

—————. *Vida de Nuestro Señor Jesucristo.* Segunda edición. Madrid: La Editorial Católica Libesa, 1954, 760p.

Ferrier, John Todd. *The Master, Known unto the World as Jesus the Christ.* Bradford; London: P. Lund, Humphries and Co., 1913, 529p.

Ferriere, Cinette. *L'Alliance ancienne et nouvelle.* Lyon; Paris: Éditions du Chalet, 1962, 304p.

—————. *Biblical Themes and Classroom Celebrations.* London; Dublin: G. Chapman, 1968, 239p.

Ferris, Theodore Parker. *The Story of Jesus.* New York: Oxford University Press, 1953, 123p.; Cincinnati: Clovernook Printing House for the Blind, 1954.

Ficarra, Aldo. *Giuda non tradì Gesù.* Milano: Sugar, 1971, 271p.

Field, Frank McCoy. *The New Where Jesus Walked.* Kansas City, Mo.: Christian Approach Mission Press, 1959, 442p.

—————. *Where Jesus Walked.* New York: Exposition Press, 1951, 243p.

Figgis, John Benjamin. *Emmanuel. Leaves from the Life and Notes on the Work of Jesus.* London: Partridge and Co., 1885, 284p.

Fillion, Louis Claude. *The Life of Christ.* 3 vols. Trans. Newton Thompson. St. Louis; London: B. Herder Book Co., 1928-29.

————. *Vie de Notre-Seigneur Jésus-Christ,* 2e édition. Paris: Letouzey et Ané, 1922, 649p.

Finegan, Jack. *Jesus, History, and You.* Richmond, Va.: John Knox Press, 1964, 144p.

First Galilean Ministry (Filmstrip). Society for Visual Education and Standard Pub. Co., 1947, 51 fr.

First Year of Christ's Ministry (Filmstrip). Society for Visual Education and Standard Pub. Co., 1947, 51 fr.

Fischer, Michael Hadwin. *The Story of Jesus.* Philadelphia: United Lutheran Publishing House, 1924, 174p.

Fisher, Samuel Ware. *Sermons on the Life of Christ.* Cincinnati: R. Clarke and Co., 1877, 465p.

Fiske, Charles. *The Christ We Know, Son of Man and Son of God: Master, Lord, and Saviour.* New York; London: Harper and Brothers, 1927, 273p.

Fiske, Charles, and Burton Scott Easton. *The Real Jesus: What He Taught; What He Did: Who He Was.* New York; London: Harper and Brothers, 1929, 261p.

Fitzgerald, John. *Scriptural Views of Our Lord Jesus Christ.* London: 1835.

Fleetwood, John. *Fleetwood's Life of Christ.* London: H. Fisher, R. Fisher, and P. Jackson, 1838, 476p.

————. *The Life of Our Blessed Lord and Savior Jesus Christ.* New York: Walker, 1820, 616p.; Philadelphia: Bradley and Co., 1866, 640p.; Philadelphia: Bradley and Co.; Alton, Ill.: Ardrey and Garretson, 1868, 750p.

————. *The Life of Our Lord and Saviour Jesus Christ.* London; New York: Virtue, 18--, 723p.; New Haven: N. Whitting, 1832, 606p.; Cincinnati: Truman and Smith, 1834, 666p.; New Haven: 1838, 608p.; New Haven: J. Galpin, 1844, 606p.; Philadelphia: J.E. Potter; Indianapolis: Stearns and Spicer, 1855, (1863), 704p.

————. *Star of Bethlehem.* Philadelphia; Chicago: National Pub. Co., 1890, 800p.

Flood, Edmund. *Jesus and His Contemporaries.* Glen Rock, N.J.: Paulist Press, 1968, 85p.

Flusser, David Gustav. *Jesus.* Trans. Ronald Walls. New York: Herder and Herder, 1969, 159p.

————. *Jesus in Selbstzeugnissen und Bilddokumenten.* Reinbek b. Hamburg: Rowohlt-Taschenbuch-Verlag, 1968, 154p.

Folliot, Katherine. *Jesus, before He Was God.* Richmond, Surrey: H and B Publications, 1978, 146p.

Fondevila, R.M. *Realidad histórica de Jesús de Nazaret.* Barcelona: Aymá, 1968, (1965), 273p.

Fonseca, Cristobal de. *Primera parte de la Vida de Christo Señor Nvestro.* Impresso en Toledo, en case de Thomas de Guzman, 1598, 342p.

Foote, Alexander Leith Ross. *Incidents in the Life of Our Saviour.* London: J. Nisbet, 1853, 381p., (1854), (1856), (1858).

Foote, Mary Hastings. *A Life of Christ for Young People in Questions and Answers.* New York: Harper and Brothers, 1895, 281p.

Footsteps of Jesus. London: 1887.

Footsteps of Jesus (Filmstrip). Church-Craft Pictures, 1950, 49 fr.

Forbush, Bliss. *Toward Understanding Jesus.* Philadelphia: Friends General Conference, 1946, 208p., (1939), 231p.

Forbush, William Byron. *The Illuminated Lessons on the Life of Jesus.* New York; London: Underwood and Underwood, 1904, 204p.

————. *The Life of Jesus.* New York: C. Scribner's Sons, 1912, 92p.

————. *The Travel Lessons on the Life of Jesus.* 2nd ed. New York; London: Underwood and Underwood, 1905, (1908), 230p.

Ford, George A. *al-Quawl al-ṣarīḥ fī sīrat Yasū' al-Masīḥ.* Bayrūt: al-Maṭba'ah al-Amīrikanīyah, 1923, 742p.

Forster, William J. *Scenes from the Wonderful Life.* London: C.H. Kelly, 1897, 128p.

Fosdick, Harry Emerson. *The Man from Nazareth as His Contemporaries Saw Him.* New York: Harper, 1949, 282p.; Westport, Conn.: Greenwood Press, 1978; Wilmington, Del.: International Academic Pub., 1979.

Foster, Rupert Clinton. *An Introduction to the Life of Christ.* Cincinnati: Standard Pub. Co., 1938, 303p.

————. *Studies in the Life of Christ.* 3 vols. Cincinnati: F.L. Rowe, 1938-68.

Fouard, Constant Henri. *The Christ the Son of God: A Life of Our Lord and Saviour Jesus Christ.* 2 vols. Trans. George F.X. Griffith. London; New York: Longmans, Green, and Co., 1890, (1891), (1892), (1908), (1919), (1927), (1930), (1941), (1944), (1946).

————. *The Life of Christ.* New York: Guild Press, 1960, 415p.

————. *La Vie de N.-S. Jésus Christ.* 2 vols. Paris: V. Lecoffre, 1880, (1882), (1884), (1888), (1891), (1895), (1904), (1905), (1907), (1910), (1913), (1919).

————. *Vita di N.S. Gesù Cristo.* 2 vols. Torino: Società editrice internazionale, 1945.

————. *Żwot Pana nawzego Jezusa Chrystusa.* 2 vols. Warszawa: Gebethner i Wolff, 1909-10.

Foucauld, Charles Eugene. *La vie de Jésus.* Grenoble: B. Arthaud, 1948, 159p.

Fox, Aley. *The Son of Man. A Simple History of the Life of Our Lord Jesus Christ.* London: Elliot Stock, 1901, 390p.; London: Christian Knowledge Society, 1911, 338p.

Frame, Hugh Fulton. *Wonderful, Counsellor; a Study in the Life of Jesus.* London: Hodder and Stoughton, 1935, 320p.

France, R.T. *I Came to Set the Earth on Fire: A Portrait of Jesus.* Downers Grove, Ill.: Inter-Varsity Press, 1975, 190p.

Francis, James Allan. *One Solitary Life.* Chicago: Le Petit Oiseau Press, 1963, 6p.

Franzolin, Ugo. *L'uomo di Nazareth.* Roma: Trevi editore, 1975, 86p.

Freeman, James Edward. *The Man and the Master.* New York: T. Whittaker, 1906, 127p.

French, Addie Marie. *The Life of Christ.* 2 vols. Harrisburg, Pa.: Christian Publications, 1941.

Frenssen, Gustav. *Das Leben des Heilands.* Berlin: G. Grote, 1907, 109p.

Friedlieb, Joseph Heinrich. *Geschichte des Lebens Jesu Christi.* Breslau: Georg Philipp Aderholz, 1855, 347p.

From the Manger to the Cross; or, Jesus of Nazareth (Motion picture). Kalem Co., 1912, 6 reels.

Furness, William Henry. *A History of Jesus*. Boston: W. Crosby and H.P. Nichols, 1850, 291p.

————. *Jesus*. Philadelphia: J.B. Lippincott, 1871, 223p.

————. *Jesus and His Biographers*. Philadelphia: Carey, Lea, and Blanchard, 1838, 450p.

————. *Thoughts on the Life and Character of Jesus of Nazareth*. Boston: Phillips, Sampson, and Co., 1859, 311p.

————. *The Unconscious Truth of the Four Gospels*. Philadelphia: J.B. Lippincott, 1868, 144p.

Fusco, Nicola. *La storia di Cristo*. New York: Vatican City Religious Book Co., 1946, 413p.

Gall, James. *A General Help to the Life of Christ*. 2nd ed. Edinburgh: 1825?, (1830?).

Galy, A. *L'Ami des Pêcheurs*. Paris: P. Téqui, 1930.

————. *The Friend of Sinners*. Trans. J.M. Lelen. New York; Cincinnati: Benziger Brothers, 1930, 274p.

Gammans, Harold Winsor. *The Autobiography of Jesus*. Boston: Bruce Humphries, 1955, 31p.

Gangitano Licata, Luigi. *Gesù nei Vangeli*. Palermo: G. Moncada, 1939, 484p.

Gardner-Smith, Percival. *The Christ of the Gospels*. Cambridge, Eng.: W. Heffer and Sons, 1938, 245p.

Garman, Wilford Ohlen Higget. *The Life and Teachings of Christ*. Philadelphia: Harris and Partridge, 1942, 152p.; Cleveland: Union Gospel Press, 1948.

Garrett, Alfred Cope. *The Man from Heaven*. Philadelphia: Engle Press, 1939, 465p.

Garvie, Alfred Ernest. *Studies in the Inner Life of Jesus*. London: Hodder and Stoughton, 1907, 543p.; New York: George H. Doran Co., 1907.

Gates, Herbert Wright. *The Life of Jesus*. Chicago: University of Chicago Press, 1921.

————. *The Life of Jesus; a Manual for Teachers*. Chicago: University Press, 1906- .

Geikie, John Cunningham. *The Life and Words of Christ*. New York: Hurst, n.d., 812p.; New York: 1877, 2 vols.; London: H.S. King, 1877, 2 vols., (1878); London: Hodder and Stoughton, 1883, 2 vols.; New York: Appleton, 1878, 2 vols., (1879), (1880), (1884), (1886), (1888), (1890), (1891), (1893), (1894), (1895), (1896), (1900), (1902), (1903),

(1905), (1906), (1913), (1916), (1922), (1925); New York: American Book Exchange, 1879, 812p., (1880), (1881); Chicago: Belford Clarke and Co., 188-?, 812p., (189-?); New York: G. Munro, 1880, 2 vols.; Strahan, 1881, 2 vols.; New York: Ward and Drummond, 1882, 812p.; New York: J.B. Alden, 1883, (1885), 612p.

————. *A Short Life of Christ for Old and Young*. New York: James Pott and Co., 1888, (1889), 486p.; London: 1898, 312p.

Geil, William Edgar. *The Man of Galilee*. London: Marshall Bros., 1904, 199p.; New York: International Committee of Young Men's Christian Associations, 1906.

Geissinger, David H. *Lessons in the Life of Our Lord Jesus Christ*. New York; Chicago: Ivison, Blakeman, Taylor, and Co., 1881, 154p.

Gence, Jean Baptiste Modeste. *Précis historique de la vie de Jésus-Christ*. Paris: Treuttel et Wurtz, 1833, 44p.

Genesis Project, Inc. *Jesus, His Life and Times*. New York: Morrow, 1979, 224p.

Genocchi, Giovanni. *Piccola vita di Gesù*. Roma: Desclee & C., 1915, 141p.

George, Bill. *His Story: The Life of Christ*. Cleveland, Tenn.: Pathway Press, 1977, 132p.

George, S.K. *The Life and Teachings of Jesus Christ*. Madras: G.A. Natesan and Co., 1942, 104p.

Gereda, José. *Assertiones historico-critico-theologicae de verbo Dei facto homine*. Guatemala: In typographia apud d. Antonium Cubillas S.O. Inquissitionis hispalensis familiarem, 1784, 30p.

Geschichte des Rabbi Jeschua ben Jossef hanootzri gennant Jesus Christus. 7. Aufl. Hamburg: L.M. Glogau Sohn, 1887, 428p.

Giacobbe, Juan Francisco. *La biografía de un hombre; el hijo del hombre*. Buenos Aires: Editorial Guadalupe, 1967, 181p.

Gialetti, Augusto. *Che cos'è la verità?* Milano: Gastaldi, 1945, 193p.

Gibson, Joseph Thompson. *Jesus Christ, the Unique Revealer of God*. New York; Chicago: Revell, 1915, 513p.

Gigot, Francis Ernest Charles. *Outlines of the Life of Our Lord*. 2 vols. Brighton, Mass.: St. John's Boston Ecclesiastical Seminary, 1896-97.

Gilbert, George Holley. *Jesus.* New York: Macmillan, 1912, 321p.

————. *Jesus for the Men of Today.* New York: Hodder and Stoughton, George H. Doran Co., 1917, 176p.

————. *The Student's Life of Jesus.* Chicago: Press of Chicago Theological Seminary, 1896, 412p.; New York; London: Macmillan, 1900, 3d ed., 418p.

Gillet, Lev. *A Day with Jesus.* Trans. by a monk of the Western Church. New York: Desclee Co., 1964, 109p.

————. *Présence du Christ.* Belgique: Edit. de Chevetogne (S.D.E.C.), 1961, 112p.

Gilmore, Albert Field. *Who Was This Nazarene?* New York: Prentice-Hall, 1940, 331p.

Giordani, Igino. *Christ, Hope of the World.* Trans. Clelia Maranzana. Boston: St. Paul Editions, 1964, 470p.

Glickman, S. Craig. *Knowing Christ.* Chicago: Moody Press, 1980, 205p.

Glorieux, Palémon. *Notre chef le Christ.* Paris: Éditions ouvrières, 1945, 251p.

Glover, Terrot Reaveley. *The Jesus of History.* New York: Association Press, 1917, 225p.

God's Wonderful Plan--Sending Jesus (Filmstrip). Mayse Studio, 1952, 26 filmstrips.

Godbey, William B. *Life of Jesus and His Apostles.* Louisville, Ky.: Pentecostal Pub. Co., 1904, 455p.

Goguel, Maurice. Jésus et les origines du christianisme. 3 vols. Paris: Payot, 1932-47; *Jésus.* Paris: Payot, 1950, 478p. (Vol. 1 of *Jésus et les origines du christianisme*).

————. *The Life of Jesus.* Trans. Olive Wyon. New York: AMS Press, 1976, (1933), 591p.; London: George Allen and Unwin, 1933.

Goodier, Alban. *Jesus Christ: Man of Sorrows.* New York: Macmillan, 1928, 88p.; London: Burns, Oates, and Washbourne, 1928.

————. *The Public Life of Our Lord Jesus Christ.* 2 vols. London: Burns, Oates, and Washbourne, 1936, 7th impression, (1930).

Goodspeed, Edgar Johnson. *A Life of Jesus.* New York: Harper, 1950; Westport, Conn.: Greenwood Press, 1979, 248p.

Gordon, Helen. *"The Way, the Truth, and the Life."* Boston; New York: E.P. Dutton, 1869, 124p.; (1872, Infant Series), 86p., (1869, Primary Series), 152p.

Gordon, W.J. *An Historical Sketch of the Life of Our Lord.* Edinburgh: 1878, 250p.

Gore, Charles. *Jesus of Nazareth.* New York: H. Holt and Co.; London: T. Butterworth, 1929, 256p.

Gorla, Pietro. *La divina misericordia e la Maddalena del Vangelo.* Milano: Casa edit. S. Lega Eucaristica, 1912, (1921), (1928); Alba: Pia società san Paolo, 1940, 603p.

The Gospel Road (Motion picture). World Wide Pictures, Made by Johnny Cash and June Cash, 1974, 63 min.

Goudge, Elizabeth. *God so Loved the World.* New York: Coward-McCann, 1951, 311p.

Goyen, William. *A Book of Jesus.* Garden City, N.Y.: Doubleday, 1973, 143p.

Graef, Richard. *Christ My Friend; Meditations for Daily Use.* Trans. John J. Coyne. Baltimore: Helicon Press, 1963, 223p.

————. *Mit Christus auf du und du. Betrachtungen.* Wurzburg: Arena-Verlag, 1957, 221p.

Graham, Eleanor. *The Story of Jesus.* Harmondsworth, Middlesex; Baltimore: Penguin Books, 1961, (1959), (1971), 264p.

Grandmaison, Léonce de. *Jesus Christ, His Person, His Message, His Credentials.* 3 vols. Trans. Dom Basil Whelan, Ada Lane, Douglas Carter. London: Sheed and Ward, 1930-34; New York: Sheed and Ward, 1961, 266p.

————. *Jésus Christ, sa personne, son message, ses preuves.* 2 vols. Paris: G. Beauchesne, 1928, (1930).

Grant, Frederick Clifton. *The Life and Times of Jesus.* New York; Cincinnati: Abingdon Press, 1921, 222p.

————. *The Life and Times of Jesus; Teacher's Manual.* New York; Cincinnati: Abingdon Press, 1922, 164p.

Grant, Michael. *Jesus.* London: Weidenfeld and Nicolson, 1977, 261p.; New York: Scribner, 1977; London: Sphere, 1978, 320p.

Grant, R.V. *Yesu Kerison yawasina teterina. A Life of Jesus Christ, Written in the Dobuan Language.* Easy Cape Papua Methodist Mission, 1949, 97p.

The Greatest Life: Aspects of the Life and Teachings of Jesus. John B. Corston and William Pope, eds. Windsor, N.S.: Lancelot Press, 1976, 120p.

Green, Doyle L. *He That Liveth; the Story of Jesus Christ the Son of God.* Salt Lake City: Deseret Book Co., 1958, 229p.

Green, Peter. *The Gospel Story; a Short Life of Christ.* London; New York: Longmans, Green, 1939, 126p.

Greg, Samuel. *Scenes from the Life of Jesus.* Edinburgh: Hamilton, 1869; London: 1875, 331p.

Gregg, Odie. *Facts of Jesus in the Gospels; a Resource Book.* Birmingham?, Ala.: 1965, 83p.

Grewen, Robert F. *Know Your King; Reflections on the Life of the Saviour.* New York: America Press, 1945, 181p.

Griffith, Arthur Leonard. *The Crucial Encounter; the Personal Ministry of Jesus.* London: Hodder and Stoughton, 1965, 158p.

Griffith, Thomas. *Studies of the Divine Master.* London: Henry S. King and Co., 1875, 447p.

Grimm, Joseph. *Das Leben Jesu nach den vier Evangelien.* 2 vols. Regensburg: F. Pustet, 1876-78, (1895-1909).

Grist, William Alexander. *The Historic Christ in the Faith of Today.* New York; Chicago: Revell, 1911, 517p.

Grou, Jean Nicolas. *L'Interieur de Jésus et de Marie.* 1794.

———. *The Interior of Jesus and Mary.* 2 vols. Trans. Miss Kennelly. New York: Catholic Publication Society Co.; London: Burns and Oates, 1891.

Grout, Henry Martyn. *The Story of Jesus, Whom They Crucified.* Boston: 1881, 36p.

Groves, Walter Alexander. *An Analysis of Obvious Outcomes in a Study of the Life of Christ Essential for Character in the Denominational Colleges.* Philadelphia: 1925, 159p.

Grundmann, Walter. *Die Geschichte Jesu Christi.* Berlin: Evangelische Verlagsanstalt, 1957, 421p.

———. *Jesus von Nazareth: Burger zwischen Gott und Menschen.* Göttingen: Musterschmidt, 1975, 111p.

Gual, Pedro. *La vida de Jesús.* 3 vols. Barcelona: Impr. del heredero de d. Pablo Riera, 1869-70.

Guardini, Romano. *Der Herr, Betrachtungen über die Person und das Leben Jesu Christi.* Wurzburg: Werkbund-verlag, 1937, 762p.

———. *The Lord.* Trans. Elinor Castendyk Briefs. Chicago: Regnery, 1954, 535p.

Guerrin, Aymé. *Jesús tal como fué visto, ensayo de reconstitución histórica y psicológica.* Trans. Boris Bureba. Paris; Madrid: Édiciones literarias, 1928, 356p.

——. *Jésus tel qu'on le vit, essai de reconstitution historique et psychologique.* Paris: Plon, 1928, 298p.

The Guide (Motion picture). Cathedral Films, 1964. Made by Ralph Hunt. 30 min.

Guignebert, Charles Alfred Honoré. *Jésus.* Paris: La Renaissance du livre, 1933, 692p.; Paris: A. Michel, 1969, 667p.

——. *Jesus.* Trans. S.H. Hooke. London: K. Paul, Trench, Trübner and Co., 1935, 563p.; New York: University Books, 1956, 563p.

——. *La vie cachée de Jésus.* Paris: E. Flammarion, 1921, 211p.

Gunsalulus, Frank Wakeley. *The Man of Galilee; a Biographical Study of the Life of Jesus Christ.* Chicago; Philadelphia: Monarch Book Co., 1899, 682p.

Guthrie, Donald. *Jesus the Messiah; an Illustrated Life of Christ.* Grand Rapids: Zondervan, 1972, 386p.

——. *A Shorter Life of Christ.* Grand Rapids: Zondervan, 1970, 186p.

Gutman, Ernest M. *The Hebrew-Christians.* Philadelphia: Dorrance, 1973, 216p.

Guy, Harold A. *The Life of Christ.* London: Macmillan, 1951, 211p.

Haas, Josef. *Jesus Christus. Sein Leben auf Erden.* München: Schnell and Steiner in Kommission, 1968, 106p.

Haïk, Farjallah. *Yésouh.* Beyrouth: Éditions Antione, 1942, 105p.

Hakim, George. *Reading the Good News in Galilee.* Trans. James E. Corbett. Baltimore: Helicon, 1965, 126p.

Hall, George. Fridolph. *What Jesus Said and Did; a Study of Luke-Acts.* Rock Island, Ill.: Augustana Press, 1947, 192p.

Hall, William Newman. *Cameos of Christ; Brief Studies in the Life of "Our Only Master."* London: J. Nisbet, 1900, 124p.

Halsey, Leroy Jones. *The Beauty of Immanuel.* Philadelphia: Presbyterian Board of Publication, 1860, 204p.

Hanish, Otoman Zar-Adusht. *Yehoshua Nazir: Jesus the Nazarite; Life of Christ.* Los Angeles: Madaznan Elector Corp., 1917, (1969), 216p.

Hanna, William. *The Close of the Ministry*. New York: Carter and Bros., 1870, 351p.

————. *The Life of Our Lord*. 6 vols. New York: R. Carter and Bros., 1870; *The Life of Christ*. New York: American Tract Society, 1871, 861p., (1913), 898p.

————. *The Ministry in Galilee*. New York: R. Carter and Bros., 1870, 360p.; London: 1869, 384p.

————. *Our Lord's Life on Earth*. 6 vols. New York: 1876; Edinburgh: Edmonston and Douglas, 1869, (1875); London; Edinburgh: Religious Tract Society, 1882, 663p.

Hannam, Wilfrid Lawson. *In the Things of My Father; A Study of the Purpose of Luke the Evangelist*. London: Hodder and Stoughton, 1935, 250p.; *Luke the Evangelist; a Study of His Purpose*. New York; Cincinnati: Abingdon Press, 1935, 238p.

Hanson, Richard Davies. *The Jesus of History*. London; Edinburgh: Williams and Norgate, 1869, 426p.

Hargrove, Charles. *Jesus of Nazareth. Lessons of His Life, Death, and Resurrection. Learnt at Oberammergau*. London: Philip Green, 1900, 80p.

Harlow, Victor Emmanuel. *Jesus the Man, an Historical Study*. Oklahoma City: Harlow Pub. Co., 1924, 256p.

Harrington, Donald Szantho. *As We Remember Him*. Boston: Beacon Press, 1965, 111p.

Harrington, Joy. *Jesus of Nazareth*. Leister, Eng.: Brockhampton Press, 1956, 191p.

Harris, Thaddeus William. *The Life and Work of Jesus Christ Our Lord*. New York; Milwaukee: Morehouse Pub. Co., 1927, 298p., (1935), 192p.

Harrison, Everett Falconer. *A Short Life of Christ*. Grand Rapids: Eerdmans, 1968, 288p.

Hart, Burdett. *Aspects of Christ; Studies of the Model Life*. New York: E.B. Treat, 1892, 288p.

Hartt, Rollin Lynde. *The Man Himself*. Garden City, N.Y.: Doubleday, Page and Co., 1923, 291p.

Harvey, William Wirt. *The Making of a Messiah*. Boston: B. Humphries, 1931, 197p.

Harwood, Edward. *The Life and Character of Jesus Christ Delineated*. London: Printed for T. Becket and P.A. de Hordt, 1772, 225p.; Philadelphia: Published by Edward Earle; T.H. Palmer, Printer, 1817, 157p.

Hase, Karl August. *Geschichte Jesu.* Leipzig: 1876, 612p., (1891).

――――. *Das Leben Jesu.* Leipzig: Breitkopf und Härtel, 1829, (1850), (1854), (1865), 233p.

――――. *Life of Jesus.* Trans. James Freeman Clarke. Boston: Walker, Wise, and Co., 1860, 267p.

Hawkes, Henry Warburton. *The Man from Nazareth; A True Life.* London: Kegan Paul and Co., 1889, 67p.

Hawthorne, Marion Olive. *Jesus among His Neighbors.* New York; Cincinnati: Abingdon Press, 1929, 194p.

――――. *Jesus among His Neighbors. Teacher's Manual.* New York; Cincinnati: Abingdon Press, 1929, 117p.

Haygood, Atticus Greene. *El hombre de Galilea.* Trans. Edna M. de Wátkins. Nashville: Casa de publicaciones de la Iglesia metodista episcopal de Sur, 1894, 195p.

――――. *Jesus, the Christ. Lessons for Bible Classes, from the Evangelists.* Macon, Ga.: J.W. Burke and Co., 1877- .

――――. *The Man of Galilee.* New York; Baltimore: J.E. Wilson and Co., 1889, 156p.; Nashville: Publishing House of the Methodist Episcopal Church, South, 1889; New York: Hunt and Eaton; Cincinnati: Cranston and Stowe, 1889; New York: Hunt and Eaton, 1890, 156p.

Hazard, Marshall Custiss, and John Luther Kilbon. *A Study of the Life of Jesus the Christ, in Fifty-two Lessons.* Boston; Chicago: Congregational Sunday-School and Pub. Society, 1892, 266p.

He Is Risen (Motion picture). NBC-TV, 1962, 27 min.

Headlam, Arthur Cayley. *The Life and Teaching of Jesus the Christ.* London: J. Murray, 1936, 338p.; New York; London: Oxford University Press, 1923, 336p.

Heckford, Sarah. *The Life of Christ and Its Bearings on Communion.* London: 1873.

Hedberg, Lydia. *Epistola de vita et passione Domini Nostri und Regula Augustini in mittelniederdeutschen Fassungen.* Lund: C.W.K. Gleerup, 1954, 231p.

Heinz, Susanna Wilder. *"Who Do Men Say That I Am?" A Study of Jesus.* Boston: Press, 1965, 176p.

Henry, Antonin Marcel. *The Triumph of Christ; the Word Made Flesh.* Notre Dame, Ind.: Fides Publishers Association, 1962, (1958), 159p.

Herbst, Winfrid. *The Savior of the World.* Ozone Park, N.Y.: Catholic Literary Guild, 1942, 199p.

Herder, Johann Gottfried. *Vom Erlöser der Menschen.* 1796; Halle: O. Handel, 1899, 121p.

Herget, John Francis. *Behold the Man; Highlights in the Life of Jesus.* Cincinnati: 1950, 105p.

Herklots, Bernard. *A Portraiture of Christ.* London: Religious Tract Society, 1924, 294p.

Herrick, Joseph. *Immanuel.* London: n.d.

Hess, Johann Jakob. *Geschichte der drei letzten Lebensjahre Jesu.* 3 vols. Leipzig: Zürich: 1768-72, (1774ff.), (1794), (1822), (1823ff.); Münster: Aschendorf, 1782, 2 Thle.; Einsiedeln: Fabricius, 1788, 2 Thle.

Hesse, Erwin. *Des Herrn Kreuz und Herrlichkeit die öffentliche Wirksamkeit Jesu in ihrem grossen Zusammenhängen.* Wien: Herder, 1940, 103p.

Hester, Hubert Inman. *The Heart of the New Testament.* Liberty, Mo.: W. Jewell Press, 1950, 350p.

Hevia Losa, Jacobo. *El gran Maestro.* Madrid: Studium, 1967, 536p.

Hifferman, John Michael. *Sketches from Our Lord's History from Our Lord's Ministry.* London: 1855.

Higgins, James. *The Story Ever New, Giving the Most Interesting Events in the Life of Jesus Christ as a Textbook in Religion for Grammar Grade Children.* New York: Macmillan, 1920, 207p.

Hill, William Bancroft. *The Life of Christ.* New York; Chicago: Revell, 1917, 328p.; Shanghai: Association Press of China, 1920.

————. *Mountain Peaks in the Life of Our Lord.* New York; Chicago: Revell, 1925, 189p.

————. *La vida de Cristo.* Trans. Gonzalo Rovero. Nashville: Imprenta Cokesbury, 1927, 435p.

Hills, Aaron Merritt. *Food for Lambs; or, Leading Children to Christ.* Cincinnati: M.W. Knapp, 1899, 202p.

Hilty, Karl. *Carl Hilty, der Christ, seine Gestalt und Lebenslehre.* Heidelberg: Kemper, 1948, 137p.

Hirschmann, Maria Anne. *Follow Me.* Huntington Beach, Calif.: SPARC Pub. Co., 1979, 223p.

The History of Our Lord and Saviour Jesus Christ. London: 1830.

The History of Our Saviour Jesus Christ. By a Lady. London: 1785.

The History of the Incarnation, Life, Doctrine, and Miracles of Jesus Christ. London: T. Cooper, 1737, 875p.; London: Printed for Arthur Bettesworth and Charles Hitch, 1738. 875p.

History of the Life of Jesus Christ. New London: 1845.

The History of the Life of Our Lord Jesus Christ. Trans. William Crathorne. London: T. Meighan, 1739, 312p.; Dublin: 1763, 220p.

Hoashi, Riichirō. *Iesu den.* Tokyo: Noguchi Shoten, 1950, 432p.

Hobbs, Herschel H. *The Life and Times of Jesus.* Grand Rapids: Zondervan, 1966, 218p.

Hodgkin, Henry Theodore. *Jesus among Men.* New York: R.R. Smith, 1930, 158p.

Höfer, Albert. *Jesus von Nazareth. Zwanzig biblische Katechesen.* Salzburg: O. Müller, 1969, 102p.

Hoenshel, Elmer Ulysses. *The Crimson Trail; or, Where the Master Trod.* New York: Every Where Pub. Co., 1912, 141p.

Hofman, Heinrich. *Come unto Me! Scenes from the Life of Christ.* New York: 1893.

————. *Come unto Me; Twelve Pictures from the Life of Our Lord.* London: 1888.

Holbach, Paul Henri Thiry. *Ecce Homo! or, A Critical Inquiry into the History of Jesus Christ.* 2d ed. Trans. George Houston. London: D.I. Eaton, 1813, 347p.; New York: Printed for the Proprietors of the Philosophical Library, 1827; New York: Gordon Press, 1976, 212p.

————. *Historia crítica de Jesucristo.* 2 vols. Trans. F. de T. Londres: En la imprenta de Davidson, 1822.

Holley, Carolyn Fizzell. *Teacher's Manual. Message of the Master.* Los Angeles, Calif.: 1935, 155p.

Holloway, Alpheus H. *The Beauty of the King.* New York: Authors' Pub. Co., 1877, 174p.

Holmes, John Mallory. *Jesus and the Young Man of Today.* New York: Macmillan, 1919, 170p.

Holmström, Rafael, Aimo T. Nikolainen, and Ilmari Tammisto. *Opas evankeliumien lukemiseen.* Helsinki: Otava, 1967, 203p.

Holt, Allan Eugene. *Behold the Bridegroom! A Life of Christ.*
Omaha: Ledyard Printing and Pub. Co., 1940- .

Holtzmann, Oskar. *Das Leben Jesu.* Tübingen; Leipzig: J.C.B.
Mohr (Paul Siebeck), 1901, 417p.

————. *The Life of Jesus.* Trans. J.T. Bealby and Maurice A.
Canney. London: A. and C. Black, 1904, 552p.

Holy Meditations and Contemplations of Jesus Christ. William
Cudworth, ed. London: Printed by Richard Cotes for John
Sweeting, 1642, (1746).

Honoré-Lainé, Geneviève, Christian Eugène, and Tugdual Magueur.
Vers toi, Terre promise, guide spirituel de Terre sainte.
Paris: Éditions franciscaines, 1971, 192p.

Hood, Alfred. *The Prophet of Nazareth and His Messages.* London: Sonnenschein and Co., 1886, 107p.

Hooke, Samuel Henry. *Christ and the Kingdom of God.* New York:
George H. Doran Co., 1917, 144p.

Hoover, Oliver Perry. *Jesus' Personal Campaign among the Gentiles.* Boston: R.G. Badger, 1930, 60p.

Horne, Herman Harrell. *Jesus--Our Standard.* New York; Cincinnati: Abingdon Press, 1918, 307p.

Horr, George Edwin. *The Great Ministry.* Boston: Bible Study
Pub. Co., 1908, 209p.

Houghton, Louise Seymour. *Das Leben Jesu in Bild und Erzählung.*
New York: Amerikanische-Traktat-Gesellschaft, 1893?, 280p.

————. *The Life of Christ in Picture and Story.* New York:
American Tract Society, 1890, 295p.

————. *The Life of the Lord Jesus.* Boston: Bible Study
Pub. Co., 1895?, 213p.

Housse, Émile. *Cristo Jesús, su vida según los documentos
más modernos.* Santiago de Chile: Zig-zag, 1943, 796p.

Hovy, J.A.L. *Het leven in Christus gropenbaard.* Amsterdam:
H.J. Paris, 1941, 231p.

Howard, Clifford. *The Story of a Young Man (a Life of Christ).*
Boston: L.C. Page and Co., 1902, 247p.

Hoyland, Geoffrey. *The Great Outlaw.* London: SCM Press, 1944,
264p.

Hubbard, Elbert. *The Man of Sorrows; Being a Little Journey
to the Home of Jesus of Nazareth.* East Aurora, N.Y.: The
Roycrofters, 1908, (1905), 121p.

Hunolt, Franz. *The Christian's Model.* 2 vols. Trans. J. Allen. New York; Cincinnati: Benziger Brothers, 1895.

Hunter, David. *Observations on the History of Jesus Christ.* 2 vols. Edinburgh: Printed E. and C. Dilly, London, and John Balfour, Edinburgh, 1770.

Hunter, Henry. *Sacred Biography; or, The History of Jesus Christ.* Walpole, N.H.: Printed for Thomas and Thomas, by D. Newhall, 1803, 273p.

Hunter, John. *From the Cradle to the Crown; or, Days with Jesus.* London: 1862.

Huonder, Anton. *At the Feet of the Divine Master; Short Meditations for Busy Parish Priests.* Trans. Horace A. Frommelt. St. Louis; London: B. Herder Book Co., 1922, 323p.

————. *Zu Füssen des Meisters; kurze Betrachtungen für vielbeschäftigte Priester.* Freiburg im Breisgau: Herder, 1917, 404p., (1914), (1915), (1922), (1925).

Hurd, Edith Start. *An Outline of the Life and Teachings of Jesus.* Utica, N.Y.: Printed by M.G. Dodge, 1941, 59p.

Hurlbut, Jesse Lyman. *Hurlbutt's Story of Jesus for Young and Old.* Philadelphia: John C. Winston Co., 1915, 496p.

Hutchinson, J.P. *The Footmarks of Jesus.* London: S.W. Partridge and Co., 1871, 67p.; London: Houghton and Co., 1878.

Huttmann, William. *The Life of Jesus Christ, Including His Apocryphal History from the Spurious Gospels' Unpublished Mss., etc.* London: 1818.

Iitsuka, Reiji. *"Kono hito o miyo"=Ecce Homo.* Tokyo: Nanboku Shoen, 1948, 341p.

Ijjas, Antal. *Jezus torgenete.* 2 vols. Budapest: Ecclesia, 1978, (1970).

Ilyās, Bulus. *Yasū' al-Masīḥ.* 2nd ed. Bayrūt: al-Maṭba'ah al-Kāthūlīkīyah, 1966, 381p.

Improved Question-Book on the Life of Christ. Philadelphia; New York: American Sunday-School Union, 1868, 134p.

Indart, M.J. *Jesús en su mundo.* Barcelona: Editorial Herder, 1963, 275p.

Irons, William Josiah. *The Sacred Life of Jesus Christ, the Son of God.* London, 1867, 56p.

Irvine, Alexander Fitzgerald. *The Carpenter and His Kingdom.* New York: C. Scribner's Sons, 1922, 247p.

Jacobs, Joseph. *As Others Saw Him; a Retrospect*. New York: Funk and Wagnalls, 1903, 230p.; London: 1894, 215p.; London: W. Heinemann, 1895; Boston: Houghton, Mifflin, 1895, (1899), (1900), 230p.

Jacobs, William J. *Jesus*. New York: Paulist Press, 1977, 124p.

Jakobi, Johann Adolph. *Die Geschichte Jesu für dekende und gemutvolle Leser*. 1816, (1818).

Jarvis, Frank Washington. *And Still Is Ours Today: The Story of Jesus*. New York: Seabury Press, 1980, 199p.

――――――. *Come and Follow; an Introduction to Christian Discipleship*. New York: Seabury Press, 1972, 252p.

Javier, Jeronimo. *Historia Christi persice conscripta, simulque multis modis contaminata*. Lvgdvni Batavorvm, ex officina Elseviriana, 1639, 636p.

Jefferys, Ulysses Morgan Grant. *The Story of the Man of the Ages*. Boston: Christopher Pub. House, 1929, 309p.

Jesus Christ: The Gospel for All Mankind (Filmstrip). Lutheran Church in America, 1968, 62 fr.

Jesus Christ, Son of God (Filmstrip). Board of Christian Education of the Presbyterian Church in the U.S.A., 1957, 39 fr.

Jesus in His Time. Hans Jurgen Schultz, ed. Trans. Brian Watchorn. Philadelphia: Fortress Press, 1971, 148p.

Jesus of Nazareth and His Contemporaries. London: 1881, 62p.

Jesus Our Saviour (Filmstrip). Eye Gate House, 1960, 45 fr.

Jesus Prepared for His Work (Filmstrip). Fibo Color, Zeist, Netherlands. Made by Bibo Color and Encyclopedia Britannica Films, 1959. 32 fr.

Johnson, Anna Jane. *Christ Unveiled; His Heavenly and Earthly Appearing*. New York: Press of J.N. Johnston, 1887, 105p., (1904).

Johnson, George B. *The Beautiful Life of Christ, and other Studies*. London: Alexander and Shepheard, 1894, 338p.

Johnson, Sherman Elbridge. *Jesus in His Homeland*. New York: Scribner, 1957, 182p.

Johnstone, J. Boston. *Life of Jesus Christ*. London: 1874.

Jomier, Jacques. *al-Masīḥ ibn Maryam*. Bayrūt: Dār al-Kalimah, 1966, 313p.

Jones, George. *Life-Scenes from the Four Gospels*. New York: J.P. Prall, 1865, 460p.; Philadelphia: J.C. Garrigues and Co., 1867, (1868), 443p.

Jones, George Curtis. *We Knew His Power.* Nashville: Abingdon, 1976, 128p.

Jones, Harry. *The Son of Man.* London: SPCK, 1897, 60p.

Jones, Rufus Matthew. *The Life of Christ.* Chicago: American Library Association, 1926, 28p.

Julie du St. Esprit. *A Book of Simple Words.* New York: P.J. Kenedy and Sons, 1942, 240p.

Jung, Emil. *Die geschichtliche persönlichkeit Jesu.* 2 Aufl. Innsbruck: Wagner, 1935, 352p.

Kallas, James G. *Jesus and the Power of Satan.* Philadelphia: Westminster Press, 1968, 215p.

Kassian, Bp. *Khristos i pervoe khristianskoe pokolenie.* Paris: YMCA-Press, 1950, 369p.

Kattackal, J. *Tyāgadīpaṃ.* Trivandrum: E. Vi. Pabḷiṣiṅg Hausá, 1967, 120p.

Keable, Robert. *The Great Galilean.* Boston: Little, Brown, and Co., 1929, 212p.

Kee, Howard Clark. *Jesus in History: an Approach to the Study of the Gospels.* New York: Harcourt, Brace, and World, 1970, 280p., (1977), 312p.

Keedy, John Lincoln. *Teachers' Book of the Heroic Christ.* Lysander, N.Y.: The author, 1905, 124p.

Keim, Theodor. *Geschichte Jesu nach den Ergebnissen heutiger Wissenschaft für weitere Kreise übersichtlich erzählt.* Zürich: Orell, Füssli, 1875, 398p.

————. *Die Geschichte Jesu von Nazara.* 3 vols. Zürich: Orell, Füssli, 1867-72.

————. *The History of Jesus of Nazara.* 6 vols. Trans. Arthur Ransom and E.M. Geldart. London; Edinburgh: Williams and Norgate, 1873-83, (1897).

Keller, Hippolyt. *Leben Jesu, dem Volke erzählt.* Freiburg/Schweiz; München: Kanisius Verlag, 1950, 171p., (1953), 237p.

————. *No Greater Life; the Story of Jesus of Nazareth.* Trans. Kathryn Sullivan. New York: Catholic Book Pub. Co., 1954, 239p.

Keller, Weldon Phillip. *Rabboni ... Which Is to Say Master.* Old Tappan, N.J.: Revell, 1977, 320p.

Kennedy, William Sloane. *Messianic Prophecy, and the Life of Christ.* New York: A.S. Barnes and Burr, 1860, 584p.

Kent, Charles Foster. *The Life and Teachings of Jesus, According to the Earliest Records.* New York: C. Scribner's Sons,
1913, 337p.

Kephart, Cyrus Jeffries. *Jesus the Nazarene; a Brief Life of
Our Saviour, with a Parallel Harmony.* Dayton: W.J. Shuey,
1894, 80p.

————. *The Life of Jesus for Children.* Dayton: W.J. Shuey,
1894, 74p.

————. *The Public Life of Christ.* Lebanon?, Pa.: The author,
1892, 16p.

Kepler, Thomas Samuel. *Jesus' Spiritual Journey--and Ours.*
Cleveland: World Pub. Co., 1952, 157p.

Kern, Paul Bentley. *The Miracle of the Galilean.* Nashville:
Cokesbury Press, 1930, 263p.

Keulers, Jos. *Kruimels van 's Meesters disch.* 2 vols. Roer-
mond-Maaseik: J.J. Romen & zonen, 1944.

Khrimian Hayrik, Catholicos of Armenia. *Hrawirak Erkrin
Aweteats'.* Jerusalem: Armenian Patriarchate, 1892, 158p.

Kienberger, Vincent Ferrer. *The Way of the Blessed Christ.*
New York; Toronto: Longmans, Green, and Co., 1942, 260p.

King, Marian. *The Ageless Story of Jesus.* Washington:
Acropolis Books, 1970, 116p.

King of Kings (Filmstrip). Society for Visual Education,
196-?, 53 fr.

King of Kings (Motion picture). Samuel Bronston Productions.
Released by Metro-Goldwyn-Mayer, 1961, 151 min.

Kingsland, John P. *The Man Called Jesus.* New York: T. Whittaker, 1903; London: Isbister, 1902, 330p.

Kinniburgh, Robert. *The Life of Jesus Christ.* Edinburgh:
1814.

Kinoshita, Junji. *Iesu den.* Tokyo: Seibunsha, 1967, 242p.

Kirkland, Winifred Margaretta. *The Man of the Hour.* New
York: Macmillan, 1942, 171p.

Kirtley, James Samuel. *The Disciple and His Lord.* Philadelphia: American Baptist Publication Society, 1906, 254p.

Kitto, John. *Life of Our Lord.* New York: 1853.

————. *Pictorial Life of Our Savior.* London: Charles Cox,
1847, 295p.; London: George Routledge and Co., 1852, 295p.

————. *The Pictorial Sunday Book.* London; New York: London Printing and Publishing Co., 1845, 516p.

Klagges, Dietrich. *Heldischer Glaube.* Leipzig: Armanen-Verlag, 1934, 103p.

Klausner, Joseph. *Jesus of Nazareth.* Trans. Herbert Danby. New York: Macmillan, 1925, 434p.

————. *Yeshu ha-Notsri.* 2 vols. Jerusalem: 1922; Tel-Aviv: 1954.

Klein, Félix. *Jesus and His Apostles.* Trans. W.P. Baines. London; New York: Longmans, Green, and Co., 1932, 363p.

————. *Jésus et ses apôtres.* Paris: Bloud & Gay, 1931, 318p.

————. *La vie humaine et divine de Jésus-Christ Notre-Seigneur.* Paris: Bloud & Gay, 1933, 475p.

Klüh, John M. *The Story of the Childhood and Passion of the Lord Jesus the Savior in the Words of the Evangelists and Traditions.* Chicago: J.M. Klüh, 1892, 70p.

Klug, Ignaz. *Der gute Meister.* Paderborn: F. Schoningh, 1930, 187p.

Kodaira, Kunio. *Kirisuto to sono jidai.* Tokyo: Kodaira Kunio Kinen Kankōlai, 1942, 540p.

Køber, Alf. *Menneskesønnen, en udogmatisk skisse av Jesu liv og glerning.* Oslo: H. Aschehoug, 1947, 206p.

Koepsel, Louis Herman. *The Life Supreme.* Parsons, Kan.: Foley Railway Printing Co., 1904, 304p.

Komroff, Manuel. *His Great Journey; the Most Beautiful Story in the World Told Anew.* New York: Zenith Publishing Corp., 1953, 159p.

————. *The Story of Jesus.* Philadelphia: Winston, 1955, 154p.; *The Story of Jesus.* Braille, grade w. Philadelphia: Winston, 1955; printed for the Library of Congress at the Clovernook Printing House for the Blind, Mt. Healthy, Cincinnati, 1955.

Kossoff, David. *The Book of Witnesses.* Large print ed. Boston: G.K. Hall, 1972, (1971), 295p.

Krabbe, Otto Carsten. *Vorlesungen über das Leben Jesu für Theologen und Nichttheologien.* Hamburg: Joh. Aug. Meissner, 1839, 542p.

Krebs, J.M. *The Private, Domestic, and Social Life of Christ, a Model for Youth.* Philadelphia: 1849.

162   The Bibliography

Kreuser, Martin. *Mein Jesus-Buch.* München; Gladbach: Volks-vereins-Verlag g. m. b. h., 1929, 164p.

Kroll, Gerhard. *Auf den Spuren Jesu.* Leipzig: St.-Benno-Verlag, 1975, 585p., (1980), 612p.

Krosney, Herbert. *Christmas in the Holyland* (Motion picture). New York: Phoenix Films, 1978, made 1971, 29 min.

Krull, Vigilius Herman. *A Prophetic Biography of Jesus Christ.* Carthagena, Ohio: Messenger Press, 1942, 97p.; Chicago: M.A. Donohue and Co., 1910, (1916), (1918).

Kuhn, Johannes von. *Das Leben Jesu, wissenschaftlich bearbeitet.* Frankfurt: Minerva, 1968, 488p.; Mainz: Kupferberg, 1838.

————. *La vie de Jésus-Christ, au point de vue de la science.* Trans. Fr. Nettement. Paris: Dufour, 1842, 294p.

Kulantaicāmi, Arul. *Ulakin oli.* Tirucci: Vīramāmunivar Ēḻuttāḻar Kaḻakam, 1967, 115p.

Kunkel, Heinrich. *Jesu liv i billeder.* København: Kristeligt Dagblad, 1967, 111p.

Lagrange, Marie Joseph. *L'evangile de Jésus-Christ.* Paris: J. Babalda et fils, 1928, 656p.

————. *The Gospel of Jesus Christ.* 2 vols. Trans. Members of the English Dominican Province. London: Burns, Oates, and Washbourne, 1938.

Lahey, Thomas Aquinas. *The Children's Friend, a Life of Christ for Children.* St. Louis: Herder, 1952, 203p.

Laine, E.C. *Das Leben Jesu auf Grundlage des vornehmsten Gebots.* Leipzig: H. Fritzsche, 1872-74; Stuttgart: J.F. Steinkopf, 1876-77.

Laird, Harold Samuel. *Portraits of Christ in the Gospel of John.* Chicago: Bible Institute Colportage Association, 1936, 126p.

Lake, Gerard. *Our Lord; an Elementary Life of Christ.* West-minster, Md.: Newman Press, 1952, 123p.

Lama, Miguel Antonio de la. *Ramillete de la redención del género humano, desde la creación del mundo hasta la asunción de María.* Lima: Librería e imprenta Gil, 1912, 746p.

LaMance, Lora Sarah (Nichols). *Jesus the Christ.* Louisville, Ky.: Pentecostal Pub. Co., 1937, 462p.

Lamsa, George Mamishisho. *The Man from Galilee; a Life of Jesus.* Garden City, N.Y.: Doubleday, 1970, 293p.

————. *My Neighbor Jesus, in the Light of His Own Language, People, and Time.* New York; London: Harper and Brothers, 1932, 148p.

Lange, A.C. *Das Leben Jesu, dargestellt in XIX einzelnen Lebensbildern.* Kiel: Schwers, 1868, 208p.

Lange, Johann Peter. *Das Leben Jesu nach den Evangelien dargestellt.* Heidelberg: R. Winter, 1844, (1847).

————. *The Life of the Lord Jesus Christ.* 4 vols. Trans. Sophia Taylor, J.E. Ryland, M.G. Huxtable, R.E. Wallis, S. Manson, Robert Smith. Edinburgh: T. and T. Clark, 1872; Philadelphia: Smith, English, and Co., 1872.

La-quad wajādnā Yasū'. Helwan, Egypt: Bayt al-Takrīs li-Khidmat al-Kirāzah al-Marqusīyah, 196-, 28p.

Larson, James Henry. *Meet the Man You Were Born to Love.* New York: Fortuny's, 1939, 196p.

Laubach, Frank Charles. *The Greatest Life; Jesus Tells His Story.* Westwood, N.J.: Revell, 1956, 192p.; *The Autobiography of Jesus.* New York: Harper and Row, 1962, 192p.

————. *Ngakiro naajokak a Yesu.* Trans. Anna Marika. Nairobi: Literacy Centre of Kenya, 196-?

————. *Yesu ŭi iyagi: Sŏnggyong esŏ ppobŭn.* Seoul: Taehan Kyemyŏng Hyŏphoe, 1962- .

Laudet, Fernand. *Histoire populaire de Jésus.* Tours; Paris: A. Mame et fils, 1924, 274p.

Laurie, Thomas. *Glimpses of Christ in Holy Scripture.* Boston: Congregational Publishing Society, 1868, 264p.; Boston: Gould and Lincoln; New York: Sheldon and Co., 1869, 264p.

Law, Edward. *A Discourse on the Life and Character of Christ.* Cambridge: 1749; 5th ed., 1818.

————. *The Life of Christ.* London: 1759.

Laymon, Charles M. *Christ in the New Testament.* New York: Abingdon Press, 1958, 256p.

————. *The Life and Teachings of Jesus.* New York: Abingdon Press, 1955, (1962), 336p.

————. *Luke's Portrait of Christ.* New York: Woman's Division of Christian Service, Board of Missions, Methodist Church, 1959, 162p.

Lea, William. *Catechisings on the Life of Our Lord.* London: 1870.

Leask, William. *Footsteps of Messiah. A Review of Passages in the History of Jesus Christ.* Philadelphia: W.S. Martien, 1850; 3rd ed., 1852?, 351p.

Leathley, Mary Elizabeth Southwell. *The Star of Promise; or, From Bethlehem to Calvary.* London: 1875.

Lebreton, Jules. *The Life and Teaching of Jesus Christ Our Lord.* 2 vols. Trans. Francis Day. London: Burns, Oates, and Washbourne, 1935.

————. *La vie et l'enseignement de Jésus Christ Notre Seigneur.* 2 vols. Paris: G. Beauchesne, 1931.

Le Camus, Émile. *The Life of Christ.* 3 vols. Trans. William A. Hickey. New York: Cathedral Library Association, 1906-08.

————. *La vie de Notre-Seigneur Jésus-Christ.* 3 vols., 6th ed. Poitiers: Oudin, 1901; Bruxelles: Téqui, 1897, (1883), 2 vols., 1st ed.; (1890), 3 vols., 4th ed.

Lee, Frederick. *Thoughts of Jesus.* Washington: Review and Herald Pub. Association, 1952, 128p.

Lee, John David. *From Bethlehem to Olivet.* New York; Nashville: Abingdon-Cokesbury Press, 1942, 120p.

Lee, Umphrey. *The Life of Christ; a Brief Outline for Students.* Nashville: Cokesbury Press, 1926, 175p.

Lee, William. *The Days of the Son of Man.* Edinburgh: W. Blackwood and Sons, 1872, 332p.

Lees, George Robinson. *The Life of Christ.* New York: Dodd, Mead, and Co., 1920, 451p.; London: S.W. Partridge and Co., 1920, 531p.

Lehmann, E. *Bilder aus dem Leben Jesu.* Leipzig: 1875.

————. *Scenes from the Life of Jesus.* Trans. Sophia Taylor. Edinburgh: T. and T. Clark, 1888, 230p.

Lenski, Richard Charles Henry. *His Footsteps; Studies for Edification from the Life of Christ.* Columbus: Lutheran Book Concern, 1898, 365p.

Leon-Dufour, Xavier. *Les Evangiles et l'histoire de Jésus.* Paris: Édit. du Seuil, 1964, 528p.

————. *The Gospels and the Jesus of History.* Trans. John McHugh. New York: Desclee Co., 1967, 288p.

Lepelletier, Almire René Jacques. *La vie de Jésus-Christ.* Paris: V. Palmé; Le Mans: Monnoyer frères, 1864, 389p.

Lepin, Marius. *Jésus Christ, sa vie et son œuvre.* 2 éd. Paris: G. Beauchesne, 1912, 269p.

Lepsius, Johannes. *Das Leben Jesu.* 2 vols. Potsdam: Tempel-verlag, 1917-18.

Lessing, Erich. *Jesus; History and Culture of the New Testament.* Trans. Stella Musulin, Robert Mahoney, and Angela Zerbe. New York: Herder and Herder, 1971, 292p.

——. *Der Mann aus Galiläa.* Freiburg/i. Br.; Basel; Wien: Herder, 1971, 300p.

Lessons on the Life of Christ. London?: 1871.

Lessons on the Life of Christ. By the author of "Hymns from the Land of Luther." New York: 1876.

Lester, Charles Stanley. *The Historic Jesus; a Study of the Synoptic Gospels.* New York; London: G.P. Putnam's Sons, 1912, 526p.

Letourneaux, Nicolas. *Histoire de la vie de Nostre Seigneur Jésus-Christ.* Paris: Elie Josset, 1681, 337p., (1686), (1687), (1698).

Leven Ons Heren Jesu Christi. Delft: Jacob Jacobszoen van der Meer and Mauricius Yemantszoen, 1479, 180 1.

Lever, Abraham Wolf. *The Life and Teaching of Jesus, and a Summary of the Twin Guides, Honest Law and Natural Religion.* Landsdowne, Pa.: A.W. Lever, 1930, 123p.

Levin, Simon S. *Jesus Alias Christ; a Theological Detection.* New York: Philosophical Library, 1969, 136p.

Levy, Rosalie Marie. *Jesus, the Divine Master.* Derby, N.Y.: Daughters of St. Paul, Apostolate of the Press, 1953?, 363p.

Lewis, Frank Warburton. *Jesus of Galilee.* London: I. Nicholson and Watson, 1931, 240p.

——. *Jesus, Saviour of Men.* London: I. Nicholson and Watson, 1933, 217p.

——. *Jesus, Son of God.* London: E. Stock, 1897, 67p.

Lewis, Walter Sunderland. *The Life of Lives; or, The Story of Jesus of Nazareth in Its Earliest Form.* London: Religious Tract Society, 1885, 184p.

Li, Mu-tsung. *Yeh-su Chi-tu ti shêng huo.* Taipei: Chiao yu sheng huo she, 1960, 391p.

The Life and Doctrine of Our Saviour Jesus Christ. London: 1656; Ghent: 1656; London: 1880.

The Life and Ministry of Our Lord (Filmstrip). Broadman Films, 1970, 52 fr.

The Life and Teaching of Jesus (Motion picture). American University, Dept. of Philosophy and Religion, and Council of Churches, National Capital Area, 1960. 14 motion pictures. Originally telecast over WMAL-TV in Washington, D.C.

The Life and Travels of Our Blessed Lord and Saviour, with a Description of the Years of His Ministry. London: 1680.

Life and Work of the Redeemer. New York: 1902, 384p.

The Life of Christ. Illustrated by Choice Passages from One Hundred and Thirty-Eight Eminent British and Foreign Divines; and Embellished with Seventy Wood Engravings after Celebrated Masters. London: Ball, Arnold, and Co., 1841, 288p.

The Life of Christ. London: 1848, 125p.

Life of Christ (Filmstrip). Christian Education Press, 1951. 2 parts, 83 fr.

The Life of Christ (Filmstrip). New Rochelle, N.Y.: Don Bosco Filmstrips, 1964, 2 rolls.

The Life of Christ in Focus (Motion picture). George Mihovich, 1964, 33 min.

The Life of Christ in Its True Humanity. London: 1860.

The Life of Christ in the Sites and Monuments of Palestine. Jerusalem: Franciscan Print. Press, 1963, 246p.

Life of Christ. London: 1876.

Life of Jesus. (Bible handbook for young people). Philadelpphia: 1905.

The Life of Jesus Christ. Dublin: 1854.

The Life of Jesus Christ. By a member of the Church of England. London: 1872.

Life of Jesus Christ, the Messiah. 2nd ed. Part I, Senior Historical Course; Part II, Junior Historical Course. Milwaukee: 1903, 126p., 134p.

The Life of Lord and Saviour Jesus Christ. Dublin: 1864.

The Life of Our Blessed Lord and Saviour Jesus Christ. London: 1847.

The Life of Our Lord. London: 1882, 32p.

The Life of Our Saviour. London: 1848.

The "Light" and the "Life"; or, The History of Him Whose Name We Bear. London: 1851.

Light of the World; or, Footprints of Christ Our Lord. New York: 1876.

Ligny, François de. *Histoire de la vie de Jésus-Christ*. 2
vols. Paris: chez l'éditeur, 1804; Sixième édition, 4 vols.
Paris: Méquignon Junior, 1830; 8 éd., 2 vols., 1844.

————. *Histoire Jésus-Christ*. Brussels: 1839.

————. *Historia da vida de Nosso Senhor Jesus-Christo*. 2 vols.
Trans. Maria do Carmo Osorio Cabral Pereira de Menezes.
Coimbra: Impr. da Universidade, 1865.

————. *History of the Life of Jesus Christ*. Trans. Mrs. J.
Sadlier. New York: D. and J. Sadlier, 1851, (1853), (1869),
749p., (1876), n.p.; New York: McDavitt and Co., 1870, 474p.

Link, Mark J. *The Seventh Trumpet: The Good News Proclaimed*.
Niles, Ill.: Argus Communications, 1978, 208p.

Lippert, Peter. *Der Menschensohn; Bilder aus dem Seelenleben
Jesu*. 4. Aufl. Regensburg: J. Habbel, 1947?, 230p.,
(1949); Mödling b. Wein: St. Gabriel, 1948, 161p.

Livingstone, William Pringle. *The Master Life; the Story of
Jesus for To-day*. London: J. Clarke and Co., 1925, 319p.;
New York: George H. Doran Co., 1925, 405p.

Llimona, Jordi. *Jesus de Natzaret*. Barcelona: Edicions 62,
1980, 354p.

Lloyd, E.M. *The Gospel History of Jesus Christ*. London: n.d.

Lloyd, Walter. *The Galilean. A Portrait of Jesus of Nazareth*.
London; Edinburgh: Williams and Norgate, 1892, 80p.

Lobingier, Henry Schell. *Man in the Book*. St. Louis: 1881,
405p.

The Locale of Jesus' Early Ministry (Filmstrip). Society for
Visual Education, 1962, 52 fr.

Lönberg, Sven. *Jésu de Nazara*. Trans. Fritiof Palmer. Paris:
M. Giard & C. Brière, 1915, 257p.

————. *Jesu från Nazara*. Stockholm: Geber, 1911, 254p.

Logan, Algernon Sydney. *Jesus in Modern Life*. Philadelphia:
Lippincott, 1888, 299p.; Philadelphia: National Pub. Co.,
1934, 253p.

Lohmann, Johann Baptist. *Betrachtungen über das Leben Jesu
Christi auf alle Tagen des Jahres*. 2 vols., 6 Aufl. Paderborn: Junfermannsche Buchhandlung, 1912.

Lokuang, Stanislao. *Chi-tu chuan*. Taipei: Chung-hua wen hua
chü pan shih yeh wei yüan hui, 1957, 270p.

Longford, Frank Pakenham. *Jesus: A Life of Christ*. Garden
City, N.Y.: Doubleday, 1975, 184p.; London: Sidgwick and
Jackson, 1974, 176p.

The Lord's Footsteps (Motion picture). Don Catlin. Released
by International Theatrical and Television Corp., 1946, 8
reels.

Lorimer, George Claude. *Jesus, the World's Savior.* Chicago:
S.C. Griggs and Co., 1883, 351p.; *The Galilean, or Jesus,
the World's Savior.* Boston; New York: Silver, Burdett and
Co., 1892, 448p.

Lotz, Benjamin. *Life and Work of Christ.* Philadelphia: Muhlenberg Press, 1957, 96p.

Lovasik, Lawrence George. *Praying the Gospels; Meditations
in Prayer on the Life of Christ According to the Four Evangelists.* New York: Macmillan, 1953, 333p.

*The Love of the Good Shepherd for His Flock. A Series of
Meditations on the Life and Sufferings of Our Lord.* Compiled
from various sources by a member of the Ursuline Community.
Cork: 1853.

Lowrie, James Gibson. *The Joyful Hours of Jesus.* New York:
Revell, 1918, 203p.

Lowrie, John Marshall. *A Week with Jesus, or, Lessons Learned
in His Company.* Philadelphia: Presbyterian Board of Publication, 1866, 360p.

Lowrie, Walter. *The Short Story of Jesus.* New York: C. Scribner's Sons, 1943, 238p.

Ludolphus de Saxonia. *Dit es dleue Ons Liefs Heeren Ihesu
Cristi.* Antwerpen: H. Eckert, 1503, 328 l., (1512), 321 l.

————. *O livro de vita Christi em lingoagem português.* Rio
de Janeiro: Ministério da Educação e Cultura, Casa de Rui
Barbosa, 1957-68?

————. *Vie de Jésus-Christ.* Trans. A. Lecoy de La Marche.
Paris: G. Hurtrel, 1870, 243p.

————. *Vita Christi.* Antwerp: Gerardus Leeu, 1487, 306 l.;
Zwolle: Pieter van Os, 1499, 345 l.

Ludowyk, H.L. *Religion and Jesus.* Kandy: Printed for the
Author at the Union Printing Works, 1940, 227p.

Ludwig, Emil. *Âdem oğlu.* Trans. Ruşen Eşref. İstanbul:
Devlet matbaasi, 1929, 321p.

————. *El Hijo del Hombre.* Trans. Ricardo Baeza. Madrid:
Biblioteca nueva, 1930, 389p.

————. *Der Menschensohn.* Berlin: E. Rowohlt; Wien: P.
Zsolnay, 273p.

————. *The Son of Man.* Trans. Eden and Cedar Paul. New York: Boni and Liveright, 1928, 315p.; Garden City, N.Y.: Sun Dial Press, 1938, 315p.; Greenwich, Conn.: Fawcett Publications, 1957, 190p.

————. *Yeshu ha-nostri.* Trans. Mark Fogelman. Warsaw: S. Goldfarb, 1930, 264p.

Luis de Granada. *Traite de la vie. de. N-S. Jésus Christ.* 2 éd. Paris: Librairie Poussielgue frères, 1868, 494p.

Luther, Martin. *Meditations on the Gospels.* Trans. Roland H. Bainton. Philadelphia: Westminster Press, 1962, 155p.

————. *Wie Luther den Deutschen das Leben Jesu erzählt hat.* 2. Aufl. Walther Köhler, ed. Leipzig: M. Heinsius, 1934, 154p.

Lyon, William P. *The Life of Our Lord.* London: Book Society, 1871.

Lytton, Victor Alexander Robert Bulwer-Lytton. *Love Incarnate.* London: P. Davies, 1945, 266p.

Ma'a al-Masīh. Helwan, Egypt: Bayt al-Takrīs li-Khidmat al-Kirāzah al-Marqusīyah, 1961, 60p.

McBirnie, William Steuart. *Preaching on the Life of Christ; Sermons on the Epochs in the Life of Christ.* Grand Rapids: Zondervan, 1958, 118p.

McCasland, Selby Vernon. *The Pioneer of Our Faith; a New Life of Jesus.* New York: McGraw-Hill, 1964, 210p.

McClelland, Adam. *The History of Our Lord.* Dubuque, Iowa: Presbyterian Pub. Co., 1898, 370p.

McConaughy, James. *Christ among Men.* New York: International Committee of Young Men's Christian Associations, 1901, (1894), 159p.

————. *The Great Events in the Life of Christ.* New York: Young Men's Christian Association Press, 1909, 210p.

————. *Outline Studies in the English Bible.* Vol. 1. Mount Hermon, Mass.: Mount Hermon School Press, 1893; New York: n.d.

McConkie, Bruce R. *The Mortal Messiah: From Bethlehem to Calvary.* 4 vols. Salt Lake City: Deseret Book Co., 1979–81.

Macdonald, Allan John. *With Jesus in Palestine.* London: Skeffington and Son, 1938, 143p.

Macduff, John Ross. *Memories of Bethany.* New York: R. Carter and Brothers, 1866, 268p., (1879).

————. *Memories of Gennesaret*. New York: R. Carter and Brothers, 1861, 388p.

Macgregor, George Hogarth Carnaby. *Gospel Glimpses; or, Short Studies in the Life of Jesus*. London: Marshall Brothers, 1895, 111p.

————. *Into His Likeness; Gospel Glimpses of the Life of Jesus*. New York; Chicago: Revell, 1899, 158p.

MacGregor, Jessie G. *Jesus the Christ, a Move by Move and Event by Event Account of the Life of Christ, Arranged Chronologically*. Hollywood, Calif.: Gospel Light Press, 1944, 459p.

Mackay, Henry Falconar Barclay. *Studies in the Ministry of Our Lord*. Milwaukee: Morehouse Pub. Co., 1932-   .

Mackay, John Alexander. *His Life and Our Life*. Philadelphia: Westminster Press, 1964, 80p.

McKendry, James Banford. *The Life of Jesus for Junior High School Pupils*. Philadelphia; Boston: Judson Press, 1928, 256p.

McKenzie, Alexander. *Christ Himself*. Boston: D. Lothrop Co., 1891, 168p.

Mackenzie, William Douglas. *The Revelation of the Christ. Familiar Studies in the Life of Jesus*. London: 1896, 303p.

McKenzie, William Scott. *Sabbath School Studies on the Life of Jesus Christ*. Boston: A.F. Graves, 18--?; New York: 1859, 4 vols.

Mackinnon, James. *The Historic Jesus*. London; New York: Longmans, Green, and Co., 1931, 407p.

Mackintosh, William. *Rabbi Jesus, Sage and Saviour*. London: 1901, 286p.

McLaren, Robert Bruce. *What's Special about Jesus?* New York: Association Press, 1963, 126p.

McNabb, Vincent Joseph. *A Life of Jesus Christ Our Lord*. New York: Sheed and Ward, 1938, 198p.

McNeil, Jesse Jai. *Moments in His Presence*. Grand Rapids: Eerdmans, 1962, 98p.

McNeile, Alan Hugh. *Concerning Christ*. Cambridge, Eng.: W. Heffer and Sons, 1924, 155p., (1923).

McWherter, Leroy. *The King of Glory*. Greenville, Tenn.: The author, 1885, 256p.

Mack, Charles A. *Twelve Lessons on the Life of Jesus.* Chicago: 1892, 16p.

Magri, Francesco. *Gesù Cristo.* Milano: Sonzogno, 1946, 686p.

Mahieu, Jerome. *Het leven van Onzen Heer Jesus-Christus.* Brugge: Moderne drukkerij D. Walleyn, 1939- .

Maïkoff, Marie. *Jésus-Christ et son temps.* Mont-Pélerin: chez l'auteur, 1971, 36p.

Malham, John. *The History and Life of Our Blessed Lord and Saviour Jesus Christ.* London: Thomas Kelly, 1810, 477p., (1811).

Malleson, Frederick Amadeus. *Jesus Christ, His Life and Work.* London: Ward, 1880, 375p., (1882), 280p., (1888), (1892), 375p.

Manco-Capac. *El Galileo.* Caracas: Empresa El Cojo, 1941, 223p.

Mann, Christopher Stephen. *The Man for All Time.* New York: Morehouse-Barlow, 1971, 126p.

Manoogian, Sion. *Awetarani patgamner.* Buenos Aires: Ararat Press, 1953, 205p.

Manson, Thomas Walter. *The Beginning of the Gospel.* London; New York: Oxford University Press, 1950, 113p.

Manzano, Braulio. *Jesús escándolo do los hombres.* Madrid: Confederación Española de Cajas Ahorros, 1974, 657p.

Map Study of the Life of Christ (Filmstrip). Church-Craft Pictures, 1953, 35 fr.

Marc, Paul. *Gospel Gems, Meditations.* Trans. Joseph A. Fredette. New York: F. Pustet Co., 1950, 226p.

————. *Le Maître vous Parle.* Paris: Éditions Siloë, 1944, 286p.

————. *Pages d'Évangile.* Paris: Lethielleux, 1937, 208p.

March, Daniel. *Days of the Son of Man.* Philadelphia: J.C. McCurdy and Co., 1882, 685p.

————. *Walks and Homes of Jesus.* Philadelphia: Presbyterian Publication Committee; New York: A.D.F. Randolph, 1866, 339p.; London: 1895.

————. *Walks with Jesus; or, Days of the Son of Man.* Philadelphia; Chicago: P.W. Ziegler and Co., 1889, 685p.

Márkus, Mihály. *Jézus.* Budapest: Kiadja a Református Zsinati Iroda Sajtóosztálya, 1977, 64p.

Marmion, Columba. *Vie de Jésus*. Paris: Flammarion, 1939, 48p.

Marnas, Mélanie. *Quel est donc cet homme?* Paris: Perrin et c^{ie}, 1927, 375p.

―――. *Who Is Then This Man?* Trans. Henry Longan Stuart. New York: E.P. Dutton and Co., 1929, 363p.

Marquis, David Calhoun. *Outline of the Life of Christ in Seven Periods*. Chicago: 1889, 32p.

Marsh, John. *Jesus in His Lifetime*. London: Sidgwick and Jackson, 1981, 262p.

Marshall, Edward A. *How Christ Lived and Labored in Palestine*. Cleveland: Tract Evangelization Society, 1925, 93p.

Marshall, Emma. *Life of Our Lord Jesus Christ*. London: Nisbet and Co., 1886, 87p.

Martin, Alfred Wilhelm. *The Life of Jesus in the Light of Higher Criticism*. New York; London: D. Appleton and Co., 1913, 280p.

Martin, Arthur Davis. *Aspects of the Way, Being Mediations and Studies in the Life of Jesus Christ*. Cambridge: University Press, 1924, 171p.

―――. *A Plain Man's Life of Christ*. London: G. Allen and Unwin, 1942, 229p., (1941); New York: Macmillan, 1947, 217p.

Martin, Hugh. *Christ's Presence in Gospel History*. London: T. Nelson and Sons, 1860, (1865), 306p.; Edinburgh: John Maclaren, 1865, 352p.

Martin, Jex. *The Words of Our Lord; the Story of Christ's Life, with Special Emphasis on the Words He Spoke*. Chicago: Catholic Press, 1961, 304p.

Martin von Cochem. *Das Leben unsers lieben Herrn und Heilandes Jesus Christus und seiner jungfräulichen Mutter Maria*. Lucas Caspar Businger, ed. Einsiedeln; New York; Cincinnati: Gebr. C. & N. Benziger, 1873, 1031p.

―――. *Life of Christ*. Adapted by Bonaventure Hammer. New York: Benziger Brothers, 1897, 314p.

―――. *Our Redeemer: A Series of Meditations Drawn from the Study of the Life of Christ and His Ever Glorious Mother Mary*. English arrangement by Frances M. Kemp. New York: A. Eichler, 1890, 1148p.

―――. *Welký žiwot Pána a Spasitele nasseho Krista Ježisse a jeho nejswětějssí a nejmilejssí Matky Marie Panny jakož i wssech jiných krewních přátel Syna Božího*. Wyd. 8. Trans. Edelberta Nymburského. W Uh. Skalici: J. Teslík, 1901, 942p.

Martinetti, Piero. *Jésus Christ et le christianisme.* Paris: Bocca frères, 1942, 642p.

Martínez, Raul V. *Yeschu.* Buenos Aires: 1932, 175p.

Mary Eleanor, Mother. *Jesus, Son of David.* Milwaukee: Bruce Pub. Co., 1955, 224p.

Mary Gonzaga, Sister. *Christ in the Old and the New Testament.* St. Louis; London: B. Herder Book Co., 1928, 697p.

Mary Viola, Sister. *The Great Knight of the Crimsoned Cross, Jesus, the God-man.* Chicago: Catholic Dept., Mentzer, Bush, and Co., 1945, 320p.

Masferrer, Alberto. *Estudios y figuraciones sobre la vida de Jesús.* San Salvador: Ministerio de Cultura, Departamento Editorial, 1956, 163p.

Masoliver, Liberata. *Dios con nosotros.* Barcelona: Jaimes-Libros, 1970, 429p.

Mason, Arthur James. *The Conditions of Our Lord's Life on Earth.* New York; London: Longmans, Green, and Co., 1896, 194p.

Mason, William. *The History of Jesus.* 7th ed. Nottingham: J. Dunn, 1809, 108p.; 4th ed. London: 1789.

Massart, H. *Jésus Notre Chef.* Maredsous: Éditions de Maredsous, 1945, 240p.

Massé, Daniel. *Jésus, ce juif sans nom.* Paris: Éditions Le Cercle du livre, 1959, 199p.

Masson, Elizabeth. *It Happened This Way.* London; New York: Regency Press, 1978, 78p.

Matheson, George. *Studies of the Portrait of Christ.* 2 vols. London: Hodder and Stoughton, 1901-02, (1899), (1900), (1903); New York: A.C. Armstrong and Son, 1900, (1903), (1907), 2 vols.

Mathews, Basil Joseph. *A Life of Jesus.* London: Oxford University Press, 1930, 470p.; New York: R.R. Smith, 1931, 519p.

Matson, Charles William. *Behold the Man.* Los Angeles: Institute Press, 1946, 94p.

Mauriac, François. *Life of Jesus.* Trans. Julie Kernan. New York; Toronto: Longmans, Green, and Co., 1937, 261p.; New York: D. McKay Co., 1951, 258p.

————. *Vie de Jésus.* Paris: E. Flammarion, 1936, 284p.

Maxwell, Lawrence. *The Man Who Loved Everybody.* Mountain View, Calif.: Pacific Press Pub. Association, 1977, 61p.

Mayer, Friedrich. *Das Leben Jesu*. Stuttgart: Quell-Verlag,
    1952, 671p.

Mears, Henrietta Cornelia. *The Life of Christ According to
    Luke*. Hollywood, Calif.: Gospel Light Press, 193-?

Meditations on Some Passages of the Life of the Son of God.
    London: 1713.

Mele evanelio. Honolulu: Pai-palapala katolika, 1880, 70p.

Memorials of Jesus of Nazareth. London?: 1876.

Mercier, Lewis. *Outlines of the Life of the Lord Jesus Christ*.
    2 vols. London: Sampson, Low, Marsten, Low, and Searle,
    1871, (1875).

Merezhkovskiĭ, Dmitriĭ Sergeevich. *Iisus Neizvi͡estnyĭ*. 2 vols.
    Belgrade: 1933?-37?

————. *Jesus der kommende*. Trans. Arthur Luther. Frauen-
    feld; Leipzig: Huber and Co., 1934, 422p.

————. *Jesus der Unbekannte*. Leipzig: Grethlein and Co.,
    1932, 431p.

————. *Jesus Manifest*. Trans. Edward Gellibrand. London:
    J. Cape, 1935, 622p.; New York: C. Scribner's Sons, 1936,
    622p.

————. *Jesus the Unknown*. Trans. H. Chrouschoff Matheson.
    London: J. Cape, 1933, 445p.; New York: C. Scribner's Sons,
    1934, 445p.

Merrick, Mary Virginia. *The Life of Christ*. St. Louis: B.
    Herder, 1909, 67p.

Merrifield, Fred. *The Rediscovery of Jesus*. New York: H. Holt
    and Co., 1929, 270p.

Merrill, George Edmands. *The Reasonable Christ*. Boston; New
    York: Silver, Burdett, and Co., 1893, 215p.

Meschler, Moritz. *Das Leben unseres Herrn Jesu Christi, des
    Sohnes Gottes, in Betrachtungen*. 2. aufl. 2 vols. Freiburg
    im Breisgau; St. Louis: Herder, 1891-92, (1912), (1919),
    (1922), (1931).

————. *The Life of Our Lord Jesus Christ, the Son of God, in
    Meditations*. 2 vols. Trans. Sister Mary Margaret. St.
    Louis; London: B. Herder Book Co., 1909, (1913), (1922),
    (1924), (1928), (1950).

Meunier, Léon. *Le vrai message de Jésus*. Paris: Les Éditions
    Jean Meyer (BPS), 1929, 376p.

Meurling, Per. *Jesus äventyr.* Stockholm: Seelig, 1967, 116p.

Meyrowitz, Alexander. *Historia Jesu Nazareni.* New York: American Tract Society, 1880, 87p.

Mezzacasa, Giacomo. *Vita di Gesù Cristo.* Torino: Società deitrice internazionale, 1945, 472p.

Micklem, Edward Romilly. *The World's Ransom.* London: SCM Press, 1946, 161p.

Mies, Frank P. *The 4 Gospel Keys.* Oak Park, Ill.: Hub Print Services, 1947, 148p.

Miles, Bernard. *God's Brainwave.* London: Hodder and Stoughton, 1970, 125p.

Miller, James Russell. *Come Ye Apart. Daily Morning Readings in the Life of Christ.* New York: R. Carter and Brothers, 1887, 369p.; *Come Ye Apart. Daily Readings in the Life of Christ.* London: Nelson, 1919, (1890), 374p.; London: Sunday School Union, 1895; London: Eyre and Spottiswoode, 1904; London: Andrew Melrose, 1905.

————. *Vir de binnekamer. Daeliske oordenkings uit de lewe van Kristus.* Trans. P.J. Marais. Stellenbosch: 1930, (1942), 373p.

Miller, Mrs. John A. *From Bethlehem to Calvary.* New York: Nelson and Phillips; Cincinnati: Hitchcock and Walden, 1876, 189p., (1878).

Miller, Lucius Hopkins. *Our Knowledge of Christ.* New York: H. Holt and Co., 1914, 166p.

Miller, T. Franklin. *Life and Teachings of Jesus.* Rev. ed. Anderson, Ind.: Warner Press, 1959, 124p.

Milne, David. *The Years and Eras of the Life of Christ.* London: Simpkin and Marshall, 1892, 62p.

Milne, W. *Looking unto Jesus. Some Aspects of His Life and Work.* London: 1901.

Milton, William Hammond. *The Cure of Soule; or, Christ's Treatment of the Individual.* New York: T. Whittaker, 1909, 227p.

Mimpriss, Robert. *The Life of Christ Harmonized from the Four Evangelists.* 2 vols. New York: M.W. Dodd, 1869-70.

————. *Studies on the Gospels in Harmony.* 2 vols. New York: Dodd and Mead, 1870-71.

————. *Teacher's Manual to Accompany the First Grade Lesson Book on the Life of Christ Harmonized from the Four Evangelists.* 2 vols. New York: M.W. Dodd, 1869-70.

————. *Teacher's Manual to Accompany the Second Grade Lesson Book on the Life of Christ Harmonized from the Four Evangelists*. 2 vols. New York: M.W. Dodd, 1869-70.

————. *Teacher's Manual to Accompany the Third Grade Lesson Book on the Life of Christ Harmonized from the Four Evangelists*. 2 vols. New York: M.W. Dodd, 1869-70.

The Ministry of Christ. London: 1886.

The Ministry of Jesus. London: 1866.

The Ministry of Jesus (Filmstrip). American Baptist Convention. Made and released by American Baptist Board of Education and Publication, 1964, 45 fr.

Monloubou, Louis. *Jésus le Galiléen*. Tours: Mame, 1968, 240p.

Montgomery, Maud. *Story of Our Lord's Life*. New York; London: Longmans, Green, and Co., 1904, 163p.

Moore, Edward Caldwell. *Notes for Readings on the Life of Jesus*. Cambridge, Mass.: Caustic-Claflin Co., 1906, 69p.

Moore, Edward W. *The Overcoming Life; or, Thoughts on the Life of Christ in the Soul of the Believer*. London: S.W. Partridge and Co., 1882.

Moore, Henry. *The Life of Our Lord and Saviour Jesus Christ*. London: 1810?

Moore, Hight C. *From Bethlehem to Olivet*. Nashville: Convention Press, 1960, 119p., (1934).

Moore, Thomas Hendrick. *The Darkness Is Passed*. New York: Declan X. McMullen Co., 1946, 176p.

————. *The Eternal Shepherd*. 4 vols. New York: Apostleship of Prayer, 1952-55.

Morador, Federico. *El Mesías perplejo*. Santiago de Chile: Zig-Zag, 1942, 268p.

More, Paul Elmer. *The Christ of the New Testament*. New York: Greenwood Press, 1969, 294p.; Princeton: Princeton University Press, 1924, 294p.

Morgan, George Campbell. *The Crises of the Christ*. New York; London: Revell, 1903, 477p.

Morgan, Richard. *The Christ of the Cross*. New York: R.R. Smith, 1950, 285p.

Moriarty, James Joseph. *All for Love; or, From the Manger to the Cross*. New York: Catholic Publication Society Co., 1882, 319p.

Morison, John Hopkins. *Scenes from the Life of Jesus.* Boston: Crosby, Nichols, and Co.; New York: C.S. Francis and Co., 1852, 137p., (1855), (1976).

Morison, Walter. *The Footprints of the Revealer.* London: J. Nisbet and Co., 1889, 296p.

Morris, Winfield Scott. *Jesus, King of Kings.* Boston: Meador Pub. Co., 1933, 152p.

Morrison, Hugh Tucker. *Mysterious Omissions; an Interpretation of Certain Unresolved Issues in the New Testament Church.* Chicago: Disciples Divinity House of the University of Chicago, 1969, 56p.

Morus, Henricus. *The Life and Doctrine of Jesus Christ.* London: Burns and Oates, 1880, (1656).

Moss, Richard Waddy. *The Scene of Our Lord's Life.* London: Hodder and Stoughton, 1903, 142p.

Mountford, Lydia Mary Olive. *Jesus Christ in His Homeland.* Cincinnati: Press of Jennings and Graham, 1911, 138p.

Müller, Karl Anton. *Evangelium Jesu.* Osnabruck: Versöhnungsverlag, 1967, 128p.

Muggeridge, Malcolm. *Jesus, the Man Who Lives.* London: Collins, 1975, 191p.; New York: Harper and Row, 1975, 191p.

————. *A Life of Christ.* Edinburgh: St. Andrew P., 1968, 32p.

Murray, James Clayton. *English Bible Studies, First Year's Course; Sixty Studies in the Life of Christ.* Cincinnati: Cranston and Stowe; New York: Hunt and Eaton, 1890, 120p.

Murray, Jane Marie. *The Life of Our Lord.* Milwaukee: Bruce Pub. Co., 1947, 370p., (1942), 314p.

Murray, William D. *The Life and Works of Jesus, According to St. Mark.* New York: International Committee of Young Men's Christian Associations, 1900, 182p.

————. *What Manner of Man Is This?* New York: Young Men's Christian Association Press, 1907, 82p.

Murry, John Middleton. *Jesus, Man of Genius.* New York; London: Harper and Brothers, 1926, 373p.

Mushakōji, Saneatsu. *Kirisuto.* Tokyo: Kōdan Sha, Shōwa 27, 1952, 188p.

My Beloved Son (Motion picture). Foundation Films Corp., 1941, 30 min.

My Beloved Son (Motion picture). Cathedral Films, 194-?
Edited and released by Blackhawk Films/Eastin-Phelan Corp.,
196-?, 21 min.

My Greatest Work (Filmstrip). Roa's Films, 1972, 35 fr.

My Land and My People (Filmstrip). Roa's Films, 1972, 35 fr.

Myers, Cortland. *Where Heaven Touched the Earth.* New York:
American Tract Society, 1912, 239p.

Myers, Mary L. *My Truth.* Nürnberg: W. Tümmels, 1965, 329p.

Nash, Augustus. *Jesus' Life; Discussions for Men's Bible
Classes.* Cleveland: 1912, 52p.

Naṭarājaṉ, A.L. *Iyecunātar vāḷkkai varalāṟu.* Madras: Pāri
Puttakappaṇṇai, 1967, 368p.

Neander, August. *Das Leben Jesu Christi in seinem geschicht-
lichen Zusammenhänge und seiner geschichtlichen Entwickelung.*
Hamburg: F. Perthes, 1837, 675p., (1839), (1845), (1852);
Gotha: F. Perthes, 1862, 599p.

————. *The Life of Jesus Christ in Its Historical Connexion
and Historical Development.* Trans. John McClintock and
Charles E. Blumenthal. New York: Harper and Brothers, 1848,
450p., (1849), (1851), (1858), (1863), (1870); New York: 1841,
(1855), (1856); London: H.G. Bohn, 1851, 499p., (1852),
(1853), (1861); Gotha: 1862; London: Bell and Daldy, 1864,
499p., (1871); London: George Bell and Sons, 1880, (1884),
(1888), (1892), (1904).

Neil, William. *The Life and Teaching of Jesus.* Philadelphia:
Lippincott, 1965, 190p.

Nelson, Samuel. *The History of Our Blessed Lord and Saviour
Jesus Christ.* London: J. Coote, 1756, 556p.

Nelson, Walter Horatius. *A Walk with Jesus.* Cincinnati:
Jennings and Pye; New York: Eaton and Mains, 1901, 463p.

Die neue Ehe und das Passional von Jesu. Augsburg: 1491,
137 1.

Neumann, Arno. *Jesus.* Trans. Maurice A. Canney. London:
A. and C. Black, 1906, 180p.

Newcome, Simon. *The Duration of Our Lord's Ministry Practically Considered.* Dublin: 1780.

Newdome, William. *Observations on Our Lord's Conduct as a
Divine Instructor; and on the Excellence of His Moral Charac-
ter.* London: J. Johnson, 1785, 516p., (1782); Charlestown:
Samuel Etheridge, 1810, 516p.; London: Oxford University
Press, 1853.

————. *Observations on the Life and Character of Jesus Christ*. Boston: Munroe and Francis, 1806, 194p.

Newman, John Henry. *According to Cardinal Newman: The Life of Christ and the Mission of His Church*. Compiled by Agnes K. Maxwell. New York: L. MacVeagh, Dial Press, 1932, 267p.

Newton, Richard Heber. *Studies of Jesus*. New York: T. Whittaker, 1880, 188p.

Nicoll, William Robertson. *The Incarnate Saviour. A Life of Jesus Christ*. Edinburgh: T. and T. Clark, 1881, 388p., (1897), (1899); London: 1897, 332p., (1898), 360p.; New York: American Tract Society, 1880; New York: Robert Carter, 1882.

Niles, Daniel Thambyrajah. *Living with the Gospel*. New York: Association Press, 1957, 92p.; London: United Society for Christian Literature, 1957, 96p.

No Greater Life (Filmstrip). American Baptist Convention. Made and released by American Baptist Board of Education and Publication, 1966, 21 fr.

Noack, Ludwig. *Die Geschichte Jesu auf Grund freier geschichtlicher Untersuchungen über das Evangelium und die Evangelien*. 2. Aufl. Strassburg: Schneider, 1876.

Nobili, Roberto de'. *Cēcunātar carittiram*. Tuttukkuti: Ilakkiyak kaḻakam, 1964, 90p.

Noel, Conrad. *The Life of Jesus*. New York: Simon and Schuster, 1937, 619p.; London: J.M. Dent and Sons, 1937, 619p.

Nolasco, Flérida de. *Cuadros del Evangelio*. Santiago, Rep. Dom.: Editorial El Diario, 1947, 134p.

Norborg, Christopher Sverre. *Christ on Main Street*. Minneapolis: Denison, 1959, 400p.

Norris, William. *Sermons on the History of Our Blessed Lord and Saviour Jesus Christ*. London: 1830.

Northrop, Henry Davenport. *The Marvelous Story of Christ and His Apostles*. Philadelphia: National Pub. Co., 1906, 352p.

Norwood, Robert Winkworth. *The Man Who Dared to Be God; a Story of Jesus*. New York; London: C. Scribner's Sons, 1929, 324p.

O le Tala ia Iesu o le alo o le Atua, ma Lana au Aposetolo. Samoa: London Missionary Society's Press, 1840, 62p.

O'Brien, Isidore. *The Life of Christ*. Paterson, N.J.: St. Anthony Guild Press, 1937, 540p., (1944), 612p., (1975).

O'Brien, John Anthony. *The Life of Christ*. New York: J.J. Crawley, 1957, 623p.

Occidentalis, Frater. *The Failure of Jesus and His Triumph.*
Red Wing, Minn.: Argus Press, 1903, 123p.

O'Connell, John P. *The Life of Christ.* Chicago: Catholic
Press, 1954, 304p.

O'Donnell, James H. *Jesus Christ: A Scriptural Study.* Boston: 1901.

Ojea, Hernando. *La venida de Christo y sv vida y milagros.*
Medina del Campo: Christoual Lasso Vaca, 1602, 68p.

Olmstead, Albert Ten Eyck. *Jesus in the Light of History.*
New York: C. Scribner's Sons, 1942, 317p.

Olmsted, Miles Newell. *Questions on the Walks and Words of
Jesus.* New York: Nelson and Phillips, 1874, 32p.

Olsen, Mahlon Ellsworth. *The Carpenter of Nazareth.* Washington: Review and Herald Publishing Association, 1930, 126p.

O'Mahony, James Edward. *Jesus the Saviour.* Westminster, Md.:
Newman Press, 1956, 145p.

Onfroy, Jean Marie. *La grande nouvelle qui vous apporte le vrai
bonheur.* Nontsurs: Résiac, 1977, 280p.

Opatovich, Stefan. *Slava na zemlîe Gospoda nashego Īisusa
Khrista.* St. Petersburg: Permanent Commission on National
Reading, 1873, 16p.

————. *Unichizhenīe na zemlîe Gospoda nashego Īisusa Khrista.*
St. Petersburg: Permanent Commission on National Reading,
1873, 21p.

Opitz, Ernst August. *Geschichte und Characterzüge Jesu.*
Jena; Leipzig: 1812, 488p.

O'Rahilly, Alfred. *Gospel Meditations.* Baltimore: Helicon
Press, 1958, 286p.

Otto, Rudolf. *Life and Ministry of Jesus According to the
Historical and Critical Method.* Trans. H.J. Whitby. Chicago: Open Court Pub. Co., 1908, 85p.

Otts, John Martin Philip. *The Fifth Gospel; the Land Where
Jesus Lived.* New York; Chicago: Revell, 1892, 367p.

Oursler, Fulton. *The Greatest Story Ever Told; a Tale of the
Greatest Life Ever Lived.* Garden City, N.Y.: Doubleday,
1950, 332p., (1949), 299p.; Boston: G.K. Hall, 1979,
617p., Large type edition; Washington: Library of Congress;
manufactured by American Printing House for the Blind, Louisville, Ky., Phonodisc., 30 s.

────. *Sarang ŭi chŭngin: Yesu.* Seoul: Shingu Munhwasa, 1967, 399p.

Page, Kirby. *The Personality of Jesus; Pathways by Which He Climbed the Heights of Life.* New York: Association Press, 1932, 176p.

Palgrave, Francis Turner. *Life of Our Lord and Saviour Jesus Christ.* London: 1885.

Pallascio-Morin, Ernest. *The Immortal Profile.* Trans. Ella-Marie Cooper. Chicago: Franciscan Herald Press, 1957, 166p.

────. *Jésus passait.* Ottawa; Montréal: Les Éditions du Lévrier, 1944, 239p.

Palmer, John. *Bethlehem to Olivet. A Course of Lessons on the Life of Jesus Christ.* London: 1880, 440p., (1883).

Paone, Anthony J. *My Life with Christ.* Garden City, N.Y.: Doubleday, 1962, 310p.

Papini, Giovanni. *Histoire du Christ.* Trans. Paul-Henri Michel. Paris: Payot, 1923, 454p.

────. *Lebensgeschichte Christi.* Trans. Max Schwarz. München: Allgemeine Verlagsanstalt, 1924, 519p.

────. *Life of Christ.* Trans. Dorothy Canfield Fisher. New York: Harcourt, Brace, and Co., 1923, 416p., (1915), (1925), (1927).

────. *Storia di Cristo.* Firenze: Vallechi, 1921, 632p., (1922), (1925), (1932), (1933), (1941), (1943), (1944), (1950), (1953), (1957), (1970), 519p.

────. *The Story of Christ.* 15th ed. Trans. Mary Prichard Agnetti. London: Hodder and Stoughton, 1924, 453p.

────. *Zivot Krista.* 4 vyd. Trans. Mikuláš Pažítka. Bratislava: Tatran, 1969, 363p.

Paradise, Frank Ilsley. *Jesus Christ and the Spirit of Youth.* London: Mills and Boon, 1923, 235p.

Parker, Joseph. *The Inner Life of Christ, as Revealed in the Gospel of Matthew.* New York: Funk and Wagnalls, 1883.

Parmly, Eleazar. *The Babe of Bethlehem, from the Cradle to the Cross, from His Conception on Earth to His Coronation in Heaven.* New York: Thomas Holman, 1861, 328p.

Pascal, Blaise. *Jésus: Abrégé de la vie de Jésus-Christ.* G. Michaut, ed. Paris: Payot, 1942, 126p.

────. *Short Life of Christ.* Trans. Emile Caillet and John C. Blankenagel. Princeton, N.J.: Princeton Theological Seminary, 1950, 39p.

Patterson, Alexander. *The Greater Life and Work of Christ.*
New York: Revell, 1896, 408p.; New York: Christian Alliance
Pub. Co., 1898?, 418p.

Patton, William. *Jesus of Nazareth? Who Was He? and What Is
He Now?* New York: R. Carter and Brothers, 1879, 320p.

Paul, Leslie Allen. *Son of Man: The Life of Christ.* London:
Hodder and Stoughton, 1961, 287p.; New York: Dutton, 1961,
287p.

Paulus, Heinrich Eberhard Gottlob. *Das Leben Jesu als Grundlage einer reinen Geschichte des Urchristentums.* 2 vols.
Heidelberg: Winter, 1828.

Pauwels, W. *Jezus Christus in de evangeliën.* Antwerpen:
Standaard, 1967, 208p.

Pax, Wolfgang E. *In the Footsteps of Jesus.* New York: Putnam,
1970, 231p.; London: Weidenfeld and Nicolson, 1970, 231p.

————. *Sur les chemins de Jésus.* Paris: Arthaud, 1971,
225p.

Paynter, Henry Martyn. *The Holy Life.* 5 vols. Chicago:
H.M. Paynter, Jr., 1886-90.

Peale, Norman Vincent. *Jesus of Nazareth; a Dramatic Interpretation of His Life from Bethlehem to Calvary.* Englewood
Cliffs, N.J.: Prentice-Hall, 1966, unpaged.

————. *The Story of Jesus.* Norwalk, Conn.: C.R. Gibson,
1976, 88p.

Pearson, Charles William. *The Carpenter Prophet; a Life of
Jesus Christ and a Discussion of His Ideals.* Chicago; New
York: H.S. Stone and Co., 1902, 288p.

Pearson, Victor Rosenius. *Life and Teachings of Christ.*
Rock Island, Ill.: Augustana Book Concern, 1940, 216p.

Pentecost, George Frederick. *Bible Studies: No. 1, The Pentateuch; No. 2, The Life of Christ.* London: 1893, 416p.;
New York: Revell, 1893, 416p.

Pentecost, J. Dwight. *The Words and Works of Jesus Christ:
A Study of the Life of Christ.* Grand Rapids: Zondervan,
1981, 629p.

Perfitt, Philip William. *The Life and Teachings of Jesus of
Nazareth.* London: G. Mainwaring, 1861, 457p.

Peters, Gershom Moore. *The Master; or, The Story of Stories
Retold.* New York; Chicago: Revell, 1911, 506p.

Peterson, Edward C., and Barbara Nan Peterson. *To Find Jesus.*
Nashville: Abingdon Press, 1967, 112p.

Petit, Joseph. *Ici Jérusalem, les Évangiles vus par des reporters.* Charenton-le-Pont: L'auteur, 1968, 136p.

Petrelli, Giuseppe. *The Redeemer.* Trenton, N.J.: Merlo, 1948, 364p.

————. *The Son of Man.* Trenton, N.J.: Merlo, 1943, 397p.

Pettis, Olive G. *The Historical Life of Jesus of Nazareth and Extracts from the Apostolic Age.* Providence, R.I.: A.C. Greene, 1870, 142p., (1871).

Peyrat, Alphonse. *Histoire élémentaire et critique de Jésus.* 2. ed. Paris: Michel Lévy frères, 1864, 351p.

Phillips, Samuel. *The History of Our Lord and Savior Jesus Christ.* Boston: Printed by S. Kneeland and T. Green for D. Henchman, 1738.

Phillips, Wendell. *An Explorer's Life of Jesus.* New York: Two Continents Pub. Group, 1975, 652p.

Phipps, William E. *The Sexuality of Jesus: Theological and Literary Perspectives.* New York: Harper and Row, 1973, 172p.

Picard, Raymundus. *De blijde boodschap, een levensweg naar het geluk.* Antwerpen: Uitgeverij 't Groeit, 1944, 94p.

Pictures from the Life of Jesus. London: 1886.

Pictures in Palestine; the Story of Jesus. New York: Fords, Howard, and Holbert, 1887?

Picucci, Giovanni. *Gesù.* Alba; Roma; Catania: Pia Società San Paolo, 1942, 373p., (1940).

Piepenbring, Charles. *The Historical Jesus.* Trans. Lilian A. Clare. London: G. Allen and Unwin; New York: Macmillan, 1924, 224p.

Pierce, William Dwight. *Jesus, Interpreter of the Eternal.* New York: Pageant Press, 1957, 565p.

Pierri, Cataldo. *Da Gesù a Gesù.* Taranto: 1961- .

Pike, John Baxter. *The Life of Christ.* London; Derby, 1844.

Pinart, Désiré. *Meditations on the Suffering Life on Earth of Our Lord and Only Saviour.* Trans. Lady E. Law; Arthur Penrose Forbes, ed. London: 1850; London: J. Masters and Son, 1853, (1875), 302p.

Piñeros Corpas, Joaquin. *Version elemental de la vida de Cristo.* Bogotá: Librería letras, n.d.

————. *Vida de Cristo.* Buenos Aires: F.A. Colombo, 1949, 109p.

Pithan, Athalicio. *O divino Mestre; narrativa singela da vida terrena de Jesús Cristo.* Pôrto Alegre: Livraria do globo, 1942, 181p.

Pittenger, William Norman. *The Life of Jesus Christ.* New York: F. Watts, 1968, 115p.

Plantier, Claude Henri Augustin. *La vraie vie de Jésus.* 2. éd. Paris: L. Giraud, 1864, 304p.

Poizat, Alfred. *La vie et l'œuvre de Jésus.* Paris: A. Michel, 1930, 397p.

Polack, Albert Isaac, and William Wynn Wimpson. *Jesus in the Background of History.* New York: R.M. McBride Co., 1959, 160p.; London: Cohen and West, 1957, 160p.

Poling, Daniel Alfred. *Between Two Worlds, the Romance of Jesus.* New York; London: Harper and Brothers, 1931, 229p.; *He Came from Galilee.* New York: Harper and Row, 1965, 246p.; *The Romance of Jesus.* New York; London: Harper and Brothers, 1939, 229p.; New York: Association Press, 1953, 236p.

Poortvliet, Rien. *Hij was een van ons.* 3e dr. Bussum: Heikema & Warendorf; Apeldoorn: Semper Agendo, 1976, 131p.

Potrel, Eugene. *Vie de N.S. Jésus-Christ.* Paris: Martin Beaupré frères, 1863, 193p.

Pott, William Hawks. *Lessons on the Life of the King.* 2nd ed. New York: J. Pott and Co., 1892.

Potter, Leo Goodwin. *My Bible Is Jesus.* St. Louis: Bethany Press, 1976, 128p.

Powell, John Walker. *The Silences of the Master.* Cincinnati: Jennings and Graham; New York: Eaton and Mains, 1904, 62p.

Practical Meditations for Every Day in the Year on the Life of Jesus Christ. By a father of the Society of Jesus. Trans. from the French. London: 1868; London: Burns, Oates, and Washbourne, 1950, 2 vols.

Prat, Ferdinand. *Jesus Christ; His Life, His Teaching, and His Work.* 2 vols. Trans. John J. Heenan. Milwaukee: Bruce, 1950.

————. *Jésus Christ, sa vie, sa doctrine, son œuvre.* 2 vols. Paris: G. Beauchesne et ses fils, 1933.

Pratapachandra, Majumdar. *The Oriental Christ.* New York: 1883.

Pressensé, Edmond Déhault de. *Desires after Jesus; or, Meditations on the Life and Passion of Our Blessed Saviour Jesus Christ.* London: 1698.

————. *Jesus Christ: His Times, Life, and Work.* Trans. Annie Harwood. London: Jackson, Walford, and Hodder, 1866, 560p., (1868), (1869), (1871), (1872), (1879); New York: Scribner, Welford, and Co., 1868, 496p.; New York: Carlton and Lanhan, 1871, 320p.; New York: 1879, 560p.

————. *Jésus Christ, son temps, sa vie, son œuvre.* Paris: Charles Meyrueis, 1866, 684p., (1865); Paris: Sandoz et Fischbacher, 1873, (1881), (1884), 694p.

————. *Jesus Christus. Seine Zeit, sein Leben, und sein Werk.* Trans. Eduard Fabarius. Halle: Buchhandlung des Waisenhauses, 1866, 503p.

————. *Jezus Christus, zijn tijd, leven en werk.* Trans. F.J.P. Moquette. Utrecht: Kemink en Zoon, 1869, 523p.

Preston, South G. *The Shadow of the King.* 2nd ed. New York; London: Abbey Press, 1901, 253p.

Price, James F. *Tabular Life of Christ.* Nashville: Cumberland Presbyterian Pub. House, 1900, 16p.

The Prince of Life; the Story of Christ for Young People. New York: Morehouse-Gorham, 1955, 240p.

Protestant Episcopal Church in the U.S.A. National Council. Dept. of Christian Education. *How to Teach the Life of Christ.* Milwaukee: Morehouse Pub. Co., 1920, 117p.

Protestant Episcopal Church in the U.S.A. New York (Diocese) Sunday School Commission. *The Life of Jesus Christ the Messiah.* 2nd ed. Milwaukee: 1905.

————. *Teachers' Notes on the Life of Jesus Christ Our Lord.* 2 vols. Milwaukee: 1904-05.

————. *Teachers' Notes on the Life of Jesus Christ the Messiah.* 2nd ed. Milwaukee: 1905.

Proudhon, Pierre Joseph. *Jésus et les origines du christianisme.* Paris: G. Havard fils, 1896, 323p.

————. *Portrait de Jésus.* Paris: P. Horay, 1951, 245p.

The Public Life of Christ (Filmstrip). J.S. van den Nieuwendijk, Zeist, Netherlands. Released in the U.S. by Encyclopedia Britannica Films, 1958, 25 fr.

Puiseux, J. *Life of Our Lord and Saviour Jesus Christ.* Trans. Roderick A. Eachen. New York; Akron, Ohio: D.H. McBride and Co., 1900, 195p.

Purinton, Carl Everett. *The Re-interpretation of Jesus in the New Testament.* New York; London: C. Scribner's Sons, 1932, 217p.

Purinton, Herbert Ronelle. *The Achievement of the Master*.
New York: C. Scribner's Sons, 1926, 206p.

Putney, Max C. *The Man of Galilee; a New Life of Jesus*.
New York: Exposition Press, 1955, 274p.

Putsykovich, F.F. *Zhizn' Gospoda nashego Iisusa Khrista*.
St. Petersburg: P.B. Lukovnikov Bookstore, 1896, 176p.

Quayle, William Alfred. *Out-of-doors with Jesus*. New York;
Cincinnati: Abingdon Press, 1924, 223p.

Quénard, Gervais. *L'évangile du royaume de Dieu*. Paris:
Maison de la Bonne Presse, 1935, 419p.

Quimby, Chester Warren. *Jesus as They Remembered Him*. New
York; Nashville: Abingdon-Cokesbury Press, 1941, 220p.

Rall, Harris Franklin. *The Life of Jesus*. New York; Cincinnati: Abingdon Press, 1917, 214p.

————. *Teacher's Manual for The Life of Jesus*. New York;
Cincinnati: Abingdon Press, 1918, 79p.

Ramsey, Joyce Sikes. *Ye Are My Friends; a Simple Study of
the Life and Teachings of Jesus*. Jacksonville?, Fla.:
1956, 329p.

Randolph, Thomas. *A View of Our Blessed Saviour's Ministry
and the Proofs of His Divine Mission Arising from Thence*.
2 vols. Oxford: J. and J. Fletcher; London: Mess. Rivington,
1784.

Rankin, John Chambers. *A Believer's Life of Christ*. Natick,
Mass.: W.A. Wilde Co., 1960, 210p.

Rauschenbusch, Walter. *Das Leben Jesu*. Cleveland: P. Ritter,
1895, 180p.

Raven, Charles Earle. *The Life and Teaching of Jesus Christ*.
Cambridge, Eng.: University Press, 1933, 263p.

Reading, William. *The History of Our Lord and Saviour Jesus
Christ*. London: Printed for J. Osborn, 1737, 584p., (1716),
(1726), (1850), (1875).

Reatz, August. *Jesus Christ: His Life, His Teaching, His
Work*. Trans. Mary Sands. London: Sands and Co.; St. Louis:
B. Herder Book Co., 1933, 374p.

————. *Jesus Christus. Sein Leben, sein Lehre, und sein
Werk*. Freiburg i Br.: Herder and Co., 1925, 395p.

Rebello da Silva, Luiz Augusto. *Fastos da Egreja. Vida de
Jesus Christo*. 4 vols. Lisboa: Empreza da Historia de
Portugal, 1907.

La regeneration; ó, El cristianismo en todas las edades. 1853?,
    183p.

Rehnborg, C.F. *Jesus and the New Age of Faith.* Corona del
    Mar?, Calif.: 1955, 573p.

Renan, Ernest. *Das Leben Jesu.* Trans. Alexander Patuzzi.
    Wien: A.A. Wenedikt, 1864, 214p.; New York: F. Gerhard, 1864,
    240p.

————. *The Life of Jesus.* London; New York: Brentano's,
    1863?, 311p.; New York; Carleton; Paris: Michel Lévy frères,
    1864, (1873), (1875), 376p., trans. Charles Edwin Wilbour;
    Boston: Roberts, 1896, 481p.; Boston: Little, Brown, and
    Co., 1899, (1924), 481p.; New York: A.L. Burt Co., 1902,
    393p.; New York: H.W. Bell, 1904, 452p.; New York: The Modern
    Library, 1927, 393p.; Cleveland; New York: World Pub. Co.,
    1941, 211p.; London: Trübner and Co., 1864, 311p., (1865),
    (1893); London: Temple Co., 1887, 192p. (abridged ed.);
    London: Watts and Co., 1904, 154p., (1935), 231p., (1947);
    London; Toronto: J.M. Dent and Sons, 1927, 244p.

————. *Renan's Life of Jesus.* Trans. W.G. Hutchison. 1897,
    289p.

————. *Vida de Jesús.* Trans. F. de la Vega. Bogotá: 1865;
    Madrid: 1869, 301p.

————. *Vie de Jésus.* Berlin: R. Schlingmann, 1864, 407p.;
    Paris: Michel Lévy frères, 1863, 462p., (1864), (1870); Paris:
    Calmann-Lévy, 1928, 559p.; Paris: 1873, (1879), (1916);
    Paris: Aubry, 1945, 375p.; Paris: Gallimard, 1974, 542p.

————. *Zhizn' Iisusa.* St. Petersburg: P. Th. Panteleev,
    1906, 199p.

Renaudière de Paulis, Domingo. *La palabra de Dios; meditaciones
    sobre el Evangelio.* Buenos Aires: 1959, 61p.

Renton, William. *Jesus.* Keswick: W. Renton, 1879, 310p.,
    (1880), 319p.

Retreat and Decision (Motion picture). Cathedral Films, 1957,
    30 min.

Reumann, John Henry Paul. *Jesus in the Church's Gospels.*
    Philadelphia: Fortress Press, 1968, 539p.

Réville, Albert. *Jesus de Nazareth.* 2 vols. Paris: Risch-
    bacher, 1897, (1906).

Rhees, Rush. *The Life of Jesus of Nazareth.* New York: C.
    Scribner's Sons, 1913, 320p., (1900), (1904), (1906), (1908),
    (1910), (1915), (1919), (1926), (1928).

Ricciotti, Giuseppe. *Life of Christ.* Trans. Alba I. Zizzamia.
Milwaukee: Bruce Pub. Co., 1952, 402p., (1957), 703p.

————. *Vita di Gesù Cristo.* Milano; Roma: Rizzoli & c.,
1942, 806p., (1941), 790p., (1946), (1948).

Richter, Josef. *Was haben wir noch von dem biblischen Jesus?*
München: Verlag Uni-Druck, 1976, 246p.

Riggenbach, Christoph Johannes. *Vorlesungen über das Leben
des Herrn Jesu.* Basel: Bahnmaier's Buchhandlung (C. Det-
loff), 1858, 724p.

Riggs, Frederick B. *Life of Christ, an Outline; Jesus Taanpetu.*
Santee Agency, Neb.: Santee Normal Training School Press,
1891, 47p.

Rihbany, Abraham Mitrie. *The Syrian Christ.* Boston; New
York: Houghton Mifflin Co., 1916, 425p.

Rimmer, Harry. *From Cana to Calvary.* Grand Rapids: Eerdmans,
1940, 136p.

Rix, Herbert. *Rabbi, Messiah, Martyr; a Modern Picture of
the Story of Jesus.* London: P. Green, 1907, 80p.

Rix, Wilton. *Jesus, Lover of Men.* New York: George H.
Doran Co., 1924, 151p.

Robbins, Ray F. *The Life and Ministry of Our Lord.* Nashville:
Convention Press, 1970, 211p.

Roberts, Richard. *The Ascending Life.* New York: Womans Press,
1924, 79p.

Robertson, Archibald Thomas. *Epochs in the Life of Jesus.*
New York: C. Scribner's Sons, 1907, 192p.; Nashville: Broadman Press, 1974, 192p.

Robinson, Alexander. *A Study of the Saviour in the Newer
Light.* London: Williams and Norgate, 1898, 404p., (1895).

Robinson, Emma Amelia. *Short Studies of Christ the Ideal
Hero.* New York: Eaton and Mains; Cincinnati: Jennings and
Graham, 1909, 153p.

Robinson, Harold McAfee. *The Kingdom of God Is at Hand; the
Life of Jesus in the Four Gospels.* Philadelphia; Chicago:
Westminster Press, 1937, 92p.

Robinson, Jennie May. *"The Comforter."* Toledo, Ohio: Press
of the B.F. Wade and Sons Co., 1928, 83p.

Robinson, L.L. *Questions on the Life of Christ.* Milwaukee:
Young Churchman Co., 1897, 142p.

————. *The Story of Jesus of Nazareth*. Milwaukee: Young Churchman Co., 1895, 270p.

Rockwell, Katharine Lambert (Richards). *Early Portraits of Jesus*. New York: Womans Press, 1937, 54p.

Rogers, Arthur Kenyon. *The Life and Teachings of Jesus*. New York; London: G.P. Putnam's Sons, 1894, 354p.

Rogers, George Albert. *Footprints of Jesus*. London: 1856, (1857), (1859), (1863).

Rogers, James Guinnes. *The Life of Christ*. London: 1849.

Rollins, Wallace Eugene. *Jesus and His Ministry*. Greenwich, Conn.: Seabury Press, 1954, 299p.

Rolt, Mary F. *A Baby's Life of Jesus Christ*. New York: Macmillan, 1924, 153p.

Roos, Magnus Friedrich. *Die Lehre und Lebensgeschichte Jesu Christi des Sohns Gottes nach den vier Evangelisten*. 2 vols. Tübingen: Ludwig Friedrich Fues, 1776-77, (1848).

Roper, Harold. *Jesus in His Own Words*. Westminster, Md.: Newman Press, 1951, 314p.

Roscamp, Robert G. *The Life of Jesus Christ*. New York; London: Abbey Press, 1902, 255p.

Ross, Alexander Wendell. *The Christ*. New York: Revell, 1938, 222p.

Ross, Pearl. *Jesus the Pagan*. New York: Philosophical Library, 1972, 73p.

Rossi, Giovanni. *Gesù*. 8. ed. Assisi: Cittadella, 1970, 202p.; Spoleto: Tip. Panetto e Petrelli, 1949, 298p., (1954).

Row, Charles Adolphus. *The Jesus of the Evangelists*. London: Williams and Norgate, 1868, 340p., (1880), (1883); New York: 1884.

Rozmyślanie o żywocie Pana Jezusa. Stefan Vrtel-Wierczynski, ed. Warszawa: Nak. Tow. Naukowego Warszawskiego, 1952, 852p.

Rubio Barrera, Diego. *Jesucristo, el gran desconocido*. Barcelona: ATE, 1978, 302p.

Rufle, Frederick Charles. *Immanuel; the Story of the Living Christ, the Lord of the Church*. Boston: Christopher Pub. House, 1954, 192p.

Russell, Josiah Cox. *Jesus of Nazareth*. New York: Pageant Press, 1967, 130p.

Russell, Ward. *The Pentecost Edition of the Man of Galilee.* Lexington, Ky.: Press of Truth Pub. Co., 1928, 186p.

Russell, William Henry. *Christ, the Leader.* Milwaukee: Bruce Pub. Co., 1937, 458p.

Rustomjee, Framroz. *An Interpretation of the Life of Jesus Christ.* Colombo: Rustomjee, 1976, 171p.

Rye, Amy Haslam. *The Beloved Son. A Life of Christ.* New York: Dodd, Mead, and Co., 1901, 145p.

————. *The Beloved Son. The Story of Jesus Christ Told to Children.* London: W. Heinemann, 1900, 121p.

Sackman, Lana. *Behold the Man; a Revelation of Christ the Master.* New York: Grafton Press, 1928, 240p.

Sacred Scenes; or, Passages in the Life of Our Saviour. New York: D. Appleton and Co.,; Philadelphia: G.S. Appleton, 1851, 283p.; London: n.d.

Sadler, John. *Sacred Records of the History of Jesus Christ.* London: 1836.

Saklatvala, Beram. *The Rebel King.* Edinburgh: Albyn Press, 1975, 222p.; New York: Coward, McCann, and Geohegan, 1975, 222p.

Salgado, Plinio. *Vida de Jesus.* 2. ed. Lisboa: Editorial Atica, 1944, 667p.

Salhab, Naṣrī. *Fī khuṭā al-Masīh.* Beirut: Catholic Printing House, 1968- .

Sallaway, George H. *Follow Me: Be Human.* Baltimore: Helicon, 1966, 174p.

Sallmon, William Henry. *Studies in the Life of Jesus for Bible Classes and Private Use.* New York: International Committee of Young Men's Christian Associations, 1903, 152p.

Salmond, Stewart Dingwall Fordyce. *The Life of Christ.* London: 1888, 100p.

Salstrand, George A.E. *What Jesus Began: The Life and Ministry of Christ.* Nashville: Broadman Press, 1976, 180p.

Salvador, Joseph. *Jésus-Christ et sa doctrine.* 2 vols. Bruxelles: Hauman et compagnie, 1838.

Salvagniac, Therese. *Jésus de Nazareth, roi des Juifs.* Paris: P. Lethielleux, 1935, 532p.

Sanday, William. *The Life of Christ in Research.* New York: Oxford University Press, 1907, 328p.

—————. *Outlines of the Life of Christ.* New York: C. Scribner's Sons, 1908, 273p., (1905), 241p., (1912), (1919); Edinburgh: T. and T. Clark, 1905, (1906), (1930).

Sanders, Frank Knight. *Historical Notes on the Life of Christ.* Boston: Bible Study Pub. Co., 1907, 202p.

—————. *The Student's Life of Christ.* Boston: Bible Study Pub. Co., 1906, 202p.

Sangster, Francis. *The Life of Our Lord.* London: E. Stock, 1881, 52p.

Santos, Miguel. *Jesus Cristo, o verdadeiro mestre da humanidade.* Rio de Janeiro: Cia. Ed. Americana, 1968, 71p.

Santucci, Luigi, and Angelo Romanò. *Chi è Costui che viene?* Milano: Mondadori, 1953, 324p.

—————. *Meeting Jesus; a New Way to Christ.* Trans. Bernard Wall. New York: Herder and Herder, 1971, 222p.

—————. *Volete andarvene anche voi? Una vita di Cristo.* Milano: A. Mondadori, 1970, 308p.; *Wrestling with Christ.* Trans. Bernard Wall. London: Collins, 1972, 222p.

Saponaro, Michele. *Gesù.* Milano: Mondadori, 1953, 331p., (1950), (1949).

Saunders, Ernest W. *Jesus in the Gospels.* Englewood Cliffs, N.J.: Prentice-Hall, 1967, 324p.

Saunderson, Henry Hallam. *His Word Was with Power.* Boston: Beacon Press, 1952, 248p.

Savage, Minot Judson. *Out of Nazareth.* Boston: American Unitarian Association, 1903, 378p.

Saville, Malcolm. *King of Kings.* Tring: Lion Publishing, 1978, 168p.; London: Nelson, 1958, 264p.

Sawyer, Elbert Henry. *Biography of Jesus.* Philadelphia; Chicago: John C. Winston Co., 1927, 188p.

Schaper, Edzard Hellmuth. *Das Leben Jesu.* Leipzig: Inselverlag, 1936, 414p.

Schell, Herman. *Das Evangelium und seine weltgeschichtliche Bedeutung.* Mainz: F. Kirchheim, 1903, 156p.

Schenkel, Daniel. *The Character of Jesus.* 2 vols. Trans. W.H. Furness. Boston: Little, Brown, and Co., 1866.

—————. *Das Charakterbild Jesu.* Wiesbaden: 1864, 405p.; Wiesbaden: Kreidel's Verlag, 1873, 433p.

Schleiermacher, Friedrich Ernst Daniel. *Das Leben Jesu.* Berlin: Georg Reimer, 1864, 511p.

————. The Life of Jesus. Trans. S. Maclean Gilmour; Jack C. Verheyden, ed. Philadelphia: Fortress Press, 1975, 481p.

Schlesinger, Hugo. Jesus era judeu. São Paulo: Edições Paulinas, 1979, 290p.

Schmidt, Nathaniel. The Prophet of Nazareth. New York; London: Macmillan, 1905, 422p.

Schmidt, Paul Wilhelm. Die Geschichte Jesu. Freiburg i. Br.: Tübingen: J.C.B. Mohr, 1899, 179p., (1900), (1904), 2 vols.

Schonfield, Hugh Joseph. Jesus, a Biography. London: Duckworth, 1939, 275p.

————. The Passover Plot. London: Hutchinson, 1965, 287p.; New York: B. Geis Associates, 1966, (1965), 287p.

Schuré, Édouard. Jesus, the Last Great Initiate. Trans. F. Rothwell. Chicago: Yogi Pub. Society, 1908?, 125p.

Schweitzer, Albert. Das Messianitäts und Leidensgeheimnis. Eine Skizze des Lebens Jesu. 3. Aufl. Tübingen: Mohr (Siebeck), 1956, 109p.

————. The Mystery of the Kingdom of God. Trans. Walter Lowrie. New York: Dodd, Mead, and Co., 1914, 275p.; New York: Macmillan, 1950, 174p.; New York: Schocken Books, 1964, 275p.

Scott, Ernest Findlay. The Crisis in the Life of Jesus. New York: Scribner, 1952, 152p.

Scott, Loa Ermina. The Life of Jesus. Chicago: New Christian Century Co., 1910, 120p.

Scott, Thomas. The English Life of Jesus. London: T. Scott, 1872, 349p.; London: Trübner and Co., 1880, 349p.

Scroggie, William Graham. Christ, the Key to Scripture. Philadelphia: Sunday School Times Co., 1924, 56p.

Scrymgeur, William. Lessons on the Life of Christ. Edinburgh: T. and T. Clark, 1883, 382p.

Sears, Edmund Hamilton. The Fourth Gospel, the Heart of Christ. 2nd ed. Boston: Noyes, Holmes, and Co., 1872, 551p., (1873), (1874), (1877), (1879), (1884), (1890), (1908).

Séché, Alphonse. Histoire merveilleuse de Jésus. Paris: A. Fayard & cie, 1926, 397p.

————. The Radiant Story of Jesus. Trans. Helen Davenport Gibbons. New York; London: Century Co., 1927, 381p.

Seeley, John Robert. *Ecce Homo; eine Darstellung von Jesu Christi Leben und Werk.* Erlangen: E. Besold, 1867, 348p.

————. *Ecce Homo; a Survey of the Life and Work of Jesus Christ.* London: Macmillan, 1866, 330p., (1868), (1874), (1876), (1888), (1895), (1908); London: J.M. Dent, 1907, (1920), (1929), (1932); Boston: Roberts Brothers, 1866, 355p., (1867), (1868), (1870), (1871), (1872), (1873), (1875), (1880), (1881), (1886), (1890), (1893); Boston: Little, Brown, 1898, 355p., (1903).

————. *Ecce homo; un esame della vita e dell' opera di Gesù Cristo.* Trans. Guglielmo Salvadori. Milano: Fratelli Bocca, n.d., 386p.

Segur, Louis Gaston Adrien de. *Jésus-Christ.* 12 ed. Paris: Tolra et Haton, 1864, 207p.

Selby, Thomas G. *The Ministry of the Lord Jesus.* London: C. Kelly, 1896, 322p.

Sell, Henry Thorne. *Bible Studies in the Life of Christ.* New York; Chicago: Revell, 1935, 160p., (1902).

Sengupta, Achintyakumar. *Amrta purusha Yīśu.* Calcutta: Sāhitya Sadana, 1974, 347p.

Senior, Donald. *God the Son.* Allen, Tex.: Argus Communications, 1981, 95p.

Sensenig, Barton. *How Jesus Showed God to the People.* Philadelphia: B. Sensenig, 1930, 222p.

Sepp, Johann Nepomuk. *Das Leben Christi.* 7 vols. Regensburg: G. Joseph Manz, 1843-46, (1853-62), 6 vols.

Seymour, Peter S., comp. *Portrait of Jesus; the Life of Christ in Poetry and Prose.* Kansas City, Mo.: Hallmark Crown Editions, 1973, 70p.

Shackleford, John D. *The Life of Jesus of Nazareth, Being an Analysis of the Biographies of Jesus, from a Lawyer's Viewpoint.* Little Rock, Ark.: 1928, 232p.

Shaffer, Charles Thomas. *The Life of Jesus Christ.* Seattle, Wash.: 1935- .

Sharman, Henry Burton. *Jesus in the Records.* New York: Association Press, 1918, 235p.

————. *Studies in the Life of Christ.* 4 vols. New York: International Committee of Young Men's Christian Associations, 1896; New York: Association Press, 1925, 222p.

————. *Studies in the Records of the Life of Jesus.* New York; London: Harper and Brothers, 1938, 155p.

Sharp, Dallas Lore. *Christ and His Time*. New York; Cincinnati: Abingdon Press, 1933, 256p.

Shaw, Elton Raymond. *The Man of Galilee*. Grand Rapids: Shaw Pub. Co., 1912, 159p.

Shearer, James William. *The Pictured Outline of the Gospel Narrative*. St. Louis, 1900, 112p.

Sheed, Francis Joseph. *The Book of the Saviour*. New York: Sheed and Ward, 1952, 420p.

————. *To Know Christ Jesus*. New York: Sheed and Ward, 1962, 377p.

Sheen, Fulton John. *The Eternal Galilean*. Garden City, N.Y.: Garden City Pub. Co., 1950, (1934), 280p.; London: D. Appleton-Century Co., 1934, 280p.

————. *The Life of Christ*. New York: Maco Magazine Corp., 1954, 126p.; New York: McGraw-Hill, 1958, 559p.; Garden City, N.Y.: Image Books, 1977, 576p.

Sheets, Herchel H. *Enemy Versions of the Gospel*. Nashville: Upper Room, 1973, 72p.

Shepard, John Watson. *The Christ of the Gospels*. Nashville: Parthenon Press, 1939, 635p.; Grand Rapids: Eerdmans, 1946, 650p.

Shilton, Lance Rupert. *Speaking from the Holy Land*. London: Oliphants, 1970, 126p.

Shunūdah, Zakī. *al-Masīh*. Matba'at Dār al-'Ālam al-'Arabī: 1975?- .

Sibbald, James. *Record of the Public Ministry of Jesus Christ*. London: 1798.

Sinclair, Upton Beall. *A Personal Jesus; Portrait and Interpretation*. New York: Evans Pub. Co., 1952, 228p.; London: Allen and Unwin, 1954, 217p.

Six, Jean François. *Jésus*. Paris: Somogy, 1972, 286p.

Skene, William Forbes. *The Gospel History; Being Lectures on the Life of Christ*. Edinburgh: 1892, 380p.

————. *The Gospel History for the Young; Being Lessons on the Life of Christ*. 3 vols. Edinburgh: D. Douglas, 1883, (1892), 401p.

Skinner, Conrad Arthur. *The Gospel of the Lord Jesus*. London: University of London Press; Hodder and Stoughton, 1937, 316p.; New York; Cincinnati: Abingdon Press, 1937, 279p.

Skoglund, John E. *Come and See.* Philadelphia: Judson Press, 1956, 96p.

Skvortsov, K. *Zhizn' Iisusa Khrista, po Evangeliiam i narodnym predaniiam.* Kiev: S.V. Kul'zhenko, 1876, 334p.

Slack, Elvira J. *Jesus, the Man of Galilee.* New York: National Board of the Young Women's Christian Association of the United States of America, 1912, 211p., (1911), 217p.

Sloyan, Gerard Stephen. *Christ the Lord.* New York: Herder and Herder, 1962, 238p.

Smeets, René. *Jesus im Bild.* München: Pfeiffer, 1975, 104p.

Smith, Mrs. C.B. *In the Early Days.* New York; Chicago: Broadway Pub. Co., 1910, 330p.

Smith, David. *The Days of His Flesh.* 2nd ed. London: Hodder and Stoughton, 1905, 549p., (1907), (1909), (1910), (1911), (1914), (1928); New York: Doran, 1910; New York: Harper, (1910), (194-?); New York: Armstrong, 1905, 549p., (1906); New York: Richard R. Smith, 1930.

————. *Our Lord's Earthly Life.* New York: George H. Doran Co., 1926, 500p.

Smith, Edward. *Life and Sayings of the Lord Jesus Christ.* London: 1708.

Smith, Edward. *The Life and Sufferings of the Lord Jesus Christ.* London: S.A. Oddy, 1815, 386p.; Dublin: Printed by William Pickering and Son, 1821, 665p.

Smith, Haskett. *The Divine Epiphany, in Ten Progressive Scenes.* London: Christian Knowledge Society, 1878.

Smith, J. Carryl. *Life of Christ: Following the Epistles and Gospels in the Book of Common Prayer.* New York: 1905, 216p.

Smith, Joseph Oswald. *Simple Meditations on the Life of Our Lord.* 3 vols. London: Catholic Truth Society, 1902, (1903), (1905), (1906), (1933).

Smith, Roy Lemon. *Toward an Understanding of the Carpenter's Son.* Nashville: Tidings, 1960, 80p.

Smith, William. *The History of the Holy Jesus.* London: 1708; London: Eben. Tracy, 1709, 191p., 6th ed., (1715), 10th ed., (1717).

Smyth, John Paterson. *A People's Life of Christ.* New York; Chicago: Revell, 1920, 505p.; London: Hodder and Stoughton, 1929, 429p.

Smyth, Julian Kennedy. *Footprints of the Saviour; Devotional Studies of the Life and Nature of Our Lord*. Boston: Roberts Brothers, 1886, 231p.; Minneapolis: Nunc Licet Press, 1907, 231p.

Snead, Littleton Upshur. *Life of Jesus, and Ministry of the Holy Ghost*. Ellisburg, Pa.: L.U. Snead and Sons, 1897, 31p.

Snowden, James Henry. *Jesus as Judged by His Enemies*. New York; Cincinnati: Abingdon Press, 1922, 246p.

———. *Scenes and Sayings in the Life of Christ*. New York; Chicago: Revell, 1903, 371p.; London: 1904.

———. *Snowden's Nine Months Course in the Life of Christ*. New York: Macmillan, 1924, 378p.

Snyder, Russell Dewey. *Jesus: His Mission and Teachings*. Philadelphia: Muhlenberg Press, 1959, 142p.

Soltau, George. *Four Portraits of the Lord Jesus Christ*. New York: C.C. Cook, 1905, 265p.

Soubigou, Louis. *Pages d'Évangile pour notre temps*. Paris: Desclée, de Brouwer & cie, 1935, 194p.

Southgate, Henry. *Christus Redemptor; Being the Life, Character, and Teachings of Our Blessed Lord Jesus Christ*. London: Southey, 1874, 312p.

Sparrow, Walter Shaw. *The Gospels in Art; the Life of Christ by Great Painters from Fra Angelico to Holman Hunt*. London: Hodder and Stoughton, 1904, 282p.

Speer, Robert Elliott. *Studies of the Man Christ Jesus*. New York; Chicago: Revell, 1896, 249p.

Sperow, Everett Hollingsworth. *The Silent Nazarene*. Boston: Gorham Press, 1917, 300p.

Spezzafumo de Faucamberge, Suzanne. *Un homme est né*. Paris: A. Michel, 1927, 252p.

Spiegel van den leven ons Heren. Doornspijk: Davaco, 1979, 129p.

Spong, John Shelby. *The Hebrew Lord*. New York: Seabury Press, 1974, 190p.

Stackhouse, Thomas. *The History of Jesus Christ, with the Lives of His Apostles and Evangelists*. Manchester: J. Harrop, 1772, 501p.

———. *The Life of Our Lord and Saviour Jesus Christ, the Apostles, and the Evangelists*. London: 1754; Dublin: Printed for W. Whitestone, 1758, 541p.; Newry: D. Car...Ter, 1761,

397p.; Aberdeen: 1768, 413p.; Macclesfield: J. Wilson, 1808, 656p.; London: Printed by C. Sympson, 1765, 584p.

Stalker, James. *Bywyd Iesu Grist.* 1898, 172p.

————. *Fra Bethlehem til Golgotha, Jesu underfulde liv.* Trans. B. Hall Tilligemed. Philadelphia; Chicago: J.C. Winston and Co., 1893, 315p.

————. *Het leven van Jezus Christus.* Amsterdam; Kaapstad: 1895, 183p.

————. *Kristi og haus apostles underfulde liv.* 1897.

————. *Das Leben Jesu.* Freiburg i.B.; Leipzig: J.C.B. Mohr, 1895, 135p.

————. *The Life of Jesus Christ.* Edinburgh: T. and T. Clark, 1879, (1880), (1881), (1885), (1891), (1918?); Chicago: H.A. Sumner and Co., 1881, 166p., (1882); New York; Chicago: Revell, 1880, 2nd ed., 166p., (1891), (1896), (1897), (1909), (1949); New York: American Tract Society, 1880, 166p., (1891).

————. *The Life of Our Lord Jesus Christ.* Philadelphia: A.J. Holman and Co., 1888.

————. *Obulamu bwa Jesu Kristo.* Kampala: Uganda Bookshop, 1931, 187p.

Stapfer, Edmond Louis. *Jesus Christ during His Ministry.* Trans. Louise Seymour Houghton. New York: C. Scribner's Sons, 1897, 265p., (1900), (1906); London: Dickinson, 1897, 265p.

————. *Jésus-Christ pendant son ministère.* Paris: Librairie Fischbacher, 1896, (1897), 352p.

Stauffer, Ethelbert. *Jesus and His Story.* Trans. Richard and Clara Winston. New York: Knopf, 1960, 243p.; London: SCM Press, 1960, 192p.

————. *Jesus: Gestalt und Geschichte.* Bern: Francke, 1957, 172p.

Steeves, Paul D. *The Character and Work of Jesus Christ.* Chicago: Inter-Varsity Press, 1967, 105p.

Steinmann, Jean. *The Life of Jesus.* Trans. Peter Green. Boston: Little, Brown, 1963, 240p.

————. *La vie de Jésus.* Paris: Denoël, 1961, 280p.

Stephen, George. *The Life of Christ.* London: Hatchards, 1871, (1875), 330p.

Stephen, Thomas. *A Gospel History of Our Lord and Saviour Jesus Christ.* London: Dean and Son, 1853, 786p.

Sterck, Leo Clement. *For All to Live By*. Milwaukee: Bruce
Pub. Co., 1946, 234p.

Stevens, Clifford J. *A Life of Christ*. Huntington, Ind.:
Our Sunday Visitor, 1983, 106p.

Stevens, William Arnold. *An Outline Handbook of the Life of
Christ from the Four Gospels*. Boston: Bible Study Pub. Co.,
1892, 45p.; Boston: Silver, Burdett and Co., 1894, 45p.,
(1896), (1898); London: 1893.

Stevenson, Herbert F. *The Road to the Cross*. Westwood, N.J.:
Revell, 1962, 128p.

Stewart, Alexander. *The Life of Christ*. London: J.M. Dent
and Co., 1906, 124p.; Philadelphia: Lippincott, 1905?, 124p.

Stewart, Desmond. *The Foreigner: A Search for the First-
Century Jesus*. London: H. Hamilton, 1981, 181p.

Stewart, George Black. *Lessons on the Life of Jesus; for
Juniors*. 2 vols. Boston: United Society of Christian
Endeavor, 1896-97.

————. *A Study of the Life of Jesus, His Words and Works*.
Boston; New York: Pilgrim Press, 1907, 182p.

Stewart, James Stuart. *The Life and Teaching of Jesus Christ*.
London: SCM Press, 1933, 209p.; New York: Abingdon Press,
195-?, 192p.

Stifler, James Madison. *The Christ of Christianity*. New
York; Chicago: Revell, 1915, 222p.

Stock, Eugene. *Lessons on the Life of Our Lord*. London:
Church of England Sunday School Institute, 1871, 140p.

————. *Lessons on the Life of Our Lord*. Adapted and translated from English into Telugu by M. Sadhuru Garu. Edited
by John Cain. Madras: SPCK, 1896-98.

Stocking, Charles, and William Wesley Totheroh. *The Business
Man of Syria*. 5 vols. Chicago: Maestro Co., 1923.

Stoke, John H. *A Man Called Jesus*. New York: Vantage Press,
1959, 231p.

Stokes, William. *Memory Pictures of the Life of Christ*. London: 1868.

*Stories from the Life of Christ for the Primary Department of
the Sunday School*. Salt Lake City, Utah: Deseret Sunday
School Union, 1916, 131p.

Stories of Jesus. Adapted from the Jerusalem Bible. Philadelphia: Fortress Press, 1973, 62p., (1968).

Storrs, Richard Salter. *The Study of the Gospels. An Introduction to the Life of Jesus Christ Our Lord.* Springfield,
Mass.: W.J. Holland and Co., 1868.

The Story of the Life of Jesus. By the author of *The Story
of the Bible.* London: 1884, 219p.

Stout, Andrew P. *The Journeys and Deeds of Jesus.* Indianapolis;
Cincinnati: F.L. Horton and Co., 1888.

Stowe, Harriet Elizabeth (Beecher). *Footsteps of the Master.*
New York: J.B. Ford and Co., 1877, 308p.

Strada, J. *Jesus.* 1902.

Strauss, David Friedrich. *Das Leben Jesu für das deutsche
Volk bearbeitet.* Leipzig: F.A. Brockhaus, 1864, 633p., (1874);
Bonn: 1877: Bonn: E. Strauss, 1895, (1902), (1904); Leipzig:
A. Kröner, 1904, (191-?), (1924); Stuttgart: A. Kröner, 1905.

————. *Das Leben Jesu, kritisch bearbeitet.* 2 vols. Tübingen: C.F. Osiander, 1835-36, (1837), (1838-39), (1840);
Darmstadt: Wissenschaftliche Buchges., 1969.

————. *The Life of Christ, or, A Critical Examination of His
History.* New York: Vale, 1843, 284p., (1845).

————. *The Life of Jesus, Critically Examined.* 4 vols.
Trans. George Eliot. Birmingham: 1842-44; London: Chapman
Brothers, 1846, 3 vols.; London: S. Sonnenschein and Co.,
1892, 784p., (1898), (1902), (1906); London: Allen and
Unwin, 1913, 784p.; London: William and Norgate, 1879, 2 vols.,
(1865); London: Hetherington, 1838-42, 2 vols.; London: SCM
Press, 1975; London: 1848, (1893); New York: C. Blanchard,
1855, 901p., (1856), (1860); St. Clair Shores, Mich.:
Scholarly Press, 1970; Philadelphia: Fortress Press, 1972,
812p.

————. *A New Life of Jesus.* 2 vols. London; Edinburgh:
William and Norgate, 1865, (1879).

————. *Nouvelle vie de Jésus.* 2 vols. Trans. A. Nefftzer
and Ch. Dolfus. Paris: J. Hetzel et A. Lacroix, 1864.

————. *Nueva vida de Jesús.* Trans. José Fernández. Buenos
Aires: Biblioteca news, 1943, 564p.

————. *Strauss' Life of Jesus. A New Translation.* Trans.
J.L. M'Ilraith. London: The Temple Co., 1892, 258p.

————. *Strauss, und die Evangelien; oder, Das Leben Jesu
von Dr. Strauss für denkende Leser aller Stände bearbeitet
von einem evangelischen Theologen.* Burgdorf: C. Langlois,
1839.

————. Vie de Jésus; ou, Examen critique de son histoire.
2 vols. Trans. E. Littré. Paris: Ladrange, 1839-40, (1853),
(1856), (1864).

Stretton, Hesba. Kristi och hans apostlars underfulla lif.
Philadelphia; Chicago: J.C. Winston and Co., 1897, 302p.

————. The Life of Christ; or, The Wonderful Life. Chicago;
Philadelphia: Monarch Book Co., 1895, 255p.

————. The Story of Jesus and the Lives of His Apostles.
Philadelphia: World Bible House, 1902, 518p.

————. The Wonderful Life. London: Hamilton, Adams, 1883,
251p., (1875), (1883), (1892).

Swank, Clavin Peter. The Lord of Life; an Account of the Life
and Teachings of the Savior for Students of High School Age.
New York: Greenwich Book Publishers, 1957, 112p.

Symington, William. Messiah the Prince, or, The Mediatorial
Dominion of Jesus Christ. London: 1840, 354p.; London: T.
Nelson and Sons, 1881; Philadelphia: 1884; New York: Carter,
1839, 261p.

Taddei, Ezio. In quinto Vangelo. Vicenza: La locustra, 1970,
96p.

Takayanagi, Isaburo. Iesu den to sono shūhen. Tokyo: Shinkyō
Shuppansha, 1975, 281p.

Talbot, Louis Thompson. Why Four Gospels? The Four-fold
Portrait of Christ in Matthew, Mark, Luke, and John. Los
Angeles: 1944, 238p.

Talmage, James Edward. Jesus the Christ; a Study of the Messiah
and His Mission According to Holy Scriptures, both Ancient
and Modern. Salt Lake City: Deseret News, 1916, 804p.,
(1915), (1922), (1928), (1948), (1951), (1955).

————. Jezus de Christus. Trans. Johanna A. Reit. 's-Gravenhage: Franklin J. Murdock, 1938.

Talmage, Thomas DeWitt. From Manger to Throne, Embracing a
New Life of Jesus the Christ, and a History of Palestine and
Its People. Philadelphia; St. Louis: Historical Pub. Co.,
1890, 656p.; Minneapolis: Hatch Pub. Co., 1890, 656p.; New
York: Christian Herald Bible House, 1893.

Tambasco, Anthony J. In the Days of Jesus; The Jewish Background and Unique Teaching of Jesus. New York: Paulist
Press, 1983, 112p.

Tanner, Obert Clark. New Testament Studies. Salt Lake City:
Dept. of Education of the Church of Jesus Christ of Latter-
Day Saints, 1932, 667p.

Tatian. *The Earliest Life of Christ Ever Compiled from the
Four Gospels, Being the Diatessaron of Tatian (circ. A.D.
160)*. Trans. J. Hamlyn Hill. Edinburgh: T. and T. Clark,
1910, 224p.

Taylor, Charles Forbes. *The Story of Jesus*. Huntington, W. Va.:
Cook Printing Co., 1940, 45p.

Taylor, Kenneth Nathaniel. *The Greatest Life Ever Lived*.
Wheaton, Ill.: Tyndale House Publishers, 1969, 59p.

Taylor, Jeremy. *Antiquitates christianæ; or, The History of
the Life and Death of the Holy Jesus*. London: Printed by
R. Norton for R. Royston, 1675, 791p., (1678), (1684),
(1691), (1694), (1703), (1742).

————. *Bishop Jeremy Taylor's Life of Our Lord and Saviour
Jesus Christ*. London: Printed by W. Johnston for G. Virtue,
1836, 705p., (1841).

————. *The Great Exemplar of Sanctity and Holy Life*. London:
Printed by R.N. for Francis Ash, 1649; London: Norton, 1651;
London: Printed by J. Flesher for R. Royston, 1653, 568p.,
(1657), (1658), (1667), (1675), (1678), (1684), (1703),
(1742); London: Printed for Luke Meredith, 1693, 432p.;
London: J. Hatchard and Son, 1835, 3 vols.; London: George
Virtue, 1845, 3 vols.; London: W. Pickering, 1849, 3 vols.;
London: Longmans, Brown, Green, and Longmans, 1850, 730p.;
New York: R. Carter and Brothers, 1859, 2 vols.

————. *The History of the Life and Death of the Holy Jesus,
the Saviour of the World*. Wolverhampton: Printed by Thomas
Smith, 1770, 234, 331p.; London: G. Routledge and Co., 1851,
714p., (1882); London: J. and C. Mozley; Oxford: J.H. Parker,
1853, 287p.; London: Routledge, Warne, and Routledge, 1860,
715p.

————. *Die Lebensgeschichte unseres Herrn und Heilands Jesu
Christi*. Lancaster: Gedruckt bey Joseph Ehrenfried, 1812,
147–209p.

————. *The Life of Christ*. London: G. Virtue, 1841, 461p.

————. *The Life of Jesus Christ* (abridged). Philadelphia:
1832; Pittsburgh: 1834.

————. *The Life of Our Blessed Saviour Jesus Christ*. Printed
at Exeter by Henry Raplet for Samuel Larkin, Portsmouth,
1724, 152p., (1794); Glasgow: Printed by John and James
Robertson for J. Gillies, 1774, 152p.; Greenfield, Mass.:
Printed by T. Dickman, 1796, 153p.; Newburyport: Printed by
Blount and March for Samuel Larkin, Portsmouth, 1796;
Philadelphia: Printed for W. Magaw by J. Rakestraw, 1809,

226p., (1810); Philadelphia: Printed by D. Dickinson, 1819,
232p.; Pittsburgh: Cook and Schayer, 1834, 243p.; Indianapolis:
Stacy and Williams, 1840; Somerset, Pa.: Reprinted by J. and
T. Patton, 1818, 299p.

————. *The Life of Our Lord and Saviour Jesus Christ.* London: 1840; London: Abridged ed., 1758, (1874).

————. *Ystyriaethau of gyflwr dyn, yn y bywyd hwn, ac yn yr hwn sy i ddyfod.* Trans. Wynn Griffith. Merthry Tydfil: J. Jenkins, 1825, 180p.

Taylor, Kenneth Nathaniel. *The Life of Christ; a Pictorial Essay from the Living Bible.* Wheaton, Ill.: Tyndale House Publishers, 1974, unpaged.

Taylor, Marion. *The Life of Christ.* Morgantown, W. Va.: Acme Pub. Co., 1909, 190p.

Taylor, Thomas Eddy, Stephen Earl Taylor, and Charles Herbert Morgan. *Studies in the Life of Christ.* Cincinnati: Jennings and Pye; New York: Eaton and Mains, 1901, 226p.

Taylor, Vincent. *The Life and Ministry of Jesus.* Nashville: Abingdon Press, 1955, 240p.; London: Macmillan, 1954, 236p.

Tennant, Charles Roger. *Christ Encountered; a Short Life of Jesus.* New York: Seabury Press, 1966, 135p., (1961).

Tenney, Edward Payson. *Our Elder Brother; His Biography.* Springfield, Mass.; Richmond: King-Richardson Co., 1899, 631p., (1897), 611p.

Terhune, Albert Payson. *The Son of God.* New York; London: Harper and Brothers, 1932, 222p.

Tesser, Carolus. *Het Lam Gods.* Maastricht: J. Schenk, 1940, 64p.

Teuschl, Wolfgang Amadé. *Da Jesus und seine Hawara.* Salzburg: Residenz Verlag, 1971, 199p.

Thayer, Erastus William. *Sketches from the Life of Jesus, Historical and Doctrinal.* Chicago; New York: Revell, 1891, 548p.

Thellier de Poncheville, Charles. *L'histoire sacerdotale de Jésus.* Paris: Éditions Spes, 1945, 591p.

Thivollier, Pierre. *Le Liberateur; vie de Jésus-Christ.* Issyles-Moulineaux: Missions ouvrières paroissiales, 1948, 334p.

Thoburn, Helen. *Studies in Knowing Jesus Christ, for Younger Girls.* New York: Womans Press, 1919, 93p., (1925), 90p.

Thomas, Thomas Glyn. *Dyddiadur Iesu o Nasareth.* Swansea: Ty John Penry, 1976, 167p.

Thomé de Jesus, Father. *Abrégé de l'ouvrage du père Thomas de Jésus les Souffrances de N.S. Jésus-Christ.* Guise: Imprimerie Baré, 1873, 517p.

————. *Les souffrances de Notre-Seigneur Jésus-Christ.* 3 vols. Trans. P. Alleaume. Lyon: J.B. Kindelem, 1820; Lyon; Paris: Perisse frères, 1858, 2 vols.

————. *The Sufferings of Our Lord Jesus Christ.* Edward Gallagher, ed. Westminster, Md.: Newman Press, 1960, 548p.

————. *Trabaios de Jesvs.* Zaragoça: 1624, 708p.

Thompson, Ebenezer, and William Charles Price. *The History of Our Blessed Lord and Saviour Jesus Christ.* 2 vols. Wilmington, Del.: Bonsal and Niles, 1805.

Thompson, Joseph Parrish. *Jesus of Nazareth: His Life for the Young.* Boston: J.R. Osgood and Co., 1876, 438p.; *The Life of Jesus of Nazareth, for Young People.* Norwich, Conn.: H. Bill, 1879, 690p.

Through Jesus to God. Chicago: American Institute of Sacred Literature, 1931, 115p.

Thumra, J.H. *Jesuwui mirin kala tamkachithei.* 2 vols. Ukhrul: TNBC, 1973.

Thurman, Thomas D. *The Jesus Years: A Chronological Study of the Life of Christ.* Cincinnati: New Life Books, 1977, 240p.

Tiden, Elwyn E. *Toward Understanding Jesus.* Englewood Cliffs, N.J.: Prentice-Hall, 1956, 289p.

Tiedemann, Karl. *The Lord of Love; Thirty Meditations on the Life of Our Lord.* London: A.R. Mowbray and Co.; Milwaukee: Morehouse Pub. Co., 1929, 195p.

Tissot, James Joseph Jacques. *The Life of Our Saviour Jesus Christ.* 2 vols. Trans. Mrs. Arthur Bell (N. d'Anvers). London: S. Low, Marston, and Co., 189-?, (1897); New York: Century Co., 1898, 2 vols.; New York: McLure-Tissot Co., 1899, 4 vols.; New York: St. Hubert Guild, 1900, 3 vols.; New York: Werner Co., 1903, 3 vols., (1913).

————. *La vie de Notre-Seigneur Jésus Christ.* 2 vols. New York: L. Weiss and Co., 1896-97.

Tondini Melgari, Amelia. *Io sono la vita; Vangelo per ragazzi.* Milano: "La Sorgente," 1952, 189p.

————. *Our Lord's Life: His Story in Reverent Words and Original Paintings.* Trans. Joy Mary Terruzzi. New York: Hawthorn Books, 1960, 167p.

Torm, Frederik Emanuel. *Forskningen over Jesu liv, tilbageblik og fremblik.* København: Universitetsbogtrykkeriet (J.H. Schultz a/s), 1918, 188p.

Torrey, Reuben Archer. *Studies in the Life and Teachings of Our Lord.* Chicago: Bible Institute Colportage Association, 1909, 347p.

————. *The Uplifted Christ.* Grand Rapids: Zondervan, 1965, 104p.

Trapp, Maria Augusta. *When the King Was Carpenter.* Harrison, Ark.: New Leaf Press, 1976, 141p.

Treasure, Geoff. *The Most Unforgettable Character You'll Ever Meet.* Chicago: Moody Press, 1977, 156p., (1973).

Trout, Ethel Wendell. *Jesus the Light of the World.* Philadelphia: Westminster Press, 1921, 127p., (1924), 2 vols.

Trovarelli, Saverio. *Vita di Gesù.* 3. ed. Vercelli: La tipografica, 1968, 358p.

Tucker, Joshua Thomas. *The Sinless One; or, The Life Manifested.* Boston: S.K. Whipple and Co., 1855, 324p.

Turnbull, Robert. *Theophony; or, The Manifestation of God in the Life, Character, and Mission of Jesus Christ.* Hartford: Brockett, Fuller, and Co.; New York: Carter and Brothers, 1849, 239p.

Ulrich, John Oliver. *The Son of Man.* Tamaqua, Pa.: Record Printing Co., 1931, 204p.

Upham, Francis W. *Saint Matthew's Witness to Words and Works of the Lord; or, Our Saviour's Life as Revealed in the Gospel of His Earliest Evangelist.* New York: Hunt and Eaton, 1891, 415p.

Vallings, James Frederick. *Jesus Christ, the Divine Man; His Life and Times.* New York; Chicago: Revell, 189-?, 229p.; New York: A.D.F. Randolph, 1889.

Valtorta, Maria. *Il poema dell'Uomo-Dio.* 10 vols. Isola del Liri: Pisani, 1970, (1961-).

Valverde, Fernando de. *Vida de Jesu-Christo Nuestro Señor Dios, hombre, maestro, y redentor del mondo.* 2 vols. Madrid: Agustín de Gordejeula, 1754.

Vanderlip, George. *Jesus, Teacher and Lord.* Valley Forge, Pa.: Judson Press, 1964, 127p.

Vandersloot, Jacob Samuel, ed. *The Inspired History of Jesus.* N.p., n.d.

Van Dyk, Fay Blix. *His Touch Is Love*. Nashville: Southern
Pub. Association, 1978, 94p.

Van Passen, Pierre. *Why Jesus Died*. New York: Dial Press,
1949, 283p.

Varenne, Gaston. *La vie merveilleuse de Jésus, selon les
textes des Évangiles*. Paris: Fasquelle, 1938, 189p.

Veach, Robert Wells. *The King and His Kingdom; Constructive
Studies in the Life of Christ for Classes and Private Use*.
New York: National Board of the Young Women's Christian
Associations of the United States of America, 1908, 150p.

Vercruysse, Bruno. *Manuel de solide piété, ou Nouvelles
méditations pratiques pour tous les jours de l'année, sur
la vie de N.S. Jésus-Christ*. Bruxelles: Lelong, 1871.

————. *Neue praktische Betrachtungen, für alle Tage des
Jahres über das Leben unsers Herrn Jesu Christi für Ordens-
leute*. 2 vols. Trans. Wilhelm Sander. Paderborn: Jung-
fermann, 1880.

————. *New Practical Mediations for Every Day on the Life
of Christ*. 2 vols. New York: Benziger Brothers, 1875,
(1954).

Vergara Cuevas, M. Antonio. *Perspectivas de Jesús*. Santiago
de Chile: 1964, 387p.

Verkuyl, Johannes. *Samakah semura agama?* Tjet. 3. Trans.
A. Simandjuntak. Djakarta: Badan Penerbit Kristen, 1965,
111p.

————. *Zijn alle godsdiensten gelijk?* Kampen: J.H. Kok,
1964, 136p.

Verschaeve, Cyriel. *Jezus*. Brugge: Iitg. Zeemeeuw, 1940,
565p.

Vetancurt, Agustin de. *Chronografia sagrada de la vida de
Christo Nuestro Redemptor*. Mexico: Maria de Benavides,
viuda de J. de Ribera, 1696, 16p.

Veuillot, Louis François. *Jésus-Christ*. Paris: Firmin-Didot
frères, fils et c^ie, 1875, 572p., (1874), (1877).

————. *The Life of Our Lord Jesus Christ*. Trans. Anthony
Farley. New York: Catholic Pub. Society, 1875, 509p.

————. *La vie de Notre-Seigneur Jésus-Christ*. 5. éd.
Paris: Périsse frères, 1864, 485p., (1870), 7th ed., (1879),
525p.

Vid, Iûrii L. *Zhite Īsusa Khrista*. Scranton, Pa.: Svoboda,
1905, 292p.

Vida de N.S. Jesucristo. Santiago de Chile: Ediciones Ercilla, 1937, 133p.

Vie de Jésus, Fils de Dieu, Sauveur des hommes (Filmstrip). Productions françaises cinématographiques, Paris. Presenté des Films St. Joseph, 1949, 20 fr.

La Vie et la passion de Jésus-Christ (Motion picture). La Société Lumière, Paris, 1898, 7 min.

La vie, mort et passion de Notre Sauveur Jésus-Christ. Troyes: J. Garnier, 17--, 120p.

Vigerius, Marcus. *Decachordvm christianvm.* Fani: H. Soncinus his caracteribus impressit, 1507, 246 1.

───────. *Marci Vigerii Decachordvm Christianvm.* Hagenau: In ædibus T. Anshelmi ac I. Alberti, expensis I. Koberger Nurenbergeñ incolae, 1517, 204 1.

Villegas Selvago, Alonso de. *Il perfetto leggendario della vita, e fatti di N.S. Giesv' Christo e di tvtti i santi.* Venetia: Appresso Nicolò Pezzana, 1682, 924p.

Villena, Isabel de. *Vita Christi.* Valéncia: Del Cénia al Segura, 1980, 612p.

Vincentius Ferrerius, Saint. *A Christology from the Sermons of St. Vincent Ferrer of the Order of Preachers.* Selected and translated by S.M.C. London: Blackfriars Publications, 1954, 211p.

The Vine (Motion picture). NBC News in cooperation with the Southern Baptist Convention Radio and Television Commission. Released by the Southern Baptist Convention Radio and Television Commission, 1967, 59 min.

Vogel, Hans. *Jesus der Helfer.* Leipzig: L. Klotz, 1937, 421p.

Vollmer, Philip. *The Life of Christ.* Philadelphia: Heidelberg Press, 1912, 353p.

Vos, Howard Frederic. *Beginnings in the Life of Christ.* Chicago: Moody Press, 1975, 176p.; *The Life of Our Divine Lord.* Grand Rapids: Zondervan, 1958, 223p.

Wace, Henry. *The Gospel and Its Witnesses. Chief Facts in the Life of Our Lord.* London: J. Murray, 1883, 211p., (1884); New York: Dutton, 1883, 211p.

───────. *Some Central Points of Our Lord's Ministry.* London: Hodder and Stoughton, 1890, 352p.; New York: T. Whittaker, 1890, 352p.

Walker, Norman Macdonald Lockhart. *Jesus Christ and His Surroundings*. London: 1898; New York; Chicago: Revell, n.d., 240p.

Walsall, Samuel. *The Life and Death of Jesus Christ the Saviour*. London: 1885.

Walser, George Henry. *The Life and Teachings of Jesus*. Boston: Sherman, French, and Co., 1909, 442p., (1908).

Walter, William Wilfred. *The Sweetest Story Ever Told*. Aurora, Ill.: W.W. Walter, 1916, 208p.

Wand, John William Charles. *The Life of Jesus Christ*. London: Methuen, 1955, 184p.; New York: Morehouse-Gorham, 1955, 208p.

Ward, Elizabeth Stuart (Phelps). *The Story of Jesus Christ*. Boston; New York: Houghton, Mifflin and Co., 1897, 413p., (1901).

Ward, John William George. *The Master and the Twelve*. New York: George H. Doran Co., 1924, 255p.

Ware, Henry. *The Life of the Saviour*. Boston: American Unitarian Association, 1873, 271p., (1868), (1884), (1892); Cambridge, Mass.: Brown, Shattuck, and Co.; Boston: Hiliard, Gray, and Co., 1833, 276p.; Cambridge, Mass.: J. Munroe and Co., 1834, 272p.

Warren, A.E. *Church Teachers' Life of Christ*. New York: Church Pub. Co., 1900, 60p.

Warshaw, Joseph. *The Historical Life of Christ*. London: T.F. Unwin, 1927, 368p.; New York: Macmillan, 1926, 368p.

Warwick, David William. *In the Fulness of Time*. London: Longmans, 1966, 117p.

Watson, John. *The Life of the Master*. New York: McClure, Phillips, and Co., 1901, 300p.

Watson, Mrs. Samuel. *The Life of Jesus Christ the Saviour*. London: Religious Tract Society, 1885.

————. *The Story of Jesus Christ the Saviour Retold from the Evangelists*. Boston: I. Bradley and Co., 1889?, 490p.

Weatherhead, Leslie Dixon. *Erlebtes Palästina*. Trans. Hedwig Schwechten. München: Methodistenkirche in Bayern, 1947, 148p.

————. *His Life and Ours: The Significance for Us of the Life of Jesus*. New York; Cincinnati: Abingdon Press, 1933, 361p.; London: Hodder and Stoughton, 1932, 384p.

————. *It Happened in Palestine.* New York; Cincinnati: Abingdon Press, 1936, 325p.

Weed, George Ludington. *A Life of Christ for the Young.* Philadelphia: G.W. Jacobs and Co., 1898, 400p.

Wegenast, Klaus. *Jesus und die Evangelien.* Gütersloh: Gütersloher Verlagshaus G. Mohn, 1966, 94p., (1965).

Weiss, Bernhard. *Das Leben Jesu.* 2 vols. Berlin: Wilhelm Hertz, 1882, (1884); Stuttgart; Berlin: J.G. Cotta, 1902, 2 vols.

————. *The Life of Christ.* 3 vols. Trans. John Walter Hope and M.G. Hope. Edinburgh: T. and T. Clark, 1883-84.

Welch, J. *Thoughts on the Devotion to the Sacred Heart and on the Life of Our Lord.* New York: 1884.

Weld, Horatio Hastings. *The Life of Christ.* Philadelphia: Hogan and Thompson, 1850, 232p.

West, Franklin Lorenzo Richards. *Jesus, His Life and Teachings.* Salt Lake City: Bookcraft, 1953, 291p.

Weston, Sidney Adams. *Discovering Jesus.* Boston; Chicago: Pilgrim Press, 1934, 137p.

Wheeler, Charlotte Bickersteth. *Our Master's Footsteps.* London: E. Stock, 1883, 408p.

Whipple, Wayne. *The Story-life of the Son of Man.* New York; Chicago: Revell, 1913, 564p.

White, Annie Randall. *My Mother's Life of Jesus.* Philadelphia: 1902.

White, Bouck. *The Call of the Carpenter.* Garden City, N.Y.: Doubleday Page and Co., 1911, 355p.

White, Ellen Gould (Harmon). *The Desire of Ages.* Oakland, Calif.; New York: Pacific Press Pub. Co., 1898, 1042p.; New York; Kansas City: Pacific Press Pub. Co., 1900, 2 vols.; Mountain View, Calif.: Pacific Press Pub. Co., 1940, 863p., (1947), (1953), (1964).

————. *Jesu Kristi liv.* Battle Creek, Mich.: Review and Herald, 1885, 624p.

————. *Das Leben Jesu.* Trans. Fritz Daniel. Hamburg; Wien: Advent-Verlag, 1934, 527p.

————. *Sketches from the Life of Christ, and the Experience of the Christian Church.* 2nd ed. Battle Creek, Mich.: Review and Herald; Oakland, Calif.: Pacific Press, 1882, 155p.

White, Reginald E.O. *The Stranger of Galilee.* Rev. ed. Evesham: James, 1978, 152p.

White, William Spranger. *History of Our Lord and Saviour Jesus Christ.* London: 1884.

Whitfield, Edward. *Jesus Christ, in the Grandeur of His Mission, the Beauty of His Life, and His Final Triumph.* London: E.T. Whitfield, 1858, 274p.

Whitfield, Frederick. *From Cana to Bethany; Gleanings from Our Lord's Life on Earth.* London: James Nisbet, 1883, 143p., (1901), 150p.

————. *Holy Footprints.* London: J. Nisbet and Co., 1883, 147p.

————. *Jesus Himself, Jesus Only.* London: 1871.

Whittemore, William Meynell. *Notes on the Life of Christ.* London: G. Stoneman, 1896, 250p.

Wickes, Thomas. *The Son of Man.* Boston: American Tract Society, 1868, 382p.

Widding, Lars. *Jesus, vem var han?* Stockholm: Diakonistyrelsens förlag, 1962, 92p.

Wild, Laura Hulda. *Selected Studies in the Life of Christ.* Chicago; New York: Revell, 1900, 121p.

Wilkinson, William Cleaver. *Concerning Jesus Christ the Son of Man.* Philadelphia; Boston: Griffith and Rowland Press, 1918, 333p., (1916), 233p.

Willam, Franz Michel. *Des Leben Jesu im Lande und Volke Israel.* Freiburg im Breisgau: Herder and Co., 1933, 513p., (1934), 548p., (1937), (1949), (1955), (1960-62), 2 vols., (1963).

————. *The Life of Jesus Christ in the Land of Israel and Among Its People.* Trans. Newton Thompson. St. Louis; London: B. Herder Book Co., 1936, 488p.

Willett, Herbert Lockwood. *Life and Teachings of Jesus.* Cleveland: Bethany C.E. Co., 1898, 163p., London: 1900, 164p.

Willett, William Marinus. *Messiah.* Boston: B.B. Russell; Philadelphia: Quaker City Pub. House, 1874, 442p.

Williams, Guilfoyle. *The Real Jesus: The Tragic Life of a Remarkable Man as Given in the Gospels.* Enfield (Middx.): Guilfoyle Publications, 1968, 153p.

Williams, John Gordon. *The Life of Our Lord.* Westminster (London): National Society, 1939, 309p.

Williams, Thomas. *The Private Life of Our Lord Jesus Christ.*
London: 1833.

Williams, William. *The Redeemer.* London: 1874.

Wills, Charles. *First Lessons in the Life of Our Lord Jesus
Christ.* London: 1863.

Wilson, Ella Calista (Handy). *Every-day Life Illustrated by
the Life of Jesus.* 2 vols. Boston: Unitarian Sunday-School
Society, 1887-88.

Wilson, Lawrence Ray. *The Triumphant Jesus.* Bartlesville?,
Okla.: 1952, 265p.

Wilson, Philip Whitwell. *The Christ We Forget; A Life of Our
Lord for Men of Today.* New York; Chicago: Revell, 1917,
328p.

————. *Is Christ Possible?* New York: Revell, 1932, 219p.

Wilson, Seth. *Learning from Jesus.* Joplin, Mo.: College
Press, 1977, 630p.

Wilton, Dean Thayer. *Through the Shadows with Jesus.* Portland, Me.: Thayer, 1949, 121p.

Winkley, Samuel Hobart. *A New Analytical Question-book on
the Life and Ministry of Jesus.* Boston: Press of J. Wilson
and Son, 1873, 78p.

————. *Question Book on the Life of Jesus.* Boston: Sunday-
School Society, 1876, (1883).

————. *Questions Concerning the Son of Man.* Boston: Unitarian Sunday-School Society, 1885, 82p., (1887).

Winslow, Robert Scott. *The Modern Man's Fully Illustrated
Life of Christ.* Albuquerque: Gloucester Art Press, 1979.

Wise, Charles C. *Windows on the Master.* Nashville: Abingdon
Press, 1968, 143p.

Wise, Daniel. *Our King and Saviour: or, The Story of Our
Lord's Life on Earth.* New York: Nelson and Phillips; Cincinnati: Hitchcock and Walden, 1875, 367p.

Wittichen, Karl. *Das Leben Jesu in urkundlicher Darstellung.*
Jena: Hermann Dufft, 1876, 397p.

Wittig, Joseph. *Leben Jesu in Palästina, Schlesien und
anderswo.* 2 vols. Gotha: Leopold Klotz, 1929; Heilbronn:
E. Salzer, 1934, 545p.; Stuttgart: Evangelische Buchgemeinde,
1966, 413p.

Wizenmann, Thomas. *Die Geschichte Jesu nach Matthäus als
Selbstbeweiss ihrer Zuverlässigkeit betrachtet.* Basel:
Bahnmaier, 1864, 511p.

Wood, H.K. *Glimpses of Christ.* Stirling: Drummond's Tract Depot, 1890, 126p.

Woodhead, Abraham. *An Historical Narrative of the Life and Death of Our Lord Jesus Christ in Two Parts.* Oxford: Printed at the Theater, 1685, 342p.

Worsnop, Abraham. *The Footsteps of Jesus; with Questions for Young People.* London: 1862.

Wright, Paul. *A Complete Life of Our Blessed Lord and Saviour Jesus Christ.* Windham: S. Webb, 1814, 404p.

————. *The Life of Our Blessed Lord and Saviour Jesus Christ.* London: n.d.

————. *The New and Complete Life of Our Blessed Lord and Saviour Jesus Christ.* 2 vols. Mill-Hill, near Trenton: D. Fenton, 1810– ; London: Alex. Hogg, 1785?, 428p.; London: Printed for Hogg and Co. by M. Allen, 1790?, 483p.; London: 1793; New York: Birdsall and Menut, 1795, 427p.; New York: Printed by Lazarus Beach, 1803?, 380p.; Philadelphia: Printed by Tertius Dunning and Walter W. Hyer, 1795, 407p.; Trenton: D. Fenton, 1810– ; Albany: Published by Elijah Torrey, 1814, 510p.; Schenectady, N.Y.: Published by Messrs. Lee and Cody, 1814, 472p.; Schenectady, N.Y.: Printed by Lazarus Black, 1815, 380p.; Winchester, Va.: Published by J.F. Archbold, 1816, 512p., (1818).

Wynne, Frederick Richard. *Fragmentary Records of Jesus of Nazareth.* London: Hodder and Stoughton, 1887, 143p.

Xavier, Jérôme. *Historia Christi.* Lvgdvni Batavorvm: 1639.

Yamagishi, Gaishi. *Ningen Kirisuto ki.* Tokyo: Makujisha, 1979, 277p.

Yanaihara, Tadao. *Iesu den.* Tokyo: Kadokawra Shoten, 1968, 384p.

Yost, Casper Salathiel. *The Carpenter of Nazareth, a Study of Jesus in the Light of His Environment and Background.* St. Louis: Bethany Press, 1938, 356p.

Young, Andrew. *The Poetic Jesus.* London: SPCK, 1972, 88p.; New York: Harper and Row, 1972, 88p.

Young, John. *The Christ of History. An Argument Founded on the Fact of His Life on Earth.* New York: R. Carter and Brothers, 1872, 260p., (1855), (1857), (1858), (1859), (1860), (1863), (1864), (1866), (1868), (1870), (1876), (1878); London: Strahan and Co., 1868; London: 1855, (1857), (1861), (1868), (1884); New York: American Tract Society, 189?, 260p.

————. *El Cristo de la historia; argumentacion baseda en los hechos de su vida sobre la tierra*. New York: American Tract Society, 1917, 268p.

Young, Peter. *Daily Readings for a Year on the Life of Our Lord and Saviour Jesus Christ*. 2 vols. London: Sidmouth, 1872, (1859), (1861), (1863).

Younghusband, Frances. *The Story of Our Lord*. London: Longmans, 1887, 267p.

Zündel, Friedrich. *Jesus in Bildern aus seinem Leben*. 2. Aufl. Zürich: S. Böhr, 1885, 436p.

Zunn, Elisabeth Rittershus. *Die Sonne, die mir lachet, das Lebensbild des Heilandes nach dem Lukasevangelium*. Berlin: Sonnenweg-Verlag, 1941, 133p.

JUVENILE WORKS

Adams, Agnes Louise Logan. *Jesus of Nazareth; Stories of the Master and His Disciples.* Illus. W.H. Margetson. New York: Oxford University Press, 1929, 96p.

Adcock, Roger. *Stories of Jesus.* Illus. Gordon King. Wheaton, Ill.: Scripture Press Publications, 1971, 77p.

Alberti, Rüdiger. *Wie ich meinen Kindern die Geschichten von Jesus erzähle.* Dresden: C.L. Ungelenk, 1934, 159p.

Alcott, William Andrus. *Travels of Our Saviour, with Some of the Leading Incidents of His Life.* Boston: Massachusetts Sabbath School Society, 1840, 311p.

Alden, Isabella (Macdonald). *Stories and Pictures from the Life of Jesus.* Boston: D. Lothrop and Co., 1886?, 122p.

Allen, Hattie Bell (McCracken). *As Jesus Passed By.* Illus. Mariel Wilhoite Turner. Philadelphia: Winston, 1954, 32p.

Allstrom, Elizabeth C. *Jesus, Friend and Helper.* Illus. Iris Beatty Johnson. New York: Abingdon Press, 1957, 47p.

Andrews, Frances King. *Fairest Lord Jesus.* Illus. John White. Nashville: Broadman Press, 1958, unpaged.

Angelini, Cesare. *Żywot Pana Jezusa.* Illus. Aurelius Borkowski. Jerozolima: Nakł. Kustodii Ziemi Świętej, 1937, 241p.

Armstrong, April (Oursler). *Stories from the Life of Jesus.* Illus. Jules Gotlieb. Garden City, N.Y.: Garden City Books, 1955, 256p.

Babcock, Emma S. *Dutch Tiles, or, Loving Words about the Saviour.* Philadelphia: Presbyterian Publication Committee; New York: A.D.F. Randolph, 1866, 171p.

Baldwin, Maud Junkin. *Stories of Jesus.* Philadelphia: United Lutheran Publication House, 1928, 189p.

Ball, Elsie. *The Greatest Name, a Life of Jesus for Juniors.* New York; Cincinnati: Abingdon Press, 1938, 149p.

————. *The Story Peter Told.* New York: H. Holt and Co., 1929, 144p.

Banks, Helen Ward. *The Life of Jesus Retold from the Gospels for Children.* Illus. Florence Choate and Elizabeth Curtis. New York: Frederick A. Stokes Co., 1922, 93p.

Barbre, Myrtle. *A Child's Book about Jesus.* Akron, Ohio; New York: Saalfield Pub. Co., 1940, 22p.

Barclay, William. *A Life of Christ.* Scripted by Iain Reid. Cartoons by Eric Fraser. New York: Harper and Row, 1977, 94p.

Barker, Elsa. *Stories from the New Testament for Children.* New York: Duffield and Co., 1911, 410p.

Barton, Lucy. *The Gospel History of Jesus Christ.* London: Fisher, 1837.

Bastin, Robert. *When Jesus Was a Man; a Catholic Child's Book.* Trans. Ann Collopy. Illus. Fred Funcken. St. Paul: Catechetical Guild Educational Society, 1958, 46p.

Bedier, Mary Juliana. *Jesus Helps Everybody.* Illus. Jack Jewell. Garden City, N.Y.: Garden City Pub. Co., 1949, unpaged.

Beebe, Catherine. *The Story of Jesus for Boys and Girls.* Illus. Robb Beebe. Paterson, N.J.: St. Anthony Guild Press, 1967, 105p.

Behnke, John. *Stories of Jesus.* Illus. Betsy Roosen Sheppard. New York: Paulist Press, 1977, 143p.

Berthier, René. *Christ, notre histoire.* Illus. Charles Front. Limoges: Droguet & Ardant, 1971, 247p.

Bird, Thomas E. *A Study of the Gospels.* Westminster, Md.: Newman Press, 1950, 270p.

Bishop, Charles Cleophus. *The Two Most Wonderful Babies Who Became the Two Greatest Men in the World.* Nashville: Consolidated Development Co., 1934, 48p.

Blackall, Christopher Rubey. *Stories about Jesus, Our Lord and Saviour.* Illus. C.R. Blackall and Emily L. Blackall. Philadelphia: B. Griffith, 1890, 271p.

Blanchard, Ferdinand Quincy. *How One Man Changed the World; a Story Told for Boys and Girls, with Questions and Topics for Study.* Boston: Pilgrim Press, 1935, 119p.

Blyton, Enid. *The Children's Life of Christ.* Illus. Eileen Soper. London: Methuen and Co., 1943, 191p.

Bowie, Walter Russell. *The Story of Jesus for Young People.* Illus. Robert Lawson. New York; London: C. Scribner's Sons, 1937, 125p.

Bradford, Barbara Taylor. *Children's Stories of Jesus from the New Testament*. Illus. László Matulay. New York: Lion Press, 1966, 127p.

Branin, John J. *The Child's Life of Christ Told in Rhyme*. Philadelphia: Chapel Pub. Co., 1895, 32p.

Brennan, Gerald Thomas. *The Man Who Never Died*. Milwaukee: Bruce Pub. Co., 1946, 96p.

Brousse, Simonne. *Ta petite histoire sainte*. Paris: Hachette, 1955, 25p.

Brown, Florence Lucy Rudston. *The Story of Jesus*. Illus. Eileen M. Watts. London: Strand Publications, 193-?, 34p.

Brown, Helen (Benjamin). *Jesus Goes to the Synagogue*. Illus. William M. Hutchinson. New York: Abingdon Press, 1960, unpaged.

Brown, Howard Nicholson. *A Life of Jesus for Children*. Boston: Unitarian Sunday-School Society, 1883, 22p.

————. *A Life of Jesus for Young People*. 15th ed. Boston: Unitarian Sunday-School Society, 1892, 183p.

Browning, Elva Ward. *The Lighted Trail; a Children's Life of Jesus*. New York: Exposition Press, 1955, 151p.

Bryant, Al. *Pictures of Jesus with Simple Stories*. Illus. Charles Zingaro and Cleveland L. Woodward. Grand Rapids: Zondervan Pub. House, 1964, unpaged.

Burt, Olive (Wooley). *They Knew Jesus; Verses and Pictures about Some of the People Who Knew Jesus*. Illus. William Heyer. Anderson, Ind.: Warner Press, 1959, unpaged.

Cake, Lu B. *The Story My Mother Told Me*. New York: L.B. Cake, 1897?, 40p.

Carriger, Sally A. *I-Can-Read-It-Myself Bible Stories*. Illus. Terry McBride. Washington: Review and Herald Pub. Assoc., 1978, 79p.

Chamberlain, Eugene. *Jesus: God's Son, Savior, Lord*. Illus. James Padgett. Nashville: Broadman Press, 1976, 47p.

Charles, Eugène. *Pour nos tout petite; l'Évangile de maman*. Paris: Desclée de Brower & c^{ie}, 1933, 201p.

Charrat, André. *The Life of Christ for Teenagers*. Trans. S.G.A. Luff. Notre Dame, Ind.: Fides Publishers, 1965, 146p.

The Child's Life of Christ. Kansas City, Mo.: Continental Pub. Co., 1889, 747p.

A Child's Life of Christ. New York: G.H. McKibbin, 1899, 192p.

A Child's Story of the New Testament in Words of One Syllable.
Philadelphia: H. Altemus Co., 1900, 112p.

Chute, Marchette Gaylord. *Jesus of Israel.* New York: Dutton,
1961, 116p.

Clark, Glenn. *"Come Follow Me."* Saint Paul: Macalester Park
Pub. Co., 1952, 206p.

Colby, Jean (Poindexter). *Jesus and the World.* Illus. Jane
Paton. New York: Hastings House, 1968, 26p.

Coleman, William L. *Jesus, My Forever Friend.* Elgin, Ill.:
D.C. Cook Pub. Co., 1981, 125p.; Elgin, Ill.: Chariot Books,
1984.

Colina, Tessa. *Bible Stories about Jesus.* Cincinnati: Standard Pub. Co., 1954, 160p.

Collins, David R. *The Wonderful Story of Jesus.* Illus. Don.
Kueker and Bill Hoyer. St. Louis: Concordia Pub. House,
1980, 48p.

Cook, Lulu Rathbun. *The Story of the Great Star.* Illus.
author. New York: Vantage Press, 1949, 64p.

Courtois, Gaston. *La plus belle histoire.* Illus. Nadir
Quinto. Paris: Fleurus, 1963, 60p.

Cousins, Mary. *More about Jesus.* Illus. Doritie Kettlewell.
Grand Rapids: Eerdmans, 1957, 172p.

Crafts, Wilbur Fisk. *Talks to Boys and Girls about Jesus.*
New York: I.K. Funk and Co., 1881, 381p.

Crawford, Mary. *Who Is This? A Life of Jesus Taken from the
Four Gospels.* Illus. Antony Lewis. Westminster: Faith
Press, 1959, 93p.

Daughters of St. Paul. *I Learn about Jesus.* Illus. Daughters
of St. Paul. Boston: St. Paul Editions, 1972, 144p.

Davis, Sadie Holcombe. *Jesus, once a Child.* Nashville:
Broadman Press, 1954, unpaged.

Day by Day with Jesus; Bible Stories for Grades 5 and 6.
Illus. Helen Torrey. Mountain View, Calif.: Mountain View
Pub. Assn., 1951, 319p.

Dearmer, Mabel (White). *A Child's Life of Christ.* Illus.
Eleanor Fortescue-Brickdale. New York: Dodd, Mead, and Co.,
1907, 309p.

Dagering, Etta B. *Once upon a Bible Time.* Illus. Vernon Nye.
Washington: Review and Herald Pub. Assn., 1976-   .

De Santis, Zerlina. *A Child's Story of the Baby Who Changed the World*. Illus. Sud. Boston: St. Paul Editions, 1968, 45p.

Dickens, Charles. *The Life of Our Lord*. Illus. Everett Shinn. New York: Garden City Pub. Co., 1939, 125p.; London: Collins, 1970, 128p.; Philadelphia: Westminster Press, 1981, 127p.; London: Associated Newspapers, 1934.

Dillard, Pauline (Hargis). *My Book about Jesus*. Illus. Anne R. Kasey. Nashville: Broadman Press, 1968, 32p.

Doonan, Grace (Wallace). *The Life on Earth of Our Blessed Lord, Told in Rhyme, Story, and Picture, for Little Catholic Children*. St. Louis: B. Herder, 1913, 80p.

Duff, Mildrid Blanche. *Slik var Jesus*. Illus. W.J. Gibbs. Oslo: Salvata kristelig forlag, 19--, 199p.

Egermeier, Elsie Emilie. *Picture-story Life of Jesus*. Anderson, Ind.: Warner Press, 1966, 127p.

Ellis, Edward Sylvester. *The Wonderful Story of Old, Told for Boys and Girls*. New York: M.W. Hazen Co., 1904, 348p.

Entwistle, Mary. *The Most Beautiful Story of All*. Wallington, Eng.: Religious Education Press, 1952, 128p.

Evans, Adelaide Bee (Cooper). *The Children's Friend; Pictures and Stories of the Life of Jesus*. Takoma Park, Washington, D.C.; South Bend, Ind.: Review and Herald Pub. Assn., 1928, 189p.

Fedderson, Jakob Friedrich. *Zhitīe Iisusa Khrista*. Trans. Petr Kalazin. St. Petersburg: Imp. Akademiīa nauk, 1809, 145p.

Fenner, Mabel B. *Stories of Jesus*. Illus. Ralph Pallen Coleman. Philadelphia: Muhlenberg Press, 1952, unpaged.

Ferrari, Erma Paul. *The Life of Jesus of Nazareth*. Illus. William Hole. New York: Simon and Schuster, 1958, 164p.

Finn, Francis James. *The Story of Jesus*. Chicago: 1924, 15p.

Fisher, Harriet Irene. *The Story of Jesus*. Findlay, Ohio: Fundamental Truth Publishers, 1935, 115p.

Fitzpatrick, Florence Baillie. *A Life of Christ for Children*. Philadelphia: Westminster Press, 1905, 170p.

Forbush, William Byron. *The Boys' Life of Christ*. New York; London: Funk and Wagnalls Co., 1906, 318p.

————. *The Life of Jesus for Young People*. New York: C. Scribner's Sons, 1917, 221p.

Fosdick, Harry Emerson. *Jesus of Nazareth*. Illus. Steele
Savage. New York: Random House, 1959, 185p.

Foster, Charles. *The Story of the Gospel and Scenes in Bible
Lands*. Philadelphia: Charles Foster Pub. Co., 1889, 374p.

————. *The Story of the Gospel; or, Our Saviour's Life on
Earth Told in Words Easy to Read and Understand*. Philadelphia: Charles Foster Pub. Co., 1909, 366p., (1881), (1884).

Fraser, Edith. *A Boy Hears about Jesus*. Illus. Kurt Werth.
New York: Abingdon Press, 1965, 94p.

Freivogel, Esther. *My Book about Jesus*. Illus. Margaret
Ayer. Philadelphia: Westminster Press, 1949, 45p.

Gales, Louis A. *A First Life of Christ for Little Catholics,
in the Words of Mary, the Mother of Jesus*. Illus. Bruno
Frost. St. Paul: Catechetical Guild Educational Society,
1952, unpaged.

Gates, Herbert Wright. *The Life of Jesus, Prepared in Outline*.
Chicago: University of Chicago Press, 1906——.

Gilbert, Rosa (Mulholland). *La vida de Nuestro Señor Jesu-
cristo, contada á los niños*. Trans. Santiago de Guatemala.
Einsiedeln y Waldshut: Benziger and Co.; New York; Cincinnati:
Benziger Brothers, 1888, 156p.

Gillie, Robert Calder. *The Story of Stories*. 2nd ed. London:
A. and C. Black, 1907, 488p.

Glover, Gloria (Diener). *The Story of Jesus*. Illus. Pris-
cilla Pointer. Chicago: Rand McNally, 1965, (1949), unpaged.

Goddard, Carrie Lou. *Jesus*. Illus. Peggy Zych. Nashville:
Abingdon, 1978, 32p.

Goldie, Agnes. *Évangile des petits*. Lyon: E. Vitte, 1931,
304p.

Gomes Leal, Antonio Duarte. *Historia de Jesus para as
creancinhas lerem*. Lisboa: Imprensa nacional, 1883, 128p.

Goodspeed, Edgar Johnson, and Edmund Warne Hicks. *The Life
of Jesus: For Young People*. New York; Boston: H.S. Goodspeed and Co., 1874, 551p.

The Gospel Story; or, The Story of Christ for the Young.
Samuel Austin Allibone, ed. Philadelphia; New York:
American Sunday-School Union, 1888, 303p.

Griffith, Robert Gladstone. *Jesus for Everychild*. London:
Skeffington and Son, 1934, 128p.

Hanser, Richard. *Jesus: What Manner of Man Is This?* New York:
Simon and Schuster, 1972, 191p.

Harrison, Eveleen. *The Life of Christ, for Boys and Girls.*
New York: Stelz Co., 1937, 96p.

Haskell, Mrs. L. *The Sweet Story of Old; a Life of Christ
for Children.* Philadelphia: Henry Altemus Co., 1904, 123p.

Hastings, Horace Lorenzo. *Bethlehem, a Children's Rhyme of
the Olden Time.* Boston: Scriptural Tract Repository, H.L.
Hastings, 1882, 70p.

Hay, Kathleen. *The Sweetest Story Told.* Rock Island, Ill.:
Augustana Book Concern, 1931, 94p.

Heath, Lucy Hannah. *From Christmas to Easter; a Story for
Boys and Girls.* Cincinnati: Jennings and Graham; New York:
Eaton and Mains, 1913, 100p.

Heinemann, Thea. *Stories of Jesus.* Illus. Don Bolognese.
Racine, Wis.: Whitman Pub. Division, Western Pub. Co., 1968,
228p.

Hemphill, Martha Locke. *A Book about Jesus.* Illus. Al Fioren-
tino. Valley Forge, Pa.: Judson Press, 1969, 24p.

Hill, Dave. *The Most Wonderful King; Luke 19:28-24:43 and
John 12:12-20:31 for Children.* Illus. Betty Wind. St. Louis:
Concordia Pub. House, 1968, unpaged.

Hock, Jánus. *Jésus élete.* Budapest: Az Athenaeum irodalmi
és nyomdai kiadása, 1905, 153p.

Hodges, George. *When the King Came; Stories from the Four
Gospels.* Illus. Frank C. Papé. Boston; New York: Houghton
Mifflin Co., 1923, 399p.

Hoffmann, Hans Peter. *Bilder für Kinder aus dem Leben Jesu.*
Illus. Johannes Grüger. Düsseldorf: Patmos-Verlag, 1966.

————. *Children's Life of Jesus.* Trans. Rosemarie McManus.
Illus. Johannes Grüger. Baltimore: Helicon, 1966, unpaged.

Holland, Cornelius Joseph. *The Divine Story; a Short Life of
Our Blessed Lord for Youth.* Illus. Gedge Harmon. St.
Meinrad, Ind.: 1954, 173p.

Holmes, Prescott. *A Child's Life of Christ in Words of One
Syllable.* Philadelphia: H. Altemus, 1899, 193p.

Horton, Robert Forman. *The Hero of Heroes; a Life of Christ
for Young People.* New York; Chicago: Revell, 1911, 326p.

Hoth, Iva. *Jesus; Matthew-John.* Illus. Andre Le Blanc.
Elgin, Ill.: D.C. Cook Pub. Co., 1973, 158p.

Hoyt, Helen Brown. *A Child's Story of the Life of Christ.*
Boston; Chicago: W.A. Wilde Co., 1902, 233p.

————. *The Story of Jesus--the Christ; Adapted for Children*. Boston; Chicago: W.A. Wilde Co., 1923, 233p.

Hug, Fritz, and Margaret Hug. *Die Esel des Herrn; eine Bilderbibel*. Zürich: Buchclub Ex Libris, 1960, 49p.

————. *In the Path of Jesus*. Edinburgh: Oliver and Boyd, 1961, unpaged.

————. *The Story of Our Lord*. New York: Random House, 1961, unpaged.

Hunsche, Klara. *Ach, bleib bei uns, Herr Jesu Christ!* Illus. Paula Jordan. Gütersloh: Der Rufer Evangelischer Verlag, 193-?, 48p.

Hunt, Marigold. *A Life of Our Lord*. Illus. Rus Anderson. New York: Sheed and Ward, 1959, 191p.

————. *A Life of Our Lord for Children*. Illus. Eleanor O. Eadie. New York: Sheed and Ward, 1944, 168p.

Hunter, Martha Angeline (Beck). *Story of the Four Gospels for Boys and Girls*. Cincinnati: Monfort and Co., 1915, 102p.

Hunting, Harold Bruce. *A Life of Christ for Young People*. New York: Minton, Balch, and Co., 1924, 182p.

Hurlbut, Jesse Lyman. *The Story of Jesus Every Child Should Know*. Philadelphia?: 1907, 256p.

Ihde, Lissy. *Der heilige Weg, das Leben Jesu für die Jugend nacherzählt*. Illus. Schnorr von Carolsfeld. Hamburg: Reich & Heidrich, 1946, 47p.

Ildefonso, frei. *História de Jesús para as criancas*. 4. ed. São Paulo: Livraria acadêmica, Saraiva & cia, 1940, 100p.

Irvin, Donald F. *The Life of Jesus*. Illus. Ralph Pallen Coleman. Philadelphia: Muhlenberg Press, 1951, 219p.

Jahsmann, Allan Hart. *It's All about Jesus*. Illus. Art Kirchoff. St. Louis: Concordia Pub. House, 1975, 157p.

James Stanislaus, Sister. *The Journeys of Jesus*. 3 vols. Boston; New York: Ginn and Co., 1927-28.

Janett, Johann Jacob. *Jesus für die erwachsene Jugend*. Cleveland: Central Pub. House, 1904, 118p.

Jesus of Nazareth (Filmstrip). Graded Press, 1965, 62 fr.

Jesus, Our Friend. Valley Forge, Pa.: Judson Press, 1976, 47p.

Jesus' Story, a Little New Testament. Illus. Maud and Miska Petersham. New York: Macmillan, 1942, 119p.

Jesus upon Earth; or, The Story of His Birth, Life, Death, and Resurrection. New York: C. Scribner, 1857, 194p.

Johnson, Ethel A. *My Book about Jesus.* Washington: Review and Herald Pub. Assn., 1962, 61p.

Jones, Mary Alice. *His Name Was Jesus.* Illus. Rafaello Busoni. Chicago: Rand McNally, 1950, 208p.

————. *Jesus Who Helped People.* Illus. Manning de V. Lee. Chicago: Rand McNally, 1965, unpaged.

————. *My First Book about Jesus.* Illus. Robert Hatch. Chicago: Rand McNally, 1953, unpaged.

————. *Tell Me about Jesus.* Illus. Dorothy Grider. Chicago: Rand McNally, 1967, 71p.

Kellogg, Caroline. *Stories from the Life of Jesus, Told for Little Children.* Illus. Harold Speakman and W.R. Lohse. Indianapolis: Bobbs-Merrill Co., 1922, 108p.

————. *What the Stars Saw, and Other Bible Stories.* Illus. Harold Speakman. Indianapolis: Bobbs-Merrill Co., 1916, 88p.

Korfker, Dena. *The Story of Jesus for Boys and Girls.* Illus. Lou Mahaeek. Grand Rapids: Zondervan Pub. House, 1954, unpaged.

Kung, Yüan-han. *Yeh-su.* Hong Kong: Chung-hua Bookstore, 1957, 37p.

Langford, Norman F. *The King Nobody Wanted.* Illus. John Lear. Philadelphia: Westminster Press, 1948, 192p.

Lathbury, Mary A. *Child's Life of Christ.* Boston: De Wolfe, Fiske, and Co., 1898, 133p.

Lathrop, Mary A. *"The Sweet Story of Old"; or, The History of Jesus.* New York; Boston: American Tract Society, 1857?, 64p.

Le Feuvre, Amy. *The Most Wonderful Story in the World; a Life of Christ for Little Children.* New York; Chicago: Revell, 1922, 219p.

A Life of Christ for Children. New York; London: Longmans, Green, and Co., 1910, 77p.

The Life of Christ Jesus in Bible Language, from the King James Version of the Bible. Arranged by Genevieve P. Olson. San Diego, Calif.: Arts and Crafts Press, 1956, 52p.

The Life of Jesus. Boston: Massachusetts Sabbath School Society, 1853, 214p.

The Life of Jesus, series 1 (Filmstrip). Catechetical Guild
Educational Society, 1965. Made by Berkey-Manhattan Labora-
tories. Released by Our Sunday Visitor, 197-, 6 filmstrips
(28 fr. each).

The Life of Jesus, series 2 (Filmstrip). Catechetical Guild
Educational Society, 1965. Made by Berkey-Manhattan Labora-
tories. Released by Our Sunday Visitor, 197-, 6 filmstrips
(28 fr. each).

Lindman, Maj. *Little Folks' Life of Jesus.* Illus. Maj Lindman. Chicago: A. Whitman, 1948, 28p.

Lindsey, Hal. *The Promise.* Illus. Norm McGary. Irvine,
Calif.: Harvest House, 1974, 100p.

Lockwood, Myna. *The Life of Our Lord.* Illus. Zac Zaccardi.
New York: Guild Press, 1963, 30p.

Lorente, Sebastian. *Compendie de la vida de N.S. Jesucristo.*
2. ed. Lima: B. Gil, 1872, 140p.

Luecke, Martin. *Biblische Symbole; oder, Bibelblätter in Bil-
dern, nebst einem Lebensbilde unseres Heilandes, in den
Hauptzügen der Jugend gezeichnet.* 2. Aufl. Chicago; Boston:
John A. Hertel Co., 1911, 182p.

McArdle, Mildred J. *Stories of Long Ago.* Illus. H.D. Gieson.
New York: T. Nelson and Sons, 1929, 128p.

McCarthy, J.J. *A Child's Life of Christ.* Philadelphia:
H. Altemus, 1895, 211p.

Macduff, John Ross. *Brighter than the Sun; or, Christ the
Light of the World. A Life of Our Lord for the Young.* Illus.
A. Rowan. New York: American Tract Society, 1892, 433p.

McFayden, Nina L. *Stories from the Life of the Wonderful.*
Los Angeles: The author, 1897, 218p.

McKeever, Harriet Burn. *Jesus on Earth.* Philadelphia: Presbyterian Publication Committee; New York: A.D.F. Randolph,
1866, 64p.

Madden, Richard C. *Father Madden's Life of Christ.* Milwaukee:
Bruce, 1960, 161p.

Madison, Marian. *Picture Stories from the Life of Christ.*
Illus. Warner Kreuter. Chicago: Wilcox and Follett Co.,
1946, 26p.

Martin, Herbert. *Vom Kind zum König.* Illus. Kurt Eichler.
Berlin: Evangelische Verlagsanstalt, 1963, 143p.

Martyn, Sarah Towne (Smith). *Jesus in Bethany.* New York:
American Tract Society, 1864, 83p.

Mary Catherine, Sister. *The Life of My Savior*. Milwaukee: Bruce Pub. Co., 1933, 195p.

Mary Josephine, Sister. *The Story of Our Lord's Life Told for Children*. New York: Cathedral Library Association, 1910, 173p.

Mary Loyola, Mother. *Jesus of Nazareth; the Story of His Life Written for Children*. New York; Cincinnati: Benziger Brothers, 1906, 101p.

Mathews, Basil Joseph. *The Story of Jesus; a Book for Young People*. New York; London: Harper and Brothers, 1934, 224p.

Matos, Marco Aurélio, and Fernando Tavares Sabino. *O Evangelho das crianças*. Rio de Janeiro: Editôra Sabiá, 1969, 90p.

Matthews, Leonard. *Tales of Jesus*. New York: Derrydale Books, 1982.

Maurice, Sister. *Journeys Beautiful*. New York; Chicago: W.H. Sadlier, 1932, 112p.

Meek, Jessie. *Jesus of Nazareth; the Life of Our Lord, Written for the Children*. Kansas City, Mo.: Publishing House of the Pentecostal Church of the Nazarene, 1914, 188p.

Melton, David. *This Man--Jesus*. Illus. David Melton. New York: McGraw-Hill, 1972, 57p.

Michel, Virgil George, and Basil Augustine Stegmann. *Jesus Our Savior*. Illus. Kate Seredy. New York: Macmillan, 1934, 134p.

Miller, Emily Clark (Huntington). *Home Talks about the Word*. New York: Hunt and Eaton; Cincinnati: Cranston and Curts, 1894, 286p.

Mitchell, Curtis. *Jesus Spreads His Gospel*. Garden City, N.Y.: Doubleday, 1961, 64p.

Modras, Ronald. *Jesus of Nazareth: A Life Worth Living*. Minneapolis: Winston Press, 1983, 122p.

Mogk, Ernst. *Kommt her, ich will erzählen! Geschichten aus dem Leben Jesu für Kinder erzählt*. Stuttgart: J.G. Oncken, 1946, 159p.

Monahan, Maud and Robin. *About Jesus, Son of God and Son of Mary*. London; New York: Longmans, Green, 1937, 50p.

Morrill, Madge Arty (Haines). *The Child's Storybook of Jesus*. Mountain View, Calif.; Portland, Ore.: Pacific Press Pub. Assn., 1940, 128p.

Morrow, Abbie Clemens. *The Old, Old Story of the Holy Child, Told Again for the Children*. Cincinnati: M.W. Knapp, 1900, 194p.

Mortimer, Favell Lee (Bevan). *More about Jesus*. New York: Harper and Brothers, 1859, 246p.

Morton, Harriet (Cave). *Talks to Children about Jesus*. Baltimore: R.H. Woodward Co., 1894, 320p.

Muir, Charles Augustus. *The Story of Jesus*. Illus. Eric Winter and Eric Wade. New York: Greystone Press, 1954, 128p.

Napoli, Guillier. *The Life of Jesus*. Illus. Napoli. Minneapolis: Augsburg Pub. House, 1971, 40p.

————. *La vie de Jésus*. Illus. Napoli. Paris: Éditions du Centurion, 1969, 39p.

Nelson, Henry Addison. *Seeing Jesus*. Philadelphia: Presbyterian Publication Committee; New York: A.D.E. Randolph and Co., 1869, 172p.

Newton, Richard. *The Life of Jesus Christ for the Young*. 4 vols. Illus. William Hole. Philadelphia: G. Barrie and Sons, 1913.

Nixdorff, George Augustus. *Scenes in the Life of Christ*. Philadelphia: Lutheran Publication Society, 1876, 202p.

Northcott, William Cecil. *The Greatest Name of All*. Illus. Denis Wrigley. Nashville: Broadman Press, 1969, 46p.

Obara, Kuniyoshi. *Iesu Sama*. Machida: Tamagawa Daigaku Shuppanbu, 1974, 137p.

Obraztsov, Petr. *Kratkaîa istorîîà stradaniĭ i smerti Khrista Spasitîîà*. St. Petersburg: Tip. Pochtovyĭ department, 1857, 116p.

O'Brien, John Anthony. *Jesus Spreads His Gospel*. Garden City, N.Y.: Doubleday, 1962, 64p.

O'Brien, William J. *The New Catholic Bible Symbols with The Story Life of Jesus*. Chicago: John A. Hertel Co., 1925.

Olson, Eudora Landstrom. *Stories of Jesus for Little Children*. Rock Island, Ill.: Augustana Book Concern, 1935- .

Osborne, Edward William. *The Children's Saviour; Instructions to Children on the Life of Our Lord and Saviour Jesus Christ*. London: Rivingtons; New York: E. and J.B. Young, 1889, 275p.

Our Blessed Lord. Charlotte, N.C.: Catholic Bible House, 1964, 287p.

Our Redemption (Filmstrip). Eye Gate House, 1958, 36 fr.

Our Saviour: or, A Brief Exposition of the Birth, Teaching, Miracles, Death, Resurrection, and Great Commission, of Jesus Christ. Philadelphia: American Baptist Publication Society, 1844, 144p.

Oursler, Fulton. *A Child's Life of Jesus.* Illus. Elinore Blaisdell. New York: F. Watts, 1951, 42p.

Parker, Jane (Marsh). *The Light of the World; or, Footprints of Christ Our Lord.* New York: Standord and Delisser, 1858, 63p.

Pell, Edward Leigh. *The Story of Jesus for Little People.* New York; Chicago: Revell, 1912, 74p.

Peterson, Edward C., and Barbara Nan Peterson. *To Find Jesus.* Illus. Jim Padgett. Nashville: Abingdon Press, 1967, 112p.

Phillips, Ethel M. *Stories of Jesus for Boys and Girls.* Anderson, Ind.: Warner Press, 1948, 64p.

Pierson, Helen W. *Bible Stories in Easy Words.* New York: McLoughlin Brothers, 1904, 134p.

————. *The Gospel Story, in Easy Words for Children.* New York: McLoughlin Brothers, 1892, 214p.

Poinsenet, Marie Dominique. *Jésus, fils de Dieu Sauveur.* Illus. Fra Angelico. Paris: Desclée De Brouwer, 1966, 93p.

Pollard, Josephine. *A Child's Life of Our Lord.* Akron, Ohio; New York: Saalfield Pub. Co., 1934, 64p.

————. *The Story of Jesus; Told in Pictures.* New York; Akron, Ohio: Werner Co., 1899, 79p.

————. *The Wonderful Story of Jesus Told in Simple Language.* New York; St. Louis: N.D. Thompson Pub. Co., 1890, 455p.

————. *Young Folks' Life of Christ Told in Pictures and in Words of Easy Reading for the Young.* St. Louis; Chicago: N.D. Thompson Pub. Co., 1902, 452p.

————. *Young Folks' Life of Jesus Christ.* New York; London: G. Routledge and Sons, 1891, 410p.

Poucel, Victor. *Vie de Jésus pour l'enfant.* Paris: E. Flammarion, 1932, 156p.

Radius, Marianne Catherine (Vos). *God with Us; a Life of Jesus for Young Readers.* Linoleum cuts by Frederick J. Ashby. Grand Rapids: Eerdmans, 1966, 286p.

Raemers, Sidney Albert. *A Teen-ager's Life of Christ.* Illus. M. Cerezo-Barredo. New York: Helios Books, 1964, 218p.

Ramsay, DeVere Maxwell. *God's Son; a Book of Stories about Jesus for Young Children*. Illus. Rita Endhoven. Grand Rapids: Eerdmans, 1964, 48p.

Rawson, Marianna S. *A Life of Jesus for Boys and Girls*. Philadelphia: Biddle Press, 1911, 115p.

Rémy, Jean S. *The Life of Christ Retold in Words of One Syllable*. Illus. Julius Schnorr. New York: A.L. Burt, 1901, 127p.

Rich, Alice Hamilton. *The Story of Jesus as Told by Grandfather John*. Chicago: R.R. Donnelley and Sons, 1900, 264p.

Rihbany, Abraham Mitrie. *The Christ Story for Boys and Girls*. Illus. Gustaf Tenggren. Boston; New York: Houghton Mifflin Co., 1923, 239p.

Robertson, Jenny. *Jesus the Leader*. Illus. Alan Parry. Grand Rapids: Zondervan Pub. House, 1980.

Robinson, Ella May (White). *When Jesus Was Here*. Nashville: Southern Pub. Assn., 1951, 240p.

Robinson, Emma Amelia. *Short Stories of Christ the Ideal Hero*. New York: Eaton and Mains; Cincinnati: Jennings and Graham, 1909, 153p.

Robinson, L.L. *The Story of Jesus of Nazareth*. Milwaukee: Young Churchman Co., 1895, 270p.

Rolt, Mary F. *A Baby's Life of Jesus Christ*. Illus. A.A. Dixon. New York: Macmillan, 1924, 153p.

Rosser, Gladys. *Our Friend of Galilee*. Illus. James Converse. Mountain View, Calif.: Pacific Press Pub. Assn., 1962, 138p.

Rye, Amy Haslam. *The Beloved Son*. New York: Dodd, Mead, 1901, 145p.

Salazar, Manuel Marcos. *Compendio de la vida de Nuestro Señor Jesucristo para las escuelas de instrucción primaria*. 2. ed. Lima: B. Gil, 1874, 69p.

Sangster, Margaret Elizabeth (Munson). *That Sweet Story of Old; a Life of Christ for the Young*. New York; Chicago: Revell, 1904, 262p.

Savage, Carol. *The Lord Jesus*. Illus. Gil Miret. Greenwich, Conn.: Seabury Press, 1962, 70p.

Schraff, Francis. *Learning about Jesus*. Illus. Jim Corbett. Liguori, Mo.: Liguori Publications, 1980, 80p.

Scriven, Gerard R. *While Angels Watch; the Life of Jesus Our King*. Illus. Fausto Conti. St. Paul: Catechetical Guild Educational Society, 1953, 192p.

Scutt, Winifred. *The Children's Master*. Illus. Winifred Scutt. New York; Chicago: Revell, 1925, 148p.

Seboldt, Roland H.A. *God's Son on Earth*. Illus. Marianne Bellenhaus. St. Louis: Concordia Pub. House, 1968, unpaged.

Ségur, Sophie (Rostopchine). *A Life of Christ for Children*. Trans. Mary Virginia Merrick. St. Louis: B. Herder, 1909, 347p.

Sentiers de joie. 1- . Paris: Apostolat des éditions, 1969- .

Sheen, Fulton John. *Jesus, Son of Mary*. Illus. Marie de John. New York: Seabury Press, 1980, 30p.

Shonkweiler, James Harvey. *Jesus*. 2 vols. Cincinnati: Standard Pub. Co., 1926.

Sill, Louise Morgan (Smith). *The Life of Lives; the Story of Our Lord Jesus Christ for Young People*. New York: George H. Doran Co., 1922, 253p.

Smallwood, Kate. *I Think about Jesus*. Illus. Esther Friend. Chicago: Rand McNally, 1958, unpaged.

Smith, Eliza Roxey (Snow). *The Story of Jesus*. Salt Lake City: Bookcraft Co., 1945, 99p.

Smith, Elwyn Allen. *Men Called Him Master*. Illus. Harold Minton. Philadelphia: Westminster Press, 1948, 186p.

Smith, Lloyd Edwin. *Children's Story of Jesus*. Racine, Wis.: Whitman Pub. Co., 1934, 24p.

————. *The Story of Jesus Retold for Children*. Illus. Henry E. Vallely. Racine, Wis.: Whitman Pub. Co., 1941, 380p.

Smither, Ethel Lisle. *Stories of Jesus*. Illus. Kurt Wiese. Nashville: Abingdon Press, 1954, 80p.

Smyth, John Paterson. *A Boys and Girls Life of Christ*. New York; Chicago: Revell, 1929, 285p.

Sockman, Ralph Washington. *The Easter Story for Children*. Illus. Gordon Laite. New York: Abingdon Press, 1966, unpaged.

A Son Is Given. Virginia Sutch, ed. Atlanta: John Knox Press, 1974, 127p.

Sousa, Osvaldo Devay de. *Jesus para os jovens*. Salvador: 1968, 76p.

Speck, Gerald Eugene. *The Story of Jesus*. Illus. Fiorenzo
Faorzi. London: Ward Lock, 1966, 60p.

Starr, Frederick Ratchford. *The Lamb of God*. Philadelphia;
New York: American Sunday-School Union, 1888, 77p.

Stevens, Clifford J. *Man of Galilee*. Huntington, Ind.: Our
Sunday Visitor, 1979, 96p.

Stevenson, Margaret J. *The Life of Jesus*. Olathe, Kan.:
M.J. Stevenson, 1925, 43p.; Topeka, Kan.: Crane and Co.,
1904, 38p.

Steward, Mary Alicia. *Our Best Friend; Stories from the Life
of Christ for Juniors*. Takoma Park, Md.; Washington, D.C.:
Review and Herald Pub. Assn., 1940, 192p.

Stewart, Mary. *A King among Men*. New York; Chicago: Revell,
1915, 128p.

————. *The Shepherd of Us All; Stories of the Christ Retold
for Children*. New York; Chicago: Revell, 1913, 255p.

Stirling, John Featherstone. *For a Little Child Like Me*.
Illus. Horace J. Knowles. New York: C. Scribner's Sons,
1934, 52p.

Stories from the Life of Christ. Janet Harvey Kelman, ed.
Illus. F.D. Bedford. New York: E.P. Dutton and Co., 1905,
113p.

The Story of Jesus; a Little New Testament. Illus. Maud and
Miska Petersham. New York: Macmillan, 1967, 103p.

The Story of Jesus for Children. Louise Castle Walbridge, ed.
New York; London: Abbey Press, 1901, 76p.

Stretton, Hesba. *The Beautiful Story of Jesus and the Lives
of His Apostles*. Philadelphia: World Bible House, 1906,
575p.

————. *The Child's Life of Christ*. Philadelphia; Chicago:
J.C. Winston and Co., 1891, 167p.

————. *The Child's Story of the Beautiful Life of Jesus Told
in Simple Language*. Hartford, Conn.: Hartford Pub. Co.,
1902, 249p.

————. *Från Betlehem till Golgata*. Trans. Fred Lönnkvist.
Philadelphia; Chicago: J.C. Winston and Co., 1893, 302p.

————. *The Gospel Story for Young People*. Philadelphia:
World Bible House, 1896, 254p.

————. *Kristi och hans apostlars underfulla lif*. Philadelphia; Chicago: J.C. Winston and Co., 1897, 302p.

————. *The New Child's Life of Christ.* Philadelphia: J.C. Winston Co., 1901, 251p.

————. *The Wonderful Story of Christ and the Apostles.* Philadelphia; Chicago: J.C. Winston and Co., 1896, 478p.

————. *The Wonderful Story of Christ and His Apostles.* Philadelphia?: 1905, 475p.

Swanston, Hamish F.G. *The Good News.* Illus. Emile Probst. Nashville: Impact Books, 1970, 26p.

Tappan, Eva March. *The Christ Story.* Boston; New York: Houghton, Mifflin and Co., 1903, 416p.

Taylor, Oliver Alden. *Brief Views of the Saviour.* Andover: Gould and Newman, 1835, 264p.

Thayne, Miria Greenwood. *When He Comes Again.* Illus. Adell Reese Palmer. Salt Lake City: Deseret Book Co., 1968, 77p.

Thurber, Robert Bruce. *The Story of Jesus.* Nashville; Atlanta: Southern Pub. Assn., 1924, 64p.

Tigchelaar, Riet. *Het hoogste woord. Verhalen uit de bijbel naverteld voor kinderen.* 's-Gravenhage: Boekencentrum, 1970– .

Trapp, Willi. *Kinderbibel.* Illus. Willi Trapp. Bern: Berchtold-Haller-Verlag, 1969, 48p.

Trent, Robbie. *The Life of Jesus.* Nashville: Broadman Press, 1965, 96p.

————. *A Star Shone.* Illus. Margaret Ayer. Philadelphia: Westminster Press, 1948, 47p.

————. *Stories of Jesus.* Illus. Paul Frame. Racine, Wis.: Whitman Pub. Co., 1954, unpaged.

————. *They Saw Jesus.* Nashville: Broadman Press, 1952, unpaged.

Van Vechten, Schuyler, comp. *The Bethlehem Star: Children's Newspaper Reports of the Life of Jesus.* New York: Walker, 1972, 60p.

Victoria, Luiz Augusto Pereira. *O profeta de Nazare.* Rio de Janeiro: 1977, 80p.

La vie de Notre Seigneur Jésus-Christ, racontée aux enfants. Einsiedeln; New York: C. & N. Benziger frères, 1882, 158p.

Villiers, Marjorie Howard. *Jesus Has Come.* Illus. Philippe Joudiou. Valley Forge, Pa.: Judson Press, 1978, (1973), 28p.

————. *Jesus with Us*. Illus. Philippe Joudiou. Valley
Forge, Pa.: Judson Press, 1978, (1973), 28p.

Wadsworth, Ernest M. *My Good Shepherd*. Illus. JoAnne Cameron.
Chicago: Moody Press, 1951, 160p.

Walker, Allen W. *Life of the Christ, Written by a Lawyer for
His Children*. Kansas City, Mo.: Franklin Hudson Pub. Co.,
1920, 132p.

Walker, Katherine Kent (Child). *From the Crib to the Cross.
A Life of Christ in Words of One Syllable*. New York: G.A.
Leavitt, 1869, 318p.

Wangerin, Walter. *My First Book about Jesus*. Illus. Jim
Cummins. Chicago: Rand McNally, 1983.

Warner, Anna Bartlett. *The Star out of Jacob*. New York:
Hurst and Co., 1891, 391p.

Watson, Elizabeth Elaine. *Tell Me about Jesus*. Illus. Don
Kueker and Assoc. St. Louis: Concordia Pub. House, 1980,
32p.

Wernström, Sven. *Kamrat Jesus*. Illus. Mats Andersson.
Stockholm: Gidlund; Solna: Sealig, 1971, 75p.

White, Mrs. Annie Randall. *Talks about Jesus with Our Little
Boys and Girls*. Illus. H. Hoffmann, Prof. Plockhorst,
George Hahn. Chicago?: Juvenile Pub. Co., 1897, 276p.

White, Ellen Gould (Harmon). *The Desire of Ages*. 2 vols.
New York; Kansas City: Pacific Press Pub. Co., 1900.

————. *Story of Jesus*. Nashville: Southern Pub. Assn.,
1949, 189p.

Wilder, John Watson. *His Name Is Jesus*. Illus. Janice Penney.
Chicago: Reilly and Lee Co., 1935, 123p.

Wilk, Gerd. *Journeys with Jesus and Paul*. Trans. Victor I.
Gruhn. Philadelphia: Fortress Press, 1970, 127p.

Witter, Evelyn. *In Jesus' Day*. Illus. Wayne Sherwood. St.
Louis: Concordia Pub. House, 1980, 32p.

Wood, S.R. *Immanuel: A Life of Jesus the Christ*. Ferndale,
Calif.: Matthews and Wooldridge, 1894, 131p.

Zanzig, Thomas. *Jesus of History, Christ of Faith: A Gospel
Portrait for Young People*. Winona, Minn.: Saint Mary's
Press, 1982, 204p.